50% OFF PSAT Test Prep Course!

Dear Customer,

We consider it an honor and a privilege that you chose our PSAT Study Guide. As a way of showing our appreciation and to help us better serve you, we have partnered with Mometrix Test Preparation to offer you **50% off their online PSAT Prep Course.** Many PSAT courses are needlessly expensive and don't deliver enough value. With their course, you get access to the best PSAT prep material, and **you only pay half price.**

Mometrix has structured their online course to perfectly complement your printed study guide. The PSAT Test Prep Course contains **in-depth lessons** that cover all the most important topics, over **950+ practice questions** to ensure you feel prepared, more than **450 flashcards** for studying on the go, and over **250 instructional videos**.

Online PSAT Prep Course

Topics Covered:
- Reading and Writing
    - Craft and Structure
    - Information and Ideas
    - Standard English Conventions
    - Expression of Ideas
- Mathematics
    - Foundational Math Concepts
    - Algebra
    - Problem-Solving and Data Analysis
    - Geometry and Trigonometry

And More!

Course Features:
- PSAT Study Guide
    - Get access to content from the best reviewed study guide available.
- Track Your Progress
    - Their customized course allows you to check off content you have studied or feel confident with.
- 9 Full-Length Practice Tests
    - With 950+ practice questions and lesson reviews, you can test yourself again and again to build confidence.
- PSAT Flashcards
    - Their course includes a flashcard mode consisting of over 475 content cards to help you study.

To receive this discount, visit them at www.mometrix.com/university/psat or simply scan this QR code with your smartphone. At the checkout page, enter the discount code: **TPBPSAT50**

If you have any questions or concerns, please contact them at universityhelp@mometrix.com.

Sincerely,

 in partnership with

Online Resources

Included with your purchase are multiple online resources. This includes the practice tests in an interactive format and a convenient study timer to help you manage your time.

Instructions for accessing these resources can be found on the last page of this book.

PSAT™ Prep 2025 and 2026
7 Digital PSAT Practice Tests and Study Guide
[9th Edition]

Lydia Morrison

Copyright © 2025 by TPB Publishing

All rights reserved. No part of this publication may be reproduced, distributed, or transmitted in any form or by any means, including photocopying, recording, or other electronic or mechanical methods, without the prior written permission of the publisher, except in the case of brief quotations embodied in critical reviews and certain other noncommercial uses permitted by copyright law.

Written and edited by TPB Publishing.

TPB Publishing is not associated with or endorsed by any official testing organization. TPB Publishing is a publisher of unofficial educational products. All test and organization names are trademarks of their respective owners. Content in this book is included for utilitarian purposes only and does not constitute an endorsement by TPB Publishing of any particular point of view.

Interested in buying more than 10 copies of our product? Contact us about bulk discounts:
bulkorders@studyguideteam.com

ISBN 13: 9781637754290

Table of Contents

Welcome *1*

Quick Overview *2*

Test-Taking Strategies *3*

Introduction to the PSAT *7*

Study Prep Plan for the PSAT *9*

Reading and Writing Section *12*

    Craft and Structure 12

    Information and Ideas 24

    Standard English Conventions 36

    Expression of Ideas 50

    Practice Quiz 60

    Answer Explanations 62

Math Section *63*

    Algebra 63

    Advanced Math 79

    Problem-Solving and Data Analysis 103

    Geometry and Trigonometry 117

    Practice Quiz 133

    Answer Explanations 134

Practice Test #1 .... *135*

    Reading and Writing 1 135

    Reading and Writing 2 144

    Math 1 152

Math 2 159

Answer Explanations #1 .... *163*
Reading and Writing 1 163
Reading and Writing 2 166
Math 1 170
Math 2 174

Practice Test #2 .... *178*
Reading and Writing 1 178
Reading and Writing 2 187
Math 1 198
Math 2 202

Answer Explanations #2 .... *208*
Reading and Writing 1 208
Reading and Writing 2 211
Math 1 215
Math 2 219

PSAT Practice Tests #3–#7 .... *223*

Online Resources *225*

Welcome

Dear Reader,

Welcome to your new Test Prep Books study guide! We are pleased that you chose us to help you prepare for your exam. There are many study options to choose from, and we appreciate you choosing us. Studying can be a daunting task, but we have designed a smart, effective study guide to help prepare you for what lies ahead.

Whether you're a parent helping your child learn and grow, a high school student working hard to get into your dream college, or a nursing student studying for a complex exam, we want to help give you the tools you need to succeed. We hope this study guide gives you the skills and the confidence to thrive, and we can't thank you enough for allowing us to be part of your journey.

In an effort to continue to improve our products, we welcome feedback from our customers. We look forward to hearing from you. Suggestions, success stories, and criticisms can all be communicated by emailing us at info@studyguideteam.com.

Sincerely,
Test Prep Books Team

Quick Overview

As you draw closer to taking your exam, effective preparation becomes more and more important. Thankfully, you have this study guide to help you get ready. Use this guide to help keep your studying on track and refer to it often.

This study guide contains several key sections that will help you be successful on your exam. The guide contains tips for what you should do the night before and the day of the test. Also included are test-taking tips. Knowing the right information is not always enough. Many well-prepared test takers struggle with exams. These tips will help equip you to accurately read, assess, and answer test questions.

A large part of the guide is devoted to showing you what content to expect on the exam and to helping you better understand that content. In this guide are practice test questions so that you can see how well you have grasped the content. Then, answer explanations are provided so that you can understand why you missed certain questions.

Don't try to cram the night before you take your exam. This is not a wise strategy for a few reasons. First, your retention of the information will be low. Your time would be better used by reviewing information you already know rather than trying to learn a lot of new information. Second, you will likely become stressed as you try to gain a large amount of knowledge in a short amount of time. Third, you will be depriving yourself of sleep. So be sure to go to bed at a reasonable time the night before. Being well-rested helps you focus and remain calm.

Be sure to eat a substantial breakfast the morning of the exam. If you are taking the exam in the afternoon, be sure to have a good lunch as well. Being hungry is distracting and can make it difficult to focus. You have hopefully spent lots of time preparing for the exam. Don't let an empty stomach get in the way of success!

When traveling to the testing center, leave earlier than needed. That way, you have a buffer in case you experience any delays. This will help you remain calm and will keep you from missing your appointment time at the testing center.

Be sure to pace yourself during the exam. Don't try to rush through the exam. There is no need to risk performing poorly on the exam just so you can leave the testing center early. Allow yourself to use all of the allotted time if needed.

Remain positive while taking the exam even if you feel like you are performing poorly. Thinking about the content you should have mastered will not help you perform better on the exam.

Once the exam is complete, take some time to relax. Even if you feel that you need to take the exam again, you will be well served by some down time before you begin studying again. It's often easier to convince yourself to study if you know that it will come with a reward!

Test-Taking Strategies

1. Predicting the Answer

When you feel confident in your preparation for a multiple-choice test, try predicting the answer before reading the answer choices. This is especially useful on questions that test objective factual knowledge. By predicting the answer before reading the available choices, you eliminate the possibility that you will be distracted or led astray by an incorrect answer choice. You will feel more confident in your selection if you read the question, predict the answer, and then find your prediction among the answer choices. After using this strategy, be sure to still read all of the answer choices carefully and completely. If you feel unprepared, you should not attempt to predict the answers. This would be a waste of time and an opportunity for your mind to wander in the wrong direction.

2. Reading the Whole Question

Too often, test takers scan a multiple-choice question, recognize a few familiar words, and immediately jump to the answer choices. Test authors are aware of this common impatience, and they will sometimes prey upon it. For instance, a test author might subtly turn the question into a negative, or he or she might redirect the focus of the question right at the end. The only way to avoid falling into these traps is to read the entirety of the question carefully before reading the answer choices.

3. Looking for Wrong Answers

Long and complicated multiple-choice questions can be intimidating. One way to simplify a difficult multiple-choice question is to eliminate all of the answer choices that are clearly wrong. In most sets of answers, there will be at least one selection that can be dismissed right away. If the test is administered on paper, the test taker could draw a line through it to indicate that it may be ignored; otherwise, the test taker will have to perform this operation mentally or on scratch paper. In either case, once the obviously incorrect answers have been eliminated, the remaining choices may be considered. Sometimes identifying the clearly wrong answers will give the test taker some information about the correct answer. For instance, if one of the remaining answer choices is a direct opposite of one of the eliminated answer choices, it may well be the correct answer. The opposite of obviously wrong is obviously right! Of course, this is not always the case. Some answers are obviously incorrect simply because they are irrelevant to the question being asked. Still, identifying and eliminating some incorrect answer choices is a good way to simplify a multiple-choice question.

4. Don't Overanalyze

Anxious test takers often overanalyze questions. When you are nervous, your brain will often run wild, causing you to make associations and discover clues that don't actually exist. If you feel that this may be a problem for you, do whatever you can to slow down during the test. Try taking a deep breath or counting to ten. As you read and consider the question, restrict yourself to the particular words used by the author. Avoid thought tangents about what the author *really* meant, or what he or she was *trying* to say. The only things that matter on a multiple-choice test are the words that are actually in the question. You must avoid reading too much into a multiple-choice question, or supposing that the writer meant

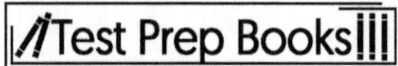

something other than what he or she wrote.

5. No Need for Panic

It is wise to learn as many strategies as possible before taking a multiple-choice test, but it is likely that you will come across a few questions for which you simply don't know the answer. In this situation, avoid panicking. Because most multiple-choice tests include dozens of questions, the relative value of a single wrong answer is small. As much as possible, you should compartmentalize each question on a multiple-choice test. In other words, you should not allow your feelings about one question to affect your success on the others. When you find a question that you either don't understand or don't know how to answer, just take a deep breath and do your best. Read the entire question slowly and carefully. Try rephrasing the question a couple of different ways. Then, read all of the answer choices carefully. After eliminating obviously wrong answers, make a selection and move on to the next question.

6. Confusing Answer Choices

When working on a difficult multiple-choice question, there may be a tendency to focus on the answer choices that are the easiest to understand. Many people, whether consciously or not, gravitate to the answer choices that require the least concentration, knowledge, and memory. This is a mistake. When you come across an answer choice that is confusing, you should give it extra attention. A question might be confusing because you do not know the subject matter to which it refers. If this is the case, don't

eliminate the answer before you have affirmatively settled on another. When you come across an answer choice of this type, set it aside as you look at the remaining choices. If you can confidently assert that one of the other choices is correct, you can leave the confusing answer aside. Otherwise, you will need to take a moment to try to better understand the confusing answer choice. Rephrasing is one way to tease out the sense of a confusing answer choice.

7. Your First Instinct

Many people struggle with multiple-choice tests because they overthink the questions. If you have studied sufficiently for the test, you should be prepared to trust your first instinct once you have carefully and completely read the question and all of the answer choices. There is a great deal of research suggesting that the mind can come to the correct conclusion very quickly once it has obtained all of the relevant information. At times, it may seem to you as if your intuition is working faster even than your reasoning mind. This may in fact be true. The knowledge you obtain while studying may be retrieved from your subconscious before you have a chance to work out the associations that support it. Verify your instinct by working out the reasons that it should be trusted.

8. Key Words

Many test takers struggle with multiple-choice questions because they have poor reading comprehension skills. Quickly reading and understanding a multiple-choice question requires a mixture of skill and experience. To help with this, try jotting down a few key words and phrases on a piece of scrap paper. Doing this concentrates the process of reading and forces the mind to weigh the relative importance of the question's parts. In selecting words and phrases to write down, the test taker thinks about the question more deeply and carefully. This is especially true for multiple-choice questions that are preceded by a long prompt.

9. Subtle Negatives

One of the oldest tricks in the multiple-choice test writer's book is to subtly reverse the meaning of a question with a word like *not* or *except*. If you are not paying attention to each word in the question, you can easily be led astray by this trick. For instance, a common question format is, "Which of the following is…?" Obviously, if the question instead is, "Which of the following is not…?," then the answer will be quite different. Even worse, the test makers are aware of the potential for this mistake and will include one answer choice that would be correct if the question were not negated or reversed. A test taker who misses the reversal will find what he or she believes to be a correct answer and will be so confident that he or she will fail to reread the question and discover the original error. The only way to avoid this is to practice a wide variety of multiple-choice questions and to pay close attention to each and every word.

10. Reading Every Answer Choice

It may seem obvious, but you should always read every one of the answer choices! Too many test takers fall into the habit of scanning the question and assuming that they understand the question because they recognize a few key words. From there, they pick the first answer choice that answers the question they believe they have read. Test takers who read all of the answer choices might discover that one of the latter answer choices is actually *more* correct. Moreover, reading all of the answer choices can remind you of facts related to the question that can help you arrive at the correct answer. Sometimes, a misstatement or incorrect detail in one of the latter answer choices will trigger your memory of the subject and will enable you to find the right answer. Failing to read all of the answer choices is like not reading all of the items on a restaurant menu: you might miss out on the perfect choice.

11. Spot the Hedges

One of the keys to success on multiple-choice tests is paying close attention to every word. This is never truer than with words like *almost*, *most*, *some*, and *sometimes*. These words are called "hedges" because they indicate that a statement is not totally true or not true in every place and time. An absolute statement will contain no hedges, but in many subjects, the answers are not always straightforward or absolute. There are always exceptions to the rules in these subjects. For this reason,

you should favor those multiple-choice questions that contain hedging language. The presence of qualifying words indicates that the author is taking special care with his or her words, which is certainly important when composing the right answer. After all, there are many ways to be wrong, but there is only one way to be right! For this reason, it is wise to avoid answers that are absolute when taking a multiple-choice test. An absolute answer is one that says things are either all one way or all another. They often include words like *every*, *always*, *best*, and *never*. If you are taking a multiple-choice test in a subject that doesn't lend itself to absolute answers, be on your guard if you see any of these words.

12. Long Answers

In many subject areas, the answers are not simple. As already mentioned, the right answer often requires hedges. Another common feature of the answers to a complex or subjective question are qualifying clauses, which are groups of words that subtly modify the meaning of the sentence. If the question or answer choice describes a rule to which there are exceptions or the subject matter is complicated, ambiguous, or confusing, the correct answer will require many words in order to be expressed clearly and accurately. In essence, you should not be deterred by answer choices that seem excessively long. Oftentimes, the author of the text will not be able to write the correct answer without offering some qualifications and modifications. Your job is to read the answer choices thoroughly and completely and to select the one that most accurately and precisely answers the question.

13. Restating to Understand

Sometimes, a question on a multiple-choice test is difficult not because of what it asks but because of how it is written. If this is the case, restate the question or answer choice in different words. This process serves a couple of important purposes. First, it forces you to concentrate on the core of the question. In order to rephrase the question accurately, you have to understand it well. Rephrasing the question will concentrate your mind on the key words and ideas. Second, it will present the information to your mind in a fresh way. This process may trigger your memory and render some useful scrap of information picked up while studying.

14. True Statements

Sometimes an answer choice will be true in itself, but it does not answer the question. This is one of the main reasons why it is essential to read the question carefully and completely before proceeding to the answer choices. Too often, test takers skip ahead to the answer choices and look for true statements. Having found one of these, they are content to select it without reference to the question above. The savvy test taker will always read the entire question before turning to the answer choices. Then, having settled on a correct answer choice, he or she will refer to the original question and ensure that the selected answer is relevant. The mistake of choosing a correct-but-irrelevant answer choice is especially common on questions related to specific pieces of objective knowledge.

15. No Patterns

One of the more dangerous ideas that circulates about multiple-choice tests is that the correct answers tend to fall into patterns. These erroneous ideas range from a belief that B and C are the most common right answers, to the idea that an unprepared test-taker should answer "A-B-A-C-A-D-A-B-A." It cannot be emphasized enough that pattern-seeking of this type is exactly the WRONG way to approach a multiple-choice test. To begin with, it is highly unlikely that the test maker will plot the correct answers according to some predetermined pattern. The questions are scrambled and delivered in a random order. Furthermore, even if the test maker was following a pattern in the assignation of correct answers, there is no reason why the test taker would know which pattern he or she was using. Any attempt to discern a pattern in the answer choices is a waste of time and a distraction from the real work of taking the test. A test taker would be much better served by extra preparation before the test than by reliance on a pattern in the answers.

Introduction to the PSAT

Function of the Test

The Preliminary SAT/National Merit Scholarship Qualifying Test (PSAT/NMSQT) is an introductory version of the SAT exam. Given by the College Board with support from the National Merit Scholarship Corporation (NMSC), the PSAT is designed to help US students get ready for the SAT or ACT. It also serves as a qualifying measure to identify students for college scholarships, including the National Merit Scholarship Program. Students taking the PSAT/NMSQT are automatically considered for the National Merit Scholarship Program, a contest that recognizes and awards scholars based on academic performance. About 50,000 pupils are acknowledged for extraordinary PSAT scores every year. Approximately 7,800 of these students become will be awarded scholarships for college.

Over 3.5 million high school students take the PSAT every year. Most are sophomore or junior high school students residing in the US. However, younger students may also register to take the PSAT. Students who are not US citizens or residents can take the PSAT as well, by locating and contacting a local school that offers it.

Test Administration

The PSAT/NMSQT is offered on dates in October throughout the United States. Some schools will pay all or part of the exam registration fee for their pupils. Since the financial responsibility of the student for the exam is different for each school, it is best to consult the school's guidance department for specifics. All the tests that fall under the SAT umbrella (including the PSAT) were made primarily digital in 2024.

Students with documented disabilities can contact the College Board to make alternative arrangements to take the PSAT. All reasonable applications are reviewed.

Test Format

The Reading and Writing portion of the PSAT measures comprehension, requiring candidates to read short passages of fiction and non-fiction, including informational visuals such as charts, tables and graphs, and answer questions based on this content. It also requires students to evaluate and edit writing to obtain an answer that correctly conveys the information given in the passage.

Four critical sectors are tested for the math section: Algebra, advanced math, problem-solving and data analysis, and geometry and trigonometry.

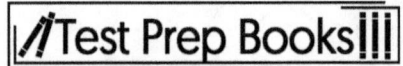

Introduction to the PSAT

The PSAT contains 98 questions divided between four modules. The first two modules are Reading and Writing, while the second two modules are Math. While most questions are multiple choice, some math questions require the user to input the answer as a number.

Section	Time (In Minutes)	Number of Questions
Reading and Writing: Module 1	32	27
Reading and Writing: Module 2	32	27
Math: Module 1	35	22
Math: Module 2	35	22
Total	134	98

Scoring

Scores for the PSAT are based on a scale of 320 to 1520, with 1520 being the best possible score. Scores range from 160-760 for the Math section and 160-760 for the Reading and Writing and Language combined. The PSAT does not penalize for incorrect answers, so you should submit an answer for every question.

Scores are usually released and available online within 4-6 weeks after the test.

Mean, or average, scores received by characteristic US test-takers, are broken down by grade level. The report ranks scores based on a percentile between 1 and 99 so students can see how they measured up to other test takers. Average (50th percentile), scores range from about 470 to 480 in each section, for a total of 940 to 960. Good scores are typically defined as higher than 50 percent. Scores in the top five percent or higher are in contention for National Merit Semifinalist and Finalist slots, but scholarships usually only go to the top one percent of 10th graders taking the PSAT.

Recent Developments

As of 2024, the PSAT/NMSQT test is now shorter than previous versions, taking only 2 hours and 14 minutes while it was previously around 3 hours. There are also substantially fewer questions, so those taking the test will have more time per question than previously.

While previous versions of the test included large passages of text with multiple questions per passage, the newer version uses shorter passages and only has one question per passage.

Additionally, the test is now completely digital, so access to an appropriate computer testing device is required.

Study Prep Plan for the PSAT

1 **Schedule -** Use one of our study schedules below or come up with one of your own.

2 **Relax -** Test anxiety can hurt even the best students. There are many ways to reduce stress. Find the one that works best for you.

3 **Execute -** Once you have a good plan in place, be sure to stick to it.

One Week Study Schedule

Day 1	Reading and Writing Section
Day 2	Standard English Conventions
Day 3	Math Section
Day 4	Advanced Math
Day 5	Problem-Solving and Data Analysis
Day 6	PSAT Practice Test 1
Day 7	Take Your Exam!

Two Week Study Schedule

Day 1	Reading and Writing Section	Day 8	Problem-Solving and Data Analysis
Day 2	Information and Ideas	Day 9	Geometry and Trigonometry
Day 3	Standard English Conventions	Day 10	PSAT Practice Test 1
Day 4	Expression of Ideas	Day 11	PSAT Practice Test 2
Day 5	Math Section	Day 12	PSAT Practice Test 3
Day 6	Advanced Math	Day 13	PSAT Practice Test 4
Day 7	Solving a System of One Linear Equation...	Day 14	Take Your Exam!

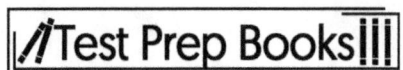

Study Prep Plan for the PSAT

One Month Study Schedule	Day 1	Reading and Writing Section	Day 11	Math Section	Day 21	Operations with Complex Numbers
	Day 2	Rhetoric and Synthesis	Day 12	Creating, Solving, and Interpreting Systems...	Day 22	Similarity, Congruence, and Triangles
	Day 3	Information and Ideas	Day 13	Algebraically Solving Systems of Two Linear...	Day 23	Practice Test 1
	Day 4	Analysis of Science Excerpts	Day 14	Advanced Math	Day 24	Practice Test 2
	Day 5	Standard English Conventions	Day 15	Solving a Quadratic Equation	Day 25	Practice Test 3
	Day 6	Shifts in Construction	Day 16	Solving a System of One Linear Equation...	Day 26	Practice Test 4
	Day 7	Logical Comparison	Day 17	Understanding a Nonlinear Relationship Between Two Variables	Day 27	Practice Test 5
	Day 8	Expression of Ideas	Day 18	Problem-Solving and Data Analysis	Day 28	Practice Test 6
	Day 9	Proposition	Day 19	Investigating Key Features of a Graph	Day 29	Practice Test 7
	Day 10	Syntax	Day 20	Geometry and Trigonometry	Day 30	Take Your Exam!

Build your own prep plan by visiting:
testprepbooks.com/prep

As you study for your test, we'd like to take the opportunity to remind you that you are capable of great things! With the right tools and dedication, you truly can do anything you set your mind to. The fact that you are holding this book right now shows how committed you are. In case no one has told you lately, you've got this! Our intention behind including this coloring page is to give you the chance to take some time to engage your creative side when you need a little brain-break from studying. As a company, we want to encourage people like you to achieve their dreams by providing good quality study materials for the tests and certifications that improve careers and change lives. As individuals, many of us have taken such tests in our careers, and we know how challenging this process can be. While we can't come alongside you and cheer you on personally, we can offer you the space to recall your purpose, reconnect with your passion, and refresh your brain through an artistic practice. We wish you every success, and happy studying!

Reading and Writing Section

The purpose of this guide is to help test takers understand the basic principles of the reading comprehension and writing questions contained in the Preliminary SAT/National Merit Qualifying Test (PSAT/NMSQT). Studying this guide will help determine the types of questions that the test contains and how best to address them, provided the test's parameters. This guide is not all-inclusive, and does not contain actual test material. This guide is, and should be used, only as preparation to improve student's reading and writing skills for the PSAT Reading Comprehension section.

Each section addresses key skills test takers need to master in order to successfully complete the Reading portion of the PSAT. Each section is further broken down into sub-skills. All of the topics and related subtopics address testable material. Careful use of this guide should fully prepare test takers for a successful test experience.

Craft and Structure

Words in Context

Identifying words in context is an important skill on the PSAT/NMSQT. This involves a set of skills that requires the test taker to answer questions about unfamiliar words within a particular text passage. Additionally, the test taker may be asked to answer critical thinking questions based on unfamiliar word meanings. Identifying the meaning of different words in context is very much like solving a puzzle. By using a variety of techniques, a test taker should be able to correctly identify the meaning of unfamiliar words and concepts with ease.

<u>Using Context Clues</u>
A context clue is a hint that an author provides to the reader in order to help define difficult or unique words. When reading a passage, a test taker should take note of any unfamiliar words, and then examine the sentence around them to look for clues to the word meanings.

Let's look at an example.

> He faced a *conundrum* in making this decision. He felt as if he had come to a crossroads. This was truly a puzzle, and what he did next would determine the course of his future.

The word *conundrum* may be unfamiliar to the reader. By looking at context clues, the reader should be able to determine its meaning. In this passage, context clues include the idea of making a decision and of being unsure. Furthermore, the author restates the definition of conundrum in using the word *puzzle* as a synonym. Therefore, the reader should be able to determine that the definition of the word *conundrum* is a difficult puzzle.

Similarly, a reader can determine difficult vocabulary by identifying antonyms. Let's look at an example.

> Her *gregarious* nature was completely opposite of her twin's, who was shy, retiring, and socially nervous.

The word *gregarious* may be unfamiliar. However, by looking at the surrounding context clues, the reader can determine that *gregarious* does not mean shy. The twins' personalities are being contrasted. Therefore, *gregarious* must mean sociable, or something similar to it.

At times, an author will provide contextual clues through a cause and effect relationship. Look at the next sentence as an example:

> The athletes were excited with *elation* when they won the tournament; unfortunately, their off-court antics caused them to forfeit the win.

The word elated may be unfamiliar to the reader. However, the author defines the word by presenting a cause and effect relationship. The athletes were so elated at the win that their behavior went overboard, and they had to forfeit. In this instance, *elated* must mean something akin to overjoyed, happy, and overexcited.

Cause and effect is one technique authors use to demonstrate relationships. A cause is why something happens. The effect is what happens as a result. For example, a reader may encounter text such as *Because he was unable to sleep, he was often restless and irritable during the day.* The cause is insomnia due to lack of sleep. The effect is being restless and irritable. When reading for a cause and effect relationship, look for words such as *if*, *then*, *such*, and *because*. By using cause and effect, an author can describe direct relationships, and convey an overall theme, particularly when taking a stance on their topic.

An author can also provide contextual clues through comparison and contrast. Let's look at an example.

> Her torpid state caused her parents, and her physician, to worry about her seemingly sluggish well-being.

The word *torpid* is probably unfamiliar to the reader. However, the author has compared *torpid* to a state of being and, moreover, one that's worrisome. Therefore, the reader should be able to determine that *torpid* is not a positive, healthy state of being. In fact, through the use of comparison, it means sluggish. Similarly, an author may contrast an unfamiliar word with an idea. In the sentence "Her torpid state was completely opposite of her usual, bubbly self," the meaning of *torpid*, or sluggish, is contrasted with the words *bubbly self*.

A test taker should be able to critically assess and determine unfamiliar word meanings through the use of an author's context clues in order to fully comprehend difficult text passages.

Relating Unfamiliar Words to Familiar Words

The PSAT/NMSQT will test a reader's ability to use context clues, and then relate unfamiliar words to more familiar ones. Using the word *torpid* as an example, the test may ask the test taker to relate the meaning of the word to a list of vocabulary options and choose the more familiar word as closest in meaning. In this case, the test may say something like the following:

> Which of the following words means the same as the word *torpid* in the above passage?

Then they will provide the test taker with a list of familiar options such as happy, disgruntled, sluggish, and animated. By using context clues, the reader has already determined the meaning of *torpid* as slow or sluggish, so the reader should be able to correctly identify the word *sluggish* as the correct answer.

One effective way to relate unfamiliar word meanings to more familiar ones is to substitute the provided word in each answer option for the unfamiliar word in question. Although this will not always lead to a correct answer every time, this strategy will help the test taker narrow answer options. Be careful when utilizing this strategy. Pay close attention to the meaning of sentences and answer choices because it's easy to mistake answer choices as correct when they are easily substituted, especially when they are the same part of speech. Does the sentence mean the same thing with the substituted word option in place or does it change entirely? Does the substituted word make sense? Does it possibly mean the same as the unfamiliar word in question?

How an Author's Word Choice Shapes Meaning, Style, and Tone

Authors choose their words carefully in order to artfully depict meaning, style, and tone, which is most commonly inferred through the use of adjectives and verbs. The *tone* is the predominant emotion present in the text, and represents the attitude or feelings that an author has towards a character or event.

To review, an adjective is a word used to describe something, and usually precedes the noun, a person, place, or object. A verb is a word describing an action. For example, the sentence "The scary woodpecker ate the spider" includes the adjective "scary," the noun "woodpecker," and the verb "ate." Reading this sentence may rouse some negative feelings, as the word "scary" carries a negative charge. The *charge* is the emotional connotation that can be derived from the adjectives and verbs and is either positive or negative. Recognizing the charge of a particular sentence or passage is an effective way to understand the meaning and tone the author is trying to convey.

Many authors have conflicting charges within the same text, but a definitive tone can be inferred by understanding the meaning of the charges relative to each other. It's important to recognize key conjunctions, or words that link sentences or clauses together. There are several types and subtypes of conjunctions. Three are most important for reading comprehension:

- *Cumulative conjunctions* add one statement to another.
- Examples: and, both, also, as well as, not only
- e.g. The juice is sweet *and* sour.
- *Adversative conjunctions* are used to contrast two clauses.
- Examples: but, while, still, yet, nevertheless
- e.g. She was tired, *but* she was happy.
- *Alternative conjunctions* express two alternatives.
- Examples: or, either, neither, nor, else, otherwise
- e.g. He must eat, *or* he will die.

Identifying the meaning and tone of a text can be accomplished with the following steps:

- Identify the adjectives and verbs.
- Recognize any important conjunctions.
- Label the adjectives and verbs as positive or negative.
- Understand what the charge means about the text.

To demonstrate these steps, examine the following passage from the classic children's poem, "The Sheep":

> Lazy sheep, pray tell me why
>
> In the pleasant fields you lie,
>
> Eating grass, and daisies white,
>
> From the morning till the night?
>
> Everything can something do,
>
> But what kind of use are you?
>
> –Taylor, Jane and Ann. "The Sheep."

This selection is a good example of conflicting charges that work together to express an overall tone. Following the first two steps, identify the adjectives, verbs, and conjunctions within the passage. For this example, the adjectives are underlined, the verbs are in **bold**, and the conjunctions *italicized*:

> <u>Lazy</u> sheep, pray **tell** me why
>
> In the <u>pleasant</u> fields you **lie**,
>
> **Eating** grass, and daisies <u>white,</u>
>
> From the morning till the night?
>
> Everything can something do,
>
> *But* what kind of use are you?

For step three, read the passage and judge whether feelings of positivity or negativity arose. Then assign a charge to each of the words that were outlined. This can be done in a table format, or simply by writing a + or − next to the word.

The word <u>lazy</u> carries a negative connotation; it usually denotes somebody unwilling to work. To **tell** someone something has an exclusively neutral connotation, as it depends on what's being told, which has not yet been revealed at this point, so a charge can be assigned later. The word <u>pleasant</u> is an inherently positive word. To **lie** could be positive or negative depending on the context, but as the subject (the sheep) is lying in a pleasant field, then this is a positive experience. **Eating** is also generally positive.

After labeling the charges for each word, it might be inferred that the tone of this poem is happy and maybe even admiring or innocuously envious. However, notice the adversative conjunction, "but" and what follows. The author has listed all the pleasant things this sheep gets to do all day, but the tone changes when the author asks, "What kind of use are you?" Asking someone to prove their value is a rather hurtful thing to do, as it implies that the person asking the question doesn't believe the subject has any value, so this could be listed under negative charges. Referring back to the verb **tell**, after

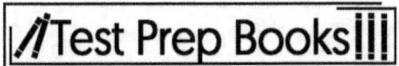

Reading and Writing Section

reading the whole passage, it can be deduced that the author is asking the sheep to tell what use the sheep is, so this has a negative charge.

+	−
<ul><li>Pleasant</li><li>Lie in fields</li><li>From morning to night</li></ul>	<ul><li>Lazy</li><li>Tell me</li><li>What kind of use are you</li></ul>

Upon examining the charges, it might seem like there's an even amount of positive and negative emotion in this selection, and that's where the conjunction "but" becomes crucial to identifying the tone. The conjunction "but" indicates there's a contrasting view to the pleasantness of the sheep's daily life, and this view is that the sheep is lazy and useless, which is also indicated by the first line, "lazy sheep, pray tell me why."

It might be helpful to look at questions pertaining to tone. For this selection, consider the following question:

The author of the poem regards the sheep with a feeling of what?
a. Respect
b. Disgust
c. Apprehension
d. Intrigue

Considering the author views the sheep as lazy with nothing to offer, Choice *A* appears to reflect the opposite of what the author is feeling.

Choice *B* seems to mirror the author's feelings towards the sheep, as laziness is considered a disreputable trait, and people (or personified animals, in this case) with unfavorable traits might be viewed with disgust.

Choice *C* doesn't make sense within context, as laziness isn't usually feared.

Choice *D* is tricky, as it may be tempting to argue that the author is intrigued with the sheep because they ask, "pray tell me why." This is another out-of-scope answer choice as it doesn't *quite* describe the feelings the author experiences and there's also a much better fit in Choice *B*.

Rhetoric and Synthesis

Rhetoric

The PSAT/NMSQT will test a reader's ability to identify an author's use of rhetoric within text passages. Rhetoric is the use of positional or persuasive language to convey one or more central ideas. The idea behind the use of rhetoric is to convince the reader of something. Its use is meant to persuade or motivate the reader. An author may choose to appeal to their audience through logic, emotion, the use of ideology, or by conveying that the central idea is timely, and thus, important to the reader. There are a variety of rhetorical techniques an author can use to achieve this goal.

An author may choose to use traditional elements of style to persuade the reader. They may also use a story's setting, mood, characters, or a central conflict to build emotion in the reader. Similarly, an author may choose to use specific techniques such as alliteration, irony, metaphor, simile, hyperbole, allegory, imagery, onomatopoeia, and personification to persuasively illustrate one or more central ideas they wish the reader to adopt. In order to be successful in a standardized reading comprehension test situation, a reader needs to be well acquainted in recognizing rhetoric and rhetorical devices.

Identifying Elements of Style

A writer's style is unique. The combinations of elements are carefully designed to create an effect on the reader. For example, the novels of J.R.R. Tolkien are very different in style than the novels of Stephen King, yet both are designed to tell a compelling tale and to entertain readers. Furthermore, the articles found in *National Geographic* are vastly different from those a reader may encounter in *People* magazine, yet both have the same objective: to inform the reader. The difference is in the elements of style.

While there are many elements of style an author can employ, it's important to look at three things: the words they choose to use, the voice an author selects, and the fluency of sentence structure. Word choice is critical in persuasive or pictorial writing. While effective authors will choose words that are succinct, different authors will choose various words based on what they are trying to accomplish. For example, a reader would not expect to encounter the same words in a gothic novel that they would read in a scholastic article on gene therapy. An author whose intent is to paint a picture of a foreboding scene, will choose different words than an author who wants to persuade the reader that a particular political party has the most sound, ideological platform. A romance novelist will sound very different than a true crime writer.

The voice an author selects is also important to note. An author's voice is that element of style that indicates their personality. It's important that authors move us as readers; therefore, they will choose a voice that helps them do that. An author's voice may be satirical or authoritative. It may be light-hearted or serious in tone. It may be silly or humorous as well. Voice, as an element of style, can be vague in nature and difficult to identify, since it's also referred to as an author's tone, but it is that element unique to the author. It is the author's "self." A reader can expect an author's voice to vary across literary genres. A non-fiction author will generally employ a more neutral voice than an author of fiction, but use caution when trying to identify voice. Do not confuse an author's voice with a particular character's voice.

Another critical element of style involves how an author structures their sentences. An effective writer—one who wants to paint a vivid picture or strongly illustrate a central idea—will use a variety of sentence structures and sentence lengths. A reader is more likely to be confused if an author uses choppy, unrelated sentences. Similarly, a reader will become bored and lose interest if an author repeatedly uses the same sentence structure. Good writing is fluent. It flows. Varying sentence structure keeps a reader engaged and helps reading comprehension. Consider the following example:

> The morning started off early. It was bright out. It was just daylight. The Moon was still in the sky. He was tired from his sleepless night.

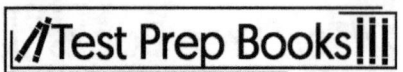

Then consider this text:

> Morning hit hard. He didn't remember the last time light hurt this bad. Sleep had been absent, and the very thought of moving towards the new day seemed like a hurdle he couldn't overcome.

Note the variety in sentence structure. The second passage is more interesting to read because the sentence fluency is more effective. Both passages paint the picture of a central character's reaction to dawn, but the second passage is more effective because it uses a variety of sentences and is more fluent than the first.

Elements of style can also include more recognizable components such as a story's setting, the type of narrative an author chooses, the mood they set, and the character conflicts employed. The ability to effectively understand the use of rhetoric demands the reader take note of an author's word choices, writing voice, and the ease of fluency employed to persuade, entertain, illustrate, or otherwise captivate a reader.

Identifying Rhetorical Devices

If a writer feels strongly about a subject, or has a passion for it, strong words and phrases can be chosen. Think of the types of rhetoric (or language) our politicians use. Each word, phrase, and idea is carefully crafted to elicit a response. Hopefully, that response is one of agreement to a certain point of view, especially among voters. Authors use the same types of language to achieve the same results. For example, the word "bad" has a certain connotation, but the words "horrid," "repugnant," and "abhorrent" paint a far better picture for the reader. They're more precise. They're interesting to read, and they should all illicit stronger feelings in the reader than the word "bad." An author generally uses other devices beyond mere word choice to persuade, convince, entertain, or otherwise engage a reader.

Rhetorical devices are those elements an author utilizes in painting sensory, and hopefully persuasive ideas to which a reader can relate. They are numerable. Test takers will likely encounter one or more standardized test questions addressing various rhetorical devices. This study guide will address the more common types: alliteration, irony, metaphor, simile, hyperbole, allegory, imagery, onomatopoeia, and personification, providing examples of each.

Alliteration is a device that uses repetitive beginning sounds in words to appeal to the reader. Classic tongue twisters are a great example of alliteration. *She sells sea shells down by the sea shore* is an extreme example of alliteration. Authors will use alliterative devices to capture a reader's attention. It's interesting to note that marketing also utilizes alliteration in the same way. A reader will likely remember products that have the brand name and item starting with the same letter. Similarly, many songs, poems, and catchy phrases use this device. It's memorable. Use of alliteration draws a reader's attention to ideas that an author wants to highlight.

Irony is a device that authors use when pitting two contrasting items or ideas against each other in order to create an effect. It's frequently used when an author wants to employ humor or convey a sarcastic tone. Additionally, it's often used in fictional works to build tension between characters, or between a particular character and the reader. An author may use *verbal irony* (sarcasm), *situational irony* (where

Reading and Writing Section

actions or events have the opposite effect than what's expected), and *dramatic irony* (where the reader knows something a character does not). Examples of irony include:

- Dramatic Irony: An author describing the presence of a hidden killer in a murder mystery, unbeknownst to the characters but known to the reader.

- Situational Irony: An author relating the tale of a fire captain who loses her home in a five-alarm conflagration.

- Verbal Irony: This is where an author or character says one thing but means another. For example, telling a police officer "Thanks a lot" after receiving a ticket.

Metaphor is a device that uses a figure of speech to paint a visual picture of something that is not literally applicable. Authors relate strong images to readers, and evoke similar strong feelings using metaphors. Most often, authors will mention one thing in comparison to another more familiar to the reader. It's important to note that metaphors do not use the comparative words "like" or "as." At times, metaphors encompass common phrases such as clichés. At other times, authors may use mixed metaphors in making identification between two dissimilar things. Examples of metaphors include:

- An author describing a character's anger as *a flaming sheet of fire.*
- An author relating a politician as having been a folding chair under close questioning.
- A novel's character telling another character to *take a flying hike.*
- Shakespeare's assertion that *all the world's a stage.*

Simile is a device that compares two dissimilar things using the words "like" and "as." When using similes, an author tries to catch a reader's attention and use comparison of unlike items to make a point. Similes are commonly used and often develop into figures of speech and catch phrases.

Examples of similes include:

- An author describing a character as having a complexion like a faded lily.

- An investigative journalist describing his interview subject as being like cold steel and with a demeanor hard as ice.

- An author asserting the current political arena is just like a three-ring circus and as dry as day old bread.

Similes and metaphors can be confusing. When utilizing simile, an author will state one thing is like another. A metaphor states one thing is another. An example of the difference would be if an author states a character is *just like a fierce tiger and twice as angry,* as opposed to stating the character *is a fierce tiger and twice as angry.*

Hyperbole is simply an exaggeration that is not taken literally. A potential test taker will have heard or employed hyperbole in daily speech, as it is a common device we all use. Authors will use hyperbole to

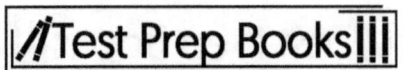

draw a reader's eye toward important points and to illicit strong emotional and relatable responses. Examples of hyperbole include:

- An author describing a character as being as big as a house and twice the circumference of a city block.

- An author stating the city's water problem as being old as the hills and more expensive than a king's ransom in spent tax dollars.

- A journalist stating the mayoral candidate died of embarrassment when her tax records were made public.

Allegories are stories or poems with hidden meanings, usually a political or moral one. Authors will frequently use allegory when leading the reader to a conclusion. Allegories are similar to parables, symbols, and analogies. Often, an author will employ the use of allegory to make political, historical, moral, or social observations. As an example, Jonathan Swift's work *Gulliver's Travels into Several Remote Nations of the World* is an allegory in and of itself. The work is a political allegory of England during Jonathan Swift's lifetime. Set in the travel journal style plot of a giant amongst smaller people, and a smaller Gulliver amongst the larger, it is a commentary on Swift's political stance of existing issues of his age. Many fictional works are entire allegories in and of themselves. George Orwell's *Animal Farm* is a story of animals that conquer man and form their own farm society with swine at the top; however, it is not a literal story in any sense. It's Orwell's political allegory of Russian society during and after the Communist revolution of 1917. Other examples of allegory in popular culture include:

- Aesop's fable "The Tortoise and the Hare," which teaches readers that being steady is more important than being fast and impulsive.

- The popular *Hunger Games* by Suzanne Collins that teaches readers that media can numb society to what is truly real and important.

- Dr. Seuss's *Yertle the Turtle* which is a warning against totalitarianism and, at the time it was written, against the despotic rule of Adolf Hitler.

Imagery is a rhetorical device that an author employs when they use visual or descriptive language to evoke a reader's emotion. Use of imagery as a rhetorical device is broader in scope than this study guide addresses, but in general, the function of imagery is to create a vibrant scene in the reader's imagination and, in turn, tease the reader's ability to identify through strong emotion and sensory experience. In the simplest of terms, imagery, as a rhetoric device, beautifies literature.

An example of poetic imagery is below:

> Pain has an element of blank
> It cannot recollect
> When it began, or if there were
> A day when it was not.
> It has no future but itself,
> Its infinite realms contain
> Its past, enlightened to perceive
> New periods of pain.

In the above poem, Emily Dickenson uses strong imagery. Pain is equivalent to an "element of blank" or of nothingness. Pain cannot recollect a beginning or end, as if it was a person (see *personification* below). Dickenson appeals to the reader's sense of a painful experience by discussing the unlikelihood that discomfort sees a future, but does visualize a past and present. She simply indicates that pain, through the use of imagery, is cyclical and never ending. Dickenson's theme is one of painful depression, and it is through the use of imagery that she conveys this to her readers.

Onomatopoeia is the author's use of words that create sound. Words like *pop* and *sizzle* are examples of onomatopoeia. When an author wants to draw a reader's attention in an auditory sense, they will use onomatopoeia. An author may also use onomatopoeia to create sounds as interjection or commentary. Examples include:

- An author describing a cat's vocalization as the kitten's chirrup echoed throughout the empty cabin.
- A description of a campfire as crackling and whining against its burning green wood.
- An author relating the sound of a car accident as *metallic screeching against crunching asphalt*.
- A description of an animal roadblock as being *a symphonic melody of groans, baas, and moans*.

Personification is a rhetorical device that an author uses to attribute human qualities to inanimate objects or animals. Once again, this device is useful when an author wants the reader to strongly relate to an idea. As in the example of George Orwell's *Animal Farm*, many of the animals are given the human abilities to speak, reason, apply logic, and otherwise interact as humans do. This helps the reader see how easily it is for any society to segregate into the haves and the have-nots through the manipulation of power. Personification is a device that enables the reader to empathize through human experience.

Examples of personification include:

- An author describing the wind as *whispering through the trees*.

- A description of a stone wall as being a hardened, unmovable creature made of cement and brick.

- An author attributing a city building as having slit eyes and an unapproachable, foreboding façade.

- An author describing spring as a beautiful bride, blooming in white, ready for summer's matrimony.

When identifying rhetorical devices, look for words and phrases that capture one's attention. Make note of the author's use of comparison between the inanimate and the animate. Consider words that make the reader feel sounds and envision imagery. Pay attention to the rhythm of fluid sentences and to the use of words that evoke emotion. The ability to identify rhetorical devices is another step in achieving successful reading comprehension and in being able to correctly answer standardized questions related to those devices.

Synthesis
Synthesis in reading involves the ability to fully comprehend text passages, and then going further by making new connections to see things in a new or different way. It involves a full thought process and requires readers to change the way they think about what they read. The PSAT/NMSQT will require a

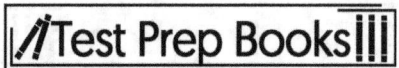

test taker to integrate new information that he or she reads during the test, and demonstrate an ability to express new thoughts.

Synthesis goes further than summary. When summarizing, a reader collects all of the information an author presents in a text passage, and restates it in an effective manner. Synthesis requires that the test taker not only summarize reading material, but be able to express new ideas based on the author's message. It is a full culmination of all reading comprehension strategies. It will require the test taker to order, recount, summarize, and recreate information into a whole new idea.

In utilizing synthesis, a reader must be able to form mental images about what they read, recall any background information they have about the topic, ask critical questions about the material, determine the importance of points an author makes, make inferences based on the reading, and finally be able to form new ideas based on all of the above skills. Synthesis requires the reader to make connections, visualize concepts, determine their importance, ask questions, make inferences, then fully synthesize all of this information into new thought.

Making Connections in Reading

There are three helpful thinking strategies to keep in mind when attempting to synthesize text passages:

- Think about how the content of a passage relates to life experience.
- Think about how the content of a passage relates to other text.
- Think about how the content of a passage relates to the world in general.

When reading a given passage, the test taker should actively think about how the content relates to their life experience. While the author's message may express an opinion different from what the reader believes, or express ideas with which the reader is unfamiliar, a good reader will try to relate any of the author's details to their own familiar ground. A reader should use context clues to understand unfamiliar terminology, and recognize familiar information they have encountered in prior experience. Bringing prior life experience and knowledge to the test-taking situation is helpful in making connections. The ability to relate an unfamiliar idea to something the reader already knows is critical in understanding unique and new ideas.

When trying to make connections while reading, keep the following questions in mind:

- How does this feel familiar in personal experience?
- How is this similar to or different from other reading?
- How is this familiar in the real world?
- How does this relate to the world in general?

A reader should ask themselves these questions during the act of reading in order to actively make connections to past and present experiences. Utilizing the ability to make connections is an important step in achieving synthesis.

Determining Importance in Reading

Being able to determine what is most important while reading is critical to synthesis. It is the difference between being able to tell what is necessary to full comprehension and that which is interesting but not necessary.

When determining the importance of an author's ideas, consider the following:

- Ask how critical an author's particular idea, assertion, or concept is to the overall message.

- Ask "is this an interesting fact or is this information essential to understanding the author's main idea?"

- Make a simple chart. On one side, list all of the important, essential points an author makes and on the other, list all of the interesting yet non-critical ideas.

- Highlight, circle, or underline any dates or data in non-fiction passages. Pay attention to headings, captions, and any graphs or diagrams.

- When reading a fictional passage, delineate important information such as theme, character, setting, conflict (what the problem is), and resolution (how the problem is fixed). Most often, these are the most important aspects contained in fictional text.

- If a non-fiction passage is instructional in nature, take physical note of any steps in the order of their importance as presented by the author. Look for words such as *first*, *next*, *then*, and *last*.

Determining the importance of an author's ideas is critical to synthesis in that it requires the test taker to parse out any unnecessary information and demonstrate they have the ability to make sound determination on what is important to the author, and what is merely a supporting or less critical detail.

Asking Questions While Reading

A reader must ask questions while reading. This demonstrates their ability to critically approach information and apply higher thinking skills to an author's content. Some of these questions have been addressed earlier in this section. A reader must ask what is or isn't important, what relates to their experience, and what relates to the world in general. However, it's important to ask other questions as well in order to make connections and synthesize reading material. Consider the following partial list of possibilities:

- What type of passage is this? Is it fiction? Non-fiction? Does it include data?

- Based on the type of passage, what information should be noted in order to make connections, visualize details, and determine importance?

- What is the author's message or theme? What is it they want the reader to understand?

- Is this passage trying to convince readers of something? What is it? If so, is the argument logical, convincing, and effective? How so? If not, how not?

- What do readers already know about this topic? Are there other viewpoints that support or contradict it?

- Is the information in this passage current and up to date?

- Is the author trying to teach readers a lesson? If so, what is it? Is there a moral to this story?

- How does this passage relate to experience?

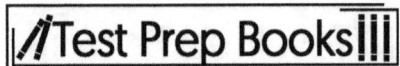

- What is not as understandable in this passage? What context clues can help with understanding?

- What conclusions can be drawn? What predictions can be made?

Again, the above should be considered only a small example of the possibilities. Any question the reader asks while reading will help achieve synthesis and full reading comprehension.

Cross-Text Connections
The PSAT/NMSQT will also test the ability to draw a conclusion by presenting the test taker with more than one passage, and then ask questions that require the reader to compare the passages in order to arrive at a logical conclusion. For example, a text passage may describe the flaws in DNA testing, and then describe the near infallibility of it in the next. The test taker then may be required to glean the evidence in both passages, then answer a question such as *would the writer of the second passage agree with the central argument of the first passage and why?* In this example, the test taker must carefully find a central concept in both passages and then rely on that information to choose the best answer.

Information and Ideas

Command of Evidence

Command of evidence, or the ability to use contextual clues, factual statements, and corroborative phrases to support an author's message or intent, is an important part of the PSAT/NMSQT. A test taker's ability to parse out factual information and draw conclusions based on evidence is important to critical reading comprehension. The test will ask students to read text passages, and then answer questions based on information contained in them. These types of questions may ask test takers to identify stated facts. They may also require test takers to draw logical conclusions, identify data based on graphs, make inferences, and to generally display analytical thinking skills.

Finding Evidence in a Passage
The basic tenet of reading comprehension is the ability to read and understand a text. One way to understand a text is to look for information that supports the author's main idea, topic, or position statement. This information may be factual, or it may be based on the author's opinion. This section will focus on the test taker's ability to identify factual information, as opposed to opinionated bias. The PSAT/NMSQT will ask test takers to read passages containing factual information, and then logically relate those passages by drawing conclusions based on evidence.

In order to identify factual information within one or more text passages, begin by looking for statements of fact. Factual statements can be either true or false. Identifying factual statements as opposed to opinion statements is important in demonstrating full command of evidence in reading. For example, the statement *The temperature outside was unbearably hot* may seem like a fact; however, it's not. While anyone can point to a temperature gauge as factual evidence, the statement itself reflects only an opinion. Some people may find the temperature unbearably hot. Others may find it comfortably warm. Thus, the sentence, *The temperature outside was unbearably hot,* reflects the opinion of the author who found it unbearable. If the text passage followed up the sentence with atmospheric conditions indicating heat indices above 140 degrees Fahrenheit, then the reader knows there is factual information that supports the author's assertion of *unbearably hot*.

In looking for information that can be proven or disproven, it's helpful to scan for dates, numbers, timelines, equations, statistics, and other similar data within any given text passage. These types of indicators will point to proven particulars. For example, the statement, *The temperature outside was unbearably hot on that summer day, July 10, 1913,* most likely indicates factual information, even if the reader is unaware that this is the hottest day on record in the United States. Be careful when reading biased words from an author. Biased words indicate opinion, as opposed to fact. The following list contains a sampling of common biased words:

- Good/bad
- Great/greatest
- Better/best/worst
- Amazing
- Terrible/bad/awful
- Beautiful/handsome/ugly
- More/most
- Exciting/dull/boring
- Favorite
- Very
- Probably/should/seem/possibly

Remember, most of what is written is actually opinion or carefully worded information that seems like fact when it isn't. To say, *duplicating DNA results is not cost-effective* sounds like it could be a scientific fact, but it isn't. Factual information can be verified through independent sources.

The simplest type of test question may provide a text passage, then ask the test taker to distinguish the correct factual supporting statement that best answers the corresponding question on the test. However, be aware that most questions may ask the test taker to read more than one text passage and identify which answer best supports an author's topic. While the ability to identify factual information is critical, these types of questions require the test taker to identify chunks of details, and then relate them to one another.

Displaying Analytical Thinking Skills

Analytical thinking involves being able to break down visual information into manageable portions in order to solve complex problems or process difficult concepts. This skill encompasses all aspects of command of evidence in reading comprehension.

A reader can approach analytical thinking in a series of steps. First, when approaching visual material, a reader should identify an author's thought process. Is the line of reasoning clear from the presented passage, or does it require inference and coming to a conclusion independent of the author? Next, a reader should evaluate the author's line of reasoning to determine if the logic is sound. Look for evidentiary clues and cited sources. Do these hold up under the author's argument? Third, look for bias. Bias includes generalized, emotional statements that will not hold up under scrutiny, as they are not based on fact. From there, a reader should ask if the presented evidence is trustworthy. Are the facts cited from reliable sources? Are they current? Is there any new factual information that has come to light since the passage was written that renders the argument useless? Next, a reader should carefully think about information that opposes the author's view. Do the author's arguments guide the reader to

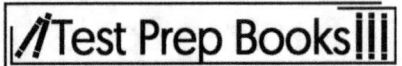

identical thoughts, or is there room for sound arguments? Finally, a reader should always be able to identify an author's conclusion and be able to weigh its effectiveness.

The ability to display analytical thinking skills while reading is key in any standardized testing situation. Test takers should be able to critically evaluate the information provided, and then answer questions related to content by using the steps above.

Making Inferences
Simply put, an inference is an educated guess drawn from evidence, logic, and reasoning. The key to making inferences is identifying clues within a passage, and then using common sense to arrive at a reasonable conclusion. Consider it "reading between the lines."

One way to make an inference is to look for main topics. When doing so, pay particular attention to any titles, headlines, or opening statements made by the author. Topic sentences or repetitive ideas can be clues in gleaning inferred ideas. For example, if a passage contains the phrase *While some consider DNA testing to be infallible, it is an inherently flawed technique,* the test taker can infer the rest of the passage will contain information that points to problems with DNA testing.

The test taker may be asked to make an inference based on prior knowledge but may also be asked to make predictions based on new ideas. For example, the test taker may have no prior knowledge of DNA other than its genetic property to replicate. However, if the reader is given passages on the flaws of DNA testing with enough factual evidence, the test taker may arrive at the inferred conclusion that the author does not support the infallibility of DNA testing in all identification cases.

When making inferences, it is important to remember that the critical thinking process involved must be fluid and open to change. While a reader may infer an idea from a main topic, general statement, or other clues, they must be open to receiving new information within a particular passage. New ideas presented by an author may require the test taker to alter an inference. Similarly, when asked questions that require making an inference, it's important to read the entire test passage and all of the answer options. Often, a test taker will need to refine a general inference based on new ideas that may be presented within the test itself.

Author's Use of Evidence to Support Claims
Authors utilize a wide range of techniques to tell a story or communicate information. Readers should be familiar with the most common of these techniques. Techniques of writing are also commonly known as rhetorical devices, and they are some of the evidence that authors use to support claims.

In nonfiction writing, authors employ argumentative techniques to present their opinion to readers in the most convincing way. Persuasive writing usually includes at least one type of appeal: an appeal to logic (logos), emotion (pathos), or credibility and trustworthiness (ethos). When a writer appeals to logic, they are asking readers to agree with them based on research, evidence, and an established line of reasoning. An author's argument might also appeal to readers' emotions, perhaps by including personal stories and anecdotes (a short narrative of a specific event). A final type of appeal, appeal to authority, asks the reader to agree with the author's argument on the basis of their expertise or credentials. Consider three different approaches to arguing the same opinion:

Logic (Logos)

Below is an example of an appeal to logic. The author uses evidence to disprove the logic of the school's rule (the rule was supposed to reduce discipline problems, but the number of problems has not been reduced; therefore, the rule is not working) and call for its repeal.

> Our school should abolish its current ban on campus cell phone use. The ban was adopted last year as an attempt to reduce class disruptions and help students focus more on their lessons. However, since the rule was enacted, there has been no change in the number of disciplinary problems in class. Therefore, the rule is ineffective and should be done away with.

Emotion (Pathos)

An author's argument might also appeal to readers' emotions, perhaps by including personal stories and anecdotes.

The next example presents an appeal to emotion. By sharing the personal anecdote of one student and speaking about emotional topics like family relationships, the author invokes the reader's empathy in asking them to reconsider the school rule.

> Our school should abolish its current ban on campus cell phone use. If students aren't able to use their phones during the school day, many of them feel isolated from their loved ones. For example, last semester, one student's grandmother had a heart attack in the morning. However, because he couldn't use his cell phone, the student didn't know about his grandmother's accident until the end of the day—when she had already passed away, and it was too late to say goodbye. By preventing students from contacting their friends and family, our school is placing undue stress and anxiety on students.

Credibility (Ethos)

Finally, an appeal to authority includes a statement from a relevant expert. In this case, the author uses a doctor in the field of education to support the argument. All three examples begin from the same opinion—the school's phone ban needs to change—but rely on different argumentative styles to persuade the reader.

> Our school should abolish its current ban on campus cell phone use. According to Dr. Bartholomew Everett, a leading educational expert, "Research studies show that cell phone usage has no real impact on student attentiveness. Rather, phones provide a valuable technological resource for learning. Schools need to learn how to integrate this new technology into their curriculum." Rather than banning phones altogether, our school should follow the advice of experts and allow students to use phones as part of their learning.

Reading for Tone, Message, and Effect

The PSAT/NMSQT does not just address a test taker's ability to find facts within a passage; it also evaluates a reader's ability to determine an author's viewpoint through the use of tone, message, and overall effect. This type of reading comprehension requires inference skills, deductive reasoning skills, the ability to draw logical conclusions, and overall critical thinking skills. Reading for factual information is straightforward. Reading for an author's tone, message, and overall effect is not. It's key to read carefully when asked test questions that address a test taker's ability to identify these writing devices. These are not questions that can be easily answered by quickly scanning for the right information.

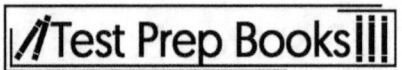

Tone

An author's *tone* is the use of particular words, phrases, and writing style to convey an overall meaning. Tone expresses the author's attitude towards a particular topic. For example, a historical reading passage may begin like the following:

> The presidential election of 1960 ushered in a new era, a new Camelot, a new phase of forward thinking in US politics that embraced brash action and unrest and responded with admirable leadership.

From this opening statement, a reader can draw some conclusions about the author's attitude towards President John F. Kennedy. Furthermore, the reader can make additional, educated guesses about the state of the Union during the 1960 presidential election. By close reading, the test taker can determine that the repeated use of the word *new* and words such as *admirable leadership* indicate the author's tone of admiration regarding President Kennedy's boldness. In addition, the author assesses that the era during President Kennedy's administration was problematic through the use of the words *brash action* and *unrest*. Therefore, if a test taker encountered a test question asking about the author's use of tone and their assessment of the Kennedy administration, the test taker should be able to identify an answer indicating admiration. Similarly, if asked about the state of the Union during the 1960s, a test taker should be able to correctly identify an answer indicating political unrest.

When identifying an author's tone, the following list of words may be helpful. This is not an inclusive list. Generally, parts of speech that indicate attitude will also indicate tone:

- Comical
- Angry
- Ambivalent
- Scary
- Lyrical
- Matter-of-fact
- Judgmental
- Sarcastic
- Malicious
- Objective
- Pessimistic
- Patronizing
- Gloomy
- Instructional
- Satirical
- Formal
- Casual

Message

An author's *message* is the same as the overall meaning of a passage. It is the main idea, or the main concept the author wishes to convey. An author's message may be stated outright, or it may be implied. Regardless, the test taker will need to use careful reading skills to identify an author's message or purpose.

Often, the message of a particular passage can be determined by thinking about why the author wrote the information. Many historical passages are written to inform and to teach readers established, factual information. However, many historical works are also written to convey biased ideas to readers. Gleaning bias from an author's message in a historical passage can be difficult, especially if the reader is presented with a variety of established facts as well. Readers tend to accept historical writing as factual. This is not always the case. Any discerning reader who has tackled historical information on topics such as United States political party agendas can attest that two or more works on the same topic may have completely different messages supporting or refuting the value of the identical policies.

Therefore, it is important to critically assess an author's message separate from factual information. One author, for example, may point to the rise of unorthodox political candidates in an election year based on the failures of the political party in office while another may point to the rise of the same candidates in the same election year based on the current party's successes. The historical facts of what has occurred leading up to an election year are not in refute. Labeling those facts as a failure or a success is a bias within an author's overall *message*, as is excluding factual information in order to further a particular point. In a standardized testing situation, a reader must be able to critically assess what the author is trying to say separate from the historical facts that surround their message.

Using the example of Lincoln's Gettysburg Address, a test question may ask the following:

> What message is the speaker trying to convey through this address?

Then they will ask the test taker to select an answer that best expresses Lincoln's *message* to his audience. Based on the options given, a test taker should be able to select the answer expressing the idea that Lincoln's audience should recognize the efforts of those who died in the war as a sacrifice to preserving human equality and self-government.

Effect
An author may want to challenge a reader's intellect, inspire imagination, or spur emotion. An author may present information to appeal to a physical, aesthetic, or transformational sense. Take the following text as an example:

> In 1963, Martin Luther King stated "I have a dream." The gathering at the Lincoln Memorial was the beginning of the Civil Rights movement and, with its reference to the Emancipation Proclamation, Dr. King's words electrified those who wanted freedom and equality while rising from hatred and slavery. It was the beginning of radical change.

The test taker may be asked about the effect this statement might have on King's audience. Through careful reading of the passage, the test taker should be able to choose an answer that best identifies an effect of grabbing the audience's attention. The historical facts are in place: King made the speech in 1963 at the Lincoln Memorial, kicked off the civil rights movement, and referenced the Emancipation Proclamation. The words *electrified* and *radical change* indicate the effect the author wants the reader to understand as a result of King's speech. In this historical passage, facts are facts. However, the author's message goes beyond the facts to indicate the effect the message had on the audience and, in addition, the effect the event should have on the reader.

When reading historical passages, the test taker should perform due diligence in their awareness of the test questions and answers up front. From there, the test taker should carefully, and critically, read all historical excerpts with an eye for detail, tone, message (biased or unbiased), and effect. Being able to synthesize these skills will result in success in a standardized testing situation.

Quantitative Information

Some writing in the test contains *infographics* such as charts, tables, or graphs. In these cases, interpret the information presented and determine how well it supports the claims made in the text. For example, if the writer makes a case that seat belts save more lives than other automobile safety measures, they might want to include a graph (like the one below) showing the number of lives saved by seat belts versus those saved by air bags.

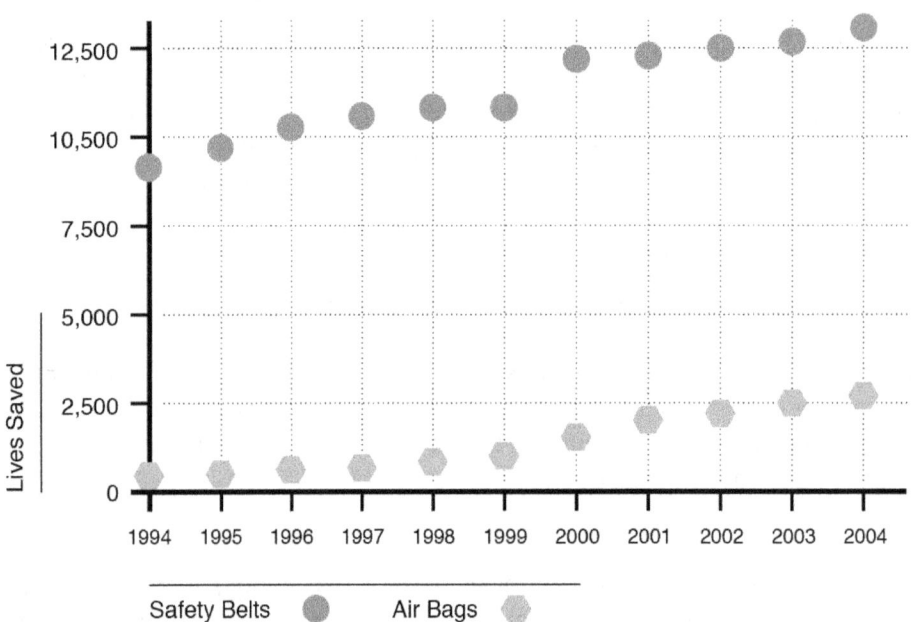

Based on data from the National Highway Traffic Safety Administration

If the graph clearly shows a higher number of lives are saved by seat belts, then it's effective. However, if the graph shows air bags save more lives than seat belts, then it doesn't support the writer's case.

Finally, graphs should be easy to understand. Their information should immediately be clear to the reader at a glance. Here are some basic things to keep in mind when interpreting infographics:

- In a *bar graph*, higher bars represent larger numbers. Lower bars represent smaller numbers.

- *Line graphs* often show trends over time. Points that are higher represent larger numbers than points that are lower. A line that consistently ascends from left to right shows a steady increase over time. A line that consistently descends from left to right shows a steady decrease over time. A line that bounces up and down represents instability or inconsistency in the trend. When interpreting a line graph, determine the point the writer is trying to make, and then see if the graph supports that point.

- *Pie charts* are used to show proportions or percentages of a whole but are less effective in showing change over time.

- *Tables* present information in numerical form, not as graphics. When interpreting a table, make sure to look for patterns in the numbers.

There can also be timelines, illustrations, or maps on the test. When interpreting these, keep in mind the writer's intentions and determine whether or not the graphic supports the case.

Analysis of Science Excerpts

The PSAT/NMSQT includes scientific passages that address the fundamental concepts of Earth science, biology, chemistry, and/or physics. While prior general knowledge of these subjects is helpful in determining correct test answers, the test taker's ability to comprehend the passages is key to success. When reading scientific excerpts, the test taker must be able to examine quantitative information, identify hypotheses, interpret data, and consider implications of the material they are presented with. This section may use the identification of hypotheses, the reading and examination of data, and the interpretation of data representation passages to determine the skill levels of test takers in the comprehension of scientific data.

Examine Hypotheses

When presented with fundamental, scientific concepts, it is important to read for understanding. The most basic skill in achieving this literacy is to understand the concept of hypothesis and, moreover, to be able to identify it in a particular passage. A hypothesis is a proposed idea that needs further investigation in order to be proven true or false. While it can be considered an educated guess, a hypothesis goes more in depth in its attempt to explain something that is not currently accepted within scientific theory. It requires further experimentation and data gathering to test its validity and is subject to change, based on scientifically conducted test results. Being able to read a science passage and understand its main purpose, including any hypotheses, helps the test taker understand data-driven evidence. It helps the test taker to be able to correctly answer questions about the science excerpt they are asked to read.

When reading to identify a hypothesis, a test taker should ask, "What is the passage trying to establish? What is the passage's main idea? What evidence does the passage contain that either supports or refutes this idea?" Asking oneself these questions will help identify a hypothesis. Additionally, hypotheses are logical statements that are testable and use very precise language.

Review the following hypothesis example:

> Consuming excess sugar in the form of beverages has a greater impact on childhood obesity and subsequent weight gain than excessive sugar from food.

While this is likely a true statement, it is still only a conceptual idea in a text passage regarding how sugar consumption affects childhood obesity, unless the passage also contains tested data that either proves or disproves the statement. A test taker could expect the rest of the passage to cite data proving that children who drink empty calories gain more weight and are more likely to be obese than children who eat sugary snacks.

A hypothesis goes further in that, given its ability to be proven or disproven, it may result in further hypotheses that require extended research. For example, the hypothesis regarding sugar consumption in drinks, after undergoing rigorous testing, may lead scientists to state another hypothesis such as the following:

> Consuming excess sugar in the form of beverages as opposed to food items is a habit found in mostly sedentary children.

This new, working hypothesis further focuses not just on the source of an excess of calories, but tries an "educated guess" that empty caloric intake has a direct, subsequent impact on physical behavior.

The data-driven chart below is similar to an illustration a test taker might see in relation to the hypothesis on sugar consumption in children:

The Effect of Excess Sugar on Activity

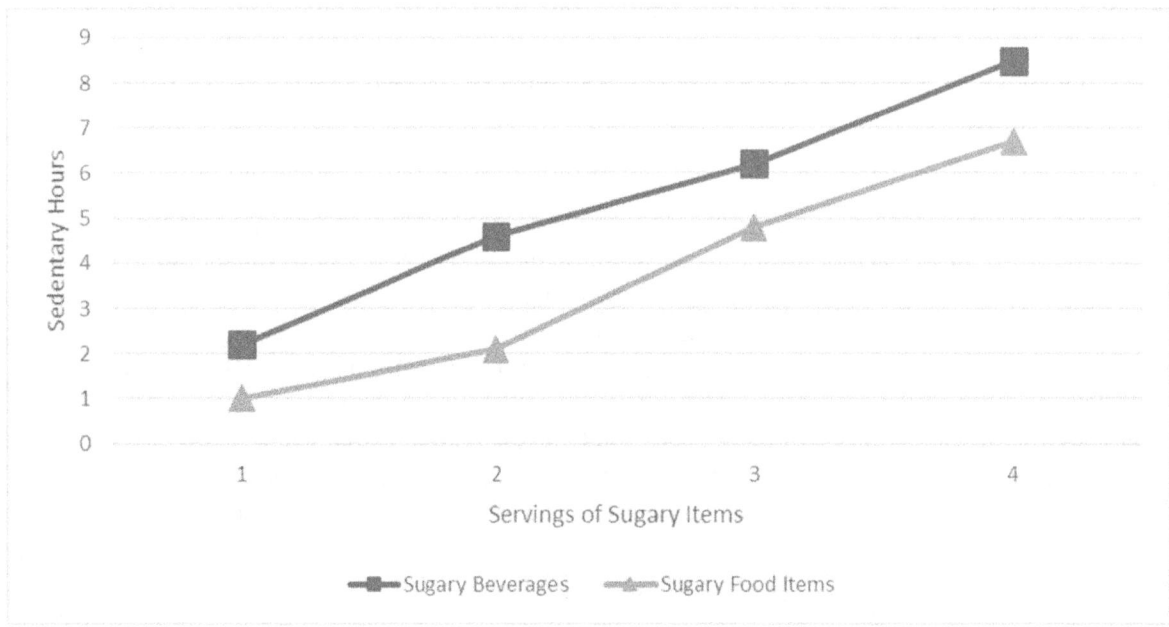

While this guide will address other data-driven passages a test taker could expect to see within a given science excerpt, note that the hypothesis regarding childhood sugar intake and rate of exercise has undergone scientific examination and yielded results that support its truth.

When reading a science passage to determine its hypothesis, a test taker should look for a concept that attempts to explain a phenomenon, is testable, is logical, is precisely worded, and yields data-driven results. The test taker should scan the presented passage for any word or data-driven clues that will help identify the hypothesis, and then be able to correctly answer test questions regarding the hypothesis by using their critical thinking skills.

Reading and Writing Section

Interpreting Data and Considering Implications

The PSAT/NMSQT is likely to contain one or more data-driven science passages that require the test taker to examine evidence within a particular type of graphic. The test taker will then be required to interpret the data and answer questions demonstrating their ability to draw logical conclusions.

In general, there are two types of data: qualitative and quantitative. Science passages may contain both, but simply put, quantitative data is reflected numerically and qualitative is not. Qualitative data is based on its qualities. In other words, qualitative data tends to present information more in subjective generalities (for example, relating to size or appearance). Quantitative data is based on numerical findings such as percentages. Quantitative data will be described in numerical terms. While both types of data are valid, the test taker will more likely be faced with having to interpret quantitative data through one or more graphic(s), and then be required to answer questions regarding the numerical data. The section of this study guide briefly addresses how data may be displayed in line graphs, bar charts, circle graphs, and scatter plots. A test taker should take the time to learn the skills it takes to interpret quantitative data.

Line Graph

An example of a line graph is as follows:

Cell Phone Use in Kiteville, 2000-2006

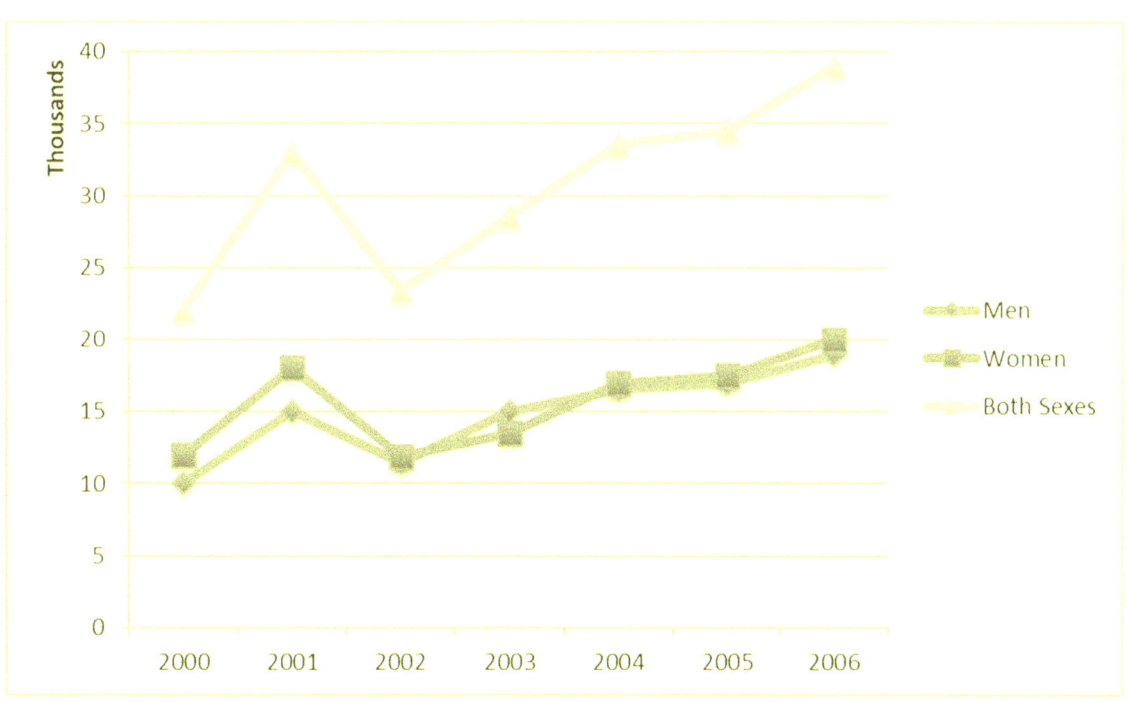

A line graph presents quantitative data on both horizontal (side to side) and vertical (up and down) axes. It requires the test taker to examine information across varying data points. When reading a line graph, a test taker should pay attention to any headings, as these indicate a title for the data it contains. In the above example, the test taker can anticipate the line graph contains numerical data regarding the use of cellphones during a certain time period. From there, a test taker should carefully read any outlying words or phrases that will help determine the meaning of data within the horizontal and vertical axes. In this example, the vertical axis displays the total number of people in increments of 5,000. Horizontally, the graph displays yearly markers, and the reader can assume the data presented accounts for a full calendar year. In addition, the line graph also uses different shapes to mark its data points. Some data points represent the number of men. Some data points represent the number of women, and a third type of data point represents the number of both sexes combined.

A test taker may be asked to read and interpret the graph's data, then answer questions about it. For example, the test may ask, *In which year did men seem to decrease cellphone use?* then require the test taker to select the correct answer. Similarly, the test taker may encounter a question such as *Which year yielded the highest number of cellphone users overall?* The test taker should be able to identify the correct answer as 2006.

Bar Graph

A bar graph presents quantitative data through the use of lines or rectangles. The height and length of these lines or rectangles corresponds to numerical data. The data presented may represent information over time, showing shaded data over time or over other defined parameters. A bar graph will also utilize horizontal and vertical axes. An example of a bar graph is as follows:

Population Growth in Major US Cities

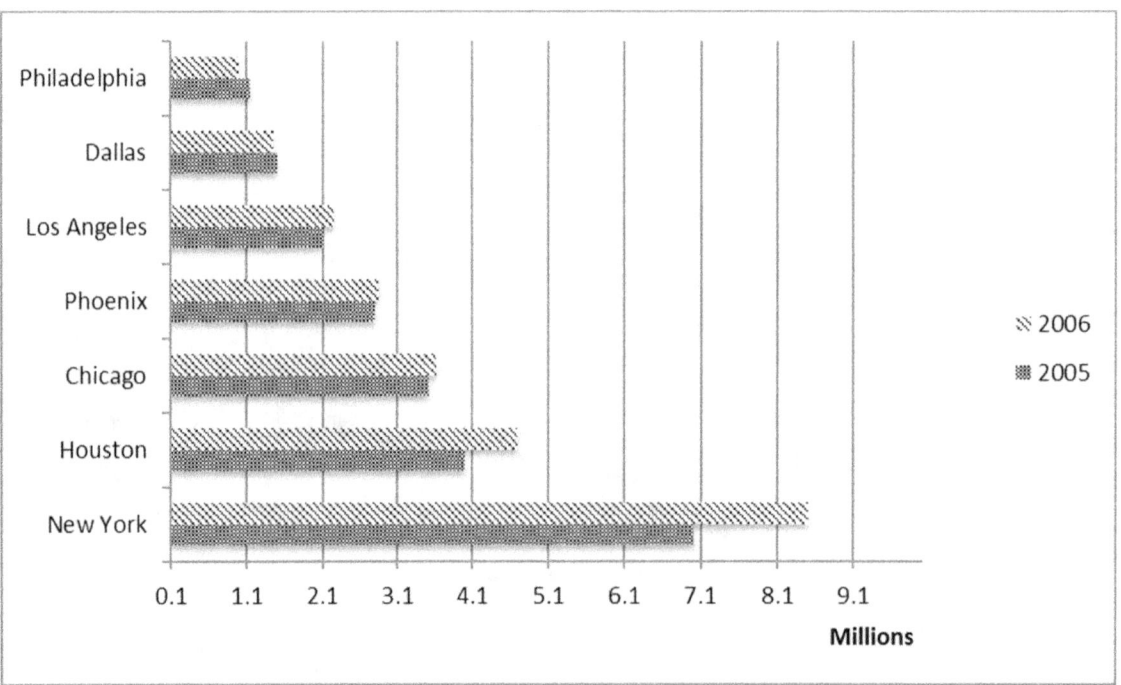

Reading the data in a bar graph is similar to the skills needed to read a line graph. The test taker should read and comprehend all heading information, as well as information provided along the horizontal and vertical axes. Note that the graph pertains to the population of some major US cities. The "values" of these cities can be found along the left side of the graph, along the vertical axis. The population values can be found along the horizontal axes. Notice how the graph uses shaded bars to depict the change in population over time, as the heading indicates. Therefore, when the test taker is asked a question such as, *Which major US city experienced the greatest amount of population growth during the depicted two year cycle,* the reader should be able to determine a correct answer of New York. It is important to pay particular attention to color, length, data points, and both axes, as well as any outlying header information in order to be able to answer graph-like test questions.

Circle Graph (Pie Chart)

A circle graph (also sometimes referred to as a pie chart) presents quantitative data in the form of a circle. The same principles apply: the test taker should look for numerical data within the confines of the circle itself but also note any outlying information that may be included in a header, footer, or to the side of the circle. A circle graph will not depict horizontal or vertical axis information, but will instead rely on the reader's ability to visually take note of segmented circle pieces and apply information accordingly. An example of a circle graph is as follows:

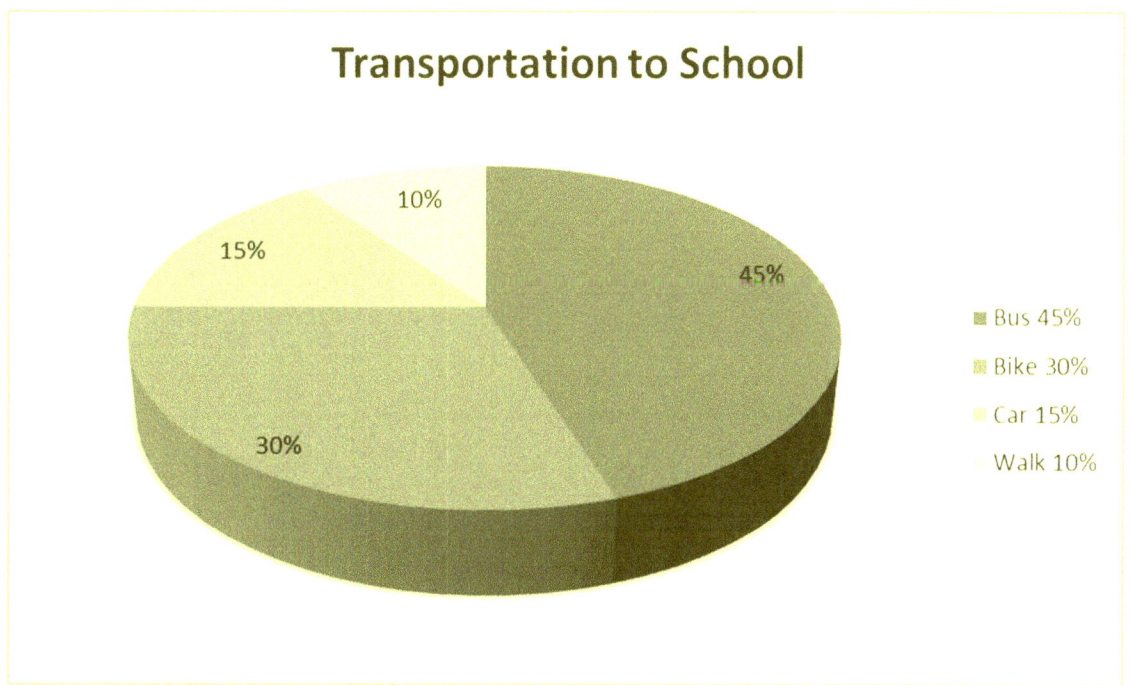

Notice the heading "Transportation to School." This should indicate to the test taker that the topic of the circle graph is how people traditionally get to school. To the right of the graph, the reader should comprehend that the data percentages contained within it directly correspond to the method of transportation. In this graph, the data is represented through the use shades and pattern. Each transportation method has its own shade. For example, if the test taker was then asked, *Which method of school transportation is most widely utilized,* the reader should be able to identify school bus as the correct answer.

Be wary of test questions that ask test takers to draw conclusions based on information that is not present. For example, it is not possible to determine, given the parameters of this circle graph, whether the population presented is of a particular gender or ethnic group. This graph does not represent data from a particular city or school district. It does not distinguish between student grade levels and, although the reader could infer that the typical student must be of driving age if cars are included, this is not necessarily the case. Elementary school students may rely on parents or others to drive them by personal methods. Therefore, do not read too much into data that is not presented. Only rely on the quantitative data that is presented in order to answer questions.

Scatter Plot

A scatter plot or scatter diagram is a graph that depicts quantitative data across plotted points. It will involve at least two sets of data. It will also involve horizontal and vertical axes.

An example of a scatter plot is as follows:

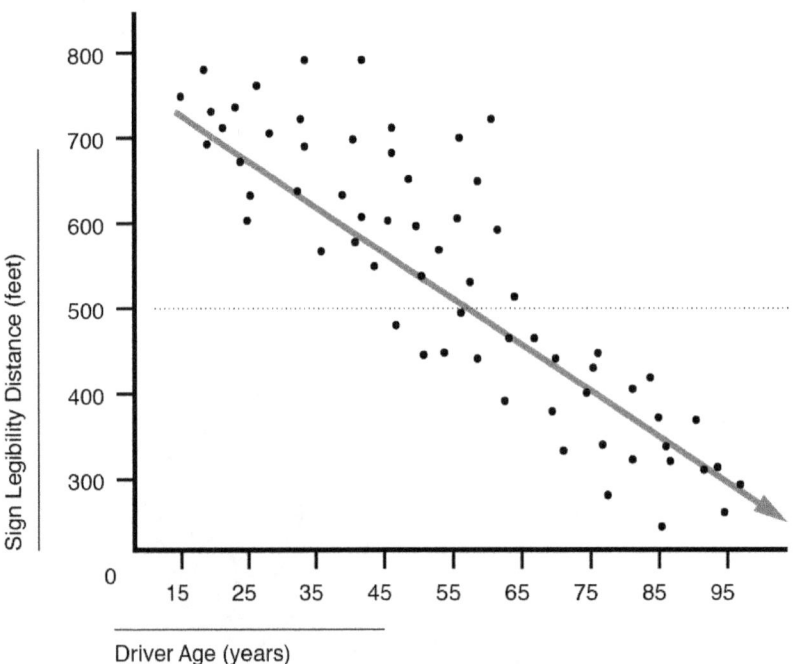

The skills needed to address a scatter plot are essentially the same as in other graph examples. Note any topic headings, as well as horizontal or vertical axis information. In the sample above, the reader can determine the data addresses a driver's ability to correctly and legibly read road signs as related to their age. Again, note the information that is absent. The test taker is not given the data to assess a time period, location, or driver gender. It simply requires the reader to note an approximate age to the ability to correctly identify road signs from a distance measured in feet. Notice that the overall graph also displays a trend. In this case, the data indicates a negative one and possibly supports the hypothesis that as a driver ages, their ability to correctly read a road sign at over 500 feet tends to decline over time. If the test taker were to be asked, *At what approximation in feet does a fifty-six-year-old driver correctly see and read a street sign,* the answer would be the option closest to 700 feet.

Reading and examining scientific data in excerpts involves all of a reader's contextual reading, data interpretation, drawing logical conclusions based only on the information presented, and their application of critical thinking skills across a set of interpretive questions. Thorough comprehension and attention to detail is necessary to achieve test success.

Standard English Conventions

Most of the topics discussed so far deal with the writer's choices and their effectiveness in a particular writing piece. In many cases, even ineffective writing can be grammatically correct. The following sections examine writing problems that actually break the rules of Standard English. These aren't questions of intent or judgment calls by the writer. These are mistakes that *must* be corrected.

Fragments and Run-Ons

A *sentence fragment* is a failed attempt to create a complete sentence because it's missing a required noun or verb. Fragments don't function properly because there isn't enough information to understand the writer's intended meaning. For example:

> Seat belt use corresponds to a lower rate of hospital visits, reducing strain on an already overburdened healthcare system. Insurance claims as well.

Look at the last sentence: *Insurance claims as well*. What does this mean? This is a fragment because it has a noun but no verb, and it leaves the reader guessing what the writer means about insurance claims. Many readers can probably infer what the writer means, but this distracts them from the flow of the writer's argument. Choosing a suitable replacement for a sentence fragment may be one of the questions on the test. The fragment is probably related to the surrounding content, so look at the overall point the writer is trying to make and choose the answer that best fits that idea.

Remember that sometimes a fragment can *look* like a complete sentence or have all the nouns and verbs it needs to make sense. Consider the following two examples:

> Seat belt use corresponds to a lower rate of hospital visits.

> Although seat belt use corresponds to a lower rate of hospital visits.

Both examples above have nouns and verbs, but only the first sentence is correct. The second sentence is a fragment, even though it's actually longer. The key is the writer's use of the word *although*. Starting a sentence with *although* turns that part into a *subordinate clause* (more on that next). Keep in mind that one doesn't have to remember that it's called a subordinate clause on the test. Just be able to recognize that the words form an incomplete thought and identify the problem as a sentence fragment.

A *run-on sentence* is, in some ways, the opposite of a fragment. It contains two or more sentences that have been improperly forced together into one. An example of a run-on sentence looks something like this:

> Seat belt use corresponds to a lower rate of hospital visits it also leads to fewer insurance claims.

Here, there are two separate ideas in one sentence. It's difficult for the reader to follow the writer's thinking because there is no transition from one idea to the next. On the test, choose the best way to correct the run-on sentence.

Here are two possibilities for the sentence above:

> Seat belt use corresponds to a lower rate of hospital visits. It also leads to fewer insurance claims.

> Seat belt use corresponds to a lower rate of hospital visits, but it also leads to fewer insurance claims.

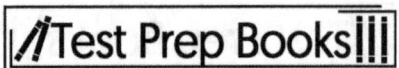

Reading and Writing Section

Both solutions are grammatically correct, so which one is the best choice? That depends on the point that the writer is trying to make. Always read the surrounding text to determine what the writer wants to demonstrate, and choose the option that best supports that thought.

Subordination and Coordination

With terms like "coordinate clause" and "subordinating conjunction," grammar terminology can scare people! So, just for a minute, forget about the terms and look at how the sentences work.

Sometimes a sentence has two ideas that work together. For example, say the writer wants to make the following points:

> Seat belt laws have saved an estimated 50,000 lives.
>
> More lives are saved by seat belts every year.

These two ideas are directly related and appear to be of equal importance. Therefore, they can be joined with a simple "and" as follows:

> Seat belt laws have saved an estimated 50,000 lives, and more lives are saved by seat belts every year.

The word *and* in the sentence helps the two ideas work together or, in other words, it "coordinates" them. It also serves as a junction where the two ideas come together, better known as a *conjunction*. Therefore, the word *and* is known as a *coordinating conjunction* (a word that helps bring two equal ideas together). Now that the ideas are joined together by a conjunction, they are known as *clauses*. Other coordinating conjunctions include *or*, *but*, and *so*.

Sometimes, however, two ideas in a sentence are *not* of equal importance:

> Seat belt laws have saved an estimated 50,000 lives.
>
> Many more lives could be saved with stronger federal seat belt laws.

In this case, combining the two with a coordinating conjunction (*and*) creates an awkward sentence:

> Seat belt laws have saved an estimated 50,000 lives, and many more lives could be saved with stronger federal seat belt laws.

Now the writer uses a word to show the reader which clause is the most important (or the "boss") of the sentence:

> Although seat belt laws have saved an estimated 50,000 lives, many more lives could be saved with stronger federal seat belt laws.

In this example, the second clause is the key point that the writer wants to make, and the first clause works to set up that point. Since the first clause "works for" the second, it's called the *subordinate clause*. The word *although* tells the reader that this idea isn't as important as the clause that follows. This word is called the *subordinating conjunction*. Other subordinating conjunctions include *after*, *because*, *if*, *since*, *unless*, and many more. As mentioned before, it's easy to spot subordinate clauses because they don't stand on their own (as shown in this previous example):

Reading and Writing Section

> Although seat belt laws have saved an estimated 50,000 lives

This is not a complete thought. It needs the other clause (called the *independent clause*) to make sense. On the test, when asked to choose the best subordinating conjunction for a sentence, look at the surrounding text. Choose the word that best allows the sentence to support the writer's argument.

Parallel Structure

Parallel structure usually has to do with lists. Look at the following sentence and spot the mistake:

> Increased seat belt legislation has been supported by the automotive industry, the insurance industry, and doctors.

Many people don't see anything wrong, but the word *doctors* breaks the sentence's parallel structure. The previous items in the list refer to an industry as a singular noun, so every item in the list must follow that same format:

> Increased seat belt legislation has been supported by the automotive industry, the insurance industry, and the healthcare industry.

Another common mistake in parallel structure might look like this:

> Before the accident, Maria enjoyed swimming, running, and played soccer.

Here, the words "played soccer" break the parallel structure. To correct it, the writer must change the final item in the list to match the format of the previous two:

> Before the accident, Maria enjoyed swimming, running, and playing soccer.

Modifier Placement

Modifiers are words or phrases (often adjectives or nouns) that add detail to, explain, or limit the meaning of other parts of a sentence. Look at the following example:

> A big pine tree is in the yard.

In the sentence, the words *big* (an adjective) and *pine* (a noun) modify *tree* (the head noun).

All related parts of a sentence must be placed together correctly. *Misplaced* and *dangling modifiers* are common writing mistakes. In fact, they're so common that many people are accustomed to seeing them and can decipher an incorrect sentence without much difficulty. On the test, expect to be asked to identify and correct this kind of error.

Misplaced Modifiers

Since *modifiers* refer to something else in the sentence (*big* and *pine* refer to *tree* in the example above), they need to be placed close to what they modify. If a modifier is so far away that the reader isn't sure what it's describing, it becomes a *misplaced modifier*. For example:

> Seat belts almost saved 5,000 lives in 2009.

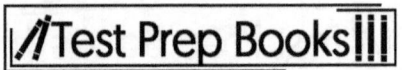

It's likely that the writer means that the total number of lives saved by seat belts in 2009 is close to 5,000. However, due to the misplaced modifier (*almost*), the sentence actually says there are 5,000 instances when seat belts *almost saved lives*. In this case, the position of the modifier is actually the difference between life and death (at least in the meaning of the sentence). A clearer way to write the sentence is:

> Seat belts saved almost 5,000 lives in 2009.

Now that the modifier is close to the 5,000 lives it references, the sentence's meaning is clearer.

Another common example of a misplaced modifier occurs when the writer uses the modifier to begin a sentence. For example:

> Having saved 5,000 lives in 2009, Senator Wilson praised the seat belt legislation.

It seems unlikely that Senator Wilson saved 5,000 lives on her own, but that's what the writer is saying in this sentence. To correct this error, the writer should move the modifier closer to the intended object it modifies. Here are two possible solutions:

> Having saved 5,000 lives in 2009, the seat belt legislation was praised by Senator Wilson.

> Senator Wilson praised the seat belt legislation, which saved 5,000 lives in 2009.

When choosing a solution for a misplaced modifier, look for an option that places the modifier close to the object or idea it describes.

Dangling Modifiers

A modifier must have a target word or phrase that it's modifying. Without this, it's a *dangling modifier*. Dangling modifiers are usually found at the beginning of sentences:

> After passing the new law, there is sure to be an improvement in highway safety.

This sentence doesn't say anything about who is passing the law. Therefore, "After passing the new law" is a dangling modifier because it doesn't modify anything in the sentence. To correct this type of error, determine what the writer intended the modifier to point to:

> After passing the new law, legislators are sure to see an improvement in highway safety.

"After passing the new law" now points to *legislators*, which makes the sentence clearer and eliminates the dangling modifier.

Shifts in Construction

It's been said several times already that *good writing must be consistent*. Another common writing mistake occurs when the writer unintentionally shifts verb tense, voice, or noun-pronoun agreement. This shift can take place within a sentence, within a paragraph, or over the course of an entire piece of writing. On the test, questions may ask that this kind of error be identified. Here are some examples.

Shift in Verb Tense

Even though test questions don't ask for verb tenses to be identified, they may cover recognizing when these tenses change unexpectedly:

> During the accident, the airbags malfunction, and the passengers were injured.

In this sentence, the writer unintentionally shifts from present tense ("airbags malfunction" is happening *now)* to past tense ("passengers were injured" has *already happened*.) This is very confusing. To correct this error, the writer must stay in the same tense throughout. Two possible solutions are:

> During the accident, the airbags malfunctioned, and the passengers were injured.

> During the accident, the airbags malfunction, and the passengers are injured.

Shift in Voice

Sometimes the writer accidentally slips from active voice to passive voice in the middle of a sentence. This is a difficult mistake to catch because it's something people often do when speaking to one another. First, it's important to understand the difference between active and passive voice. Most sentences are written in *active voice*, which means that the noun is doing what the verb in the sentence says. For example:

> Seat belts save lives.

Here, the noun (*seat belt*) is doing the saving. However, in *passive voice*, the verb is doing something to the noun:

> Lives are saved.

In this case, the noun (*lives*) is the thing *being saved*. Passive voice is difficult for many people to identify and understand, but there's a simple (and memorable) way to check: simply add "by zombies" to the end of the verb and, if it makes sense, then the verb is written in passive voice. For example: "My car was wrecked...by zombies." Also, in the above example, "Lives are saved...by zombies." If the zombie trick doesn't work, then the sentence is in active voice.

Here's what a shift in voice looks like in a sentence:

> When Amy buckled her seat belt, a satisfying click was heard.

The writer shifts from active voice in the beginning of the sentence to passive voice after the comma (remember, "a satisfying click was heard...by zombies"). To fix this mistake, the writer must remain in active voice throughout:

> When Amy buckled her seat belt, she heard a satisfying click.

This sentence is now grammatically correct, easier to read...and zombie free!

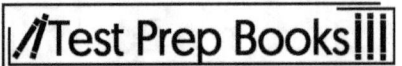

Reading and Writing Section

Shift in Noun-Pronoun Agreement

Pronouns are used to replace nouns so sentences don't have a lot of unnecessary repetition. This repetition can make a sentence seem awkward as in the following example:

> Seat belts are important because seat belts save lives, but seat belts can't do so unless seat belts are used.

Replacing some of the nouns (*seat belts*) with a pronoun (*they*) improves the flow of the sentence:

> Seat belts are important because they save lives, but they can't do so unless they are used.

A pronoun should agree in number (singular or plural) with the noun that precedes it. Another common writing error is the shift in *noun-pronoun agreement*. Here's an example:

> When people are getting in a car, he should always remember to buckle his seatbelt.

The first half of the sentence talks about a plural (*people*), while the second half refers to a singular person (*he* and *his*). These don't agree, so the sentence should be rewritten as:

> When people are getting in a car, they should always remember to buckle their seatbelt.

Pronouns

Pronoun Person

Pronoun person refers to the narrative voice the writer uses in a piece of writing. A great deal of nonfiction is written in third person, which uses pronouns like *he, she, it,* and *they* to convey meaning. Occasionally a writer uses first person (*I, me, we*, etc.) or second person (*you*). Any choice of pronoun person can be appropriate for a particular situation, but the writer must remain consistent and logical.

Test questions may cover examining samples that should stay in a single pronoun person, be it first, second, or third. Look out for shifts between words like *you* and *I* or *he* and *they.*

Pronoun Clarity

Pronouns always refer back to a noun. However, as the writer composes longer, more complicated sentences, the reader may be unsure which noun the pronoun should replace. For example:

> An amendment was made to the bill, but now it has been voted down.

Was the amendment voted down or the entire bill? It's impossible to tell from this sentence. To correct this error, the writer needs to restate the appropriate noun rather than using a pronoun:

> An amendment was made to the bill, but now the bill has been voted down.

Pronouns in Combination

Writers often make mistakes when choosing pronouns to use in combination with other nouns. The most common mistakes are found in sentences like this:

> Please join Senator Wilson and I at the event tomorrow.

Reading and Writing Section

Notice anything wrong? Though many people think the sentence sounds perfectly fine, the use of the pronoun *I* is actually incorrect. To double-check this, take the other person out of the sentence:

> Please join I at the event tomorrow.

Now the sentence is obviously incorrect, as it should read, "Please join *me* at the event tomorrow." Thus, the first sentence should replace *I* with *me*:

> Please join Senator Wilson and me at the event tomorrow.

For many people, this sounds wrong because they're used to hearing and saying it incorrectly. Take extra care when answering this kind of question and follow the double-checking procedure.

Agreement

In English writing, certain words connect to other words. People often learn these connections (or *agreements*) as young children and use the correct combinations without a second thought. However, the questions on the test dealing with agreement probably aren't simple ones.

Subject-Verb Agreement

Which of the following sentences is correct?

> A large crowd of protesters was on hand.

> A large crowd of protesters were on hand.

Many people would say the second sentence is correct, but they'd be wrong. However, they probably wouldn't be alone. Most people just look at two words: *protesters were*. Together they make sense. They sound right. The problem is that the verb *were* doesn't refer to the word *protesters*. Here, the word *protesters* is part of a prepositional phrase that clarifies the actual subject of the sentence (*crowd*). Take the phrase "of protesters" away and re-examine the sentences:

> A large crowd was on hand.

> A large crowd were on hand.

Without the prepositional phrase to separate the subject and verb, the answer is obvious. The first sentence is correct. On the test, look for confusing prepositional phrases when answering questions about subject-verb agreement. Take the phrase away, and then recheck the sentence.

Noun Agreement

Nouns that refer to other nouns must also match in number. Take the following example:

> John and Emily both served as an intern for Senator Wilson.

Two people are involved in this sentence: John and Emily. Therefore, the word *intern* should be plural to match. Here is how the sentence should read:

> John and Emily both served as interns for Senator Wilson.

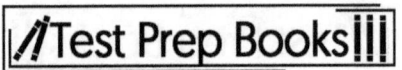

Frequently Confused Words

The English language is interesting because many of its words sound so similar or identical that they confuse readers and writers alike. Errors involving these words are hard to spot because they *sound* right even when they're wrong. Also, because these mistakes are so pervasive, many people think they're correct. Here are a few examples that may be encountered on the test:

They're vs. Their vs. There

This set of words is probably the all-time winner of misuse. The word *they're* is a contraction of "they are." Remember that contractions combine two words, using an apostrophe to replace any eliminated letters. If a question asks whether the writer is using the word *they're* correctly, change the word to "they are" and reread the sentence. Look at the following example:

Legislators can be proud of they're work on this issue.

This sentence *sounds* correct, but replace the contraction *they're* with "they are" to see what happens:

Legislators can be proud of they are work on this issue.

The result doesn't make sense, which shows that it's an incorrect use of the word *they're*. Did the writer mean to use the word *their* instead? The word *their* indicates possession because it shows that something *belongs* to something else. Now put the word *their* into the sentence:

Legislators can be proud of their work on this issue.

To check the answer, find the word that comes right after the word *their* (which in this case is *work*). Pose this question: whose *work* is it? If the question can be answered in the sentence, then the word signifies possession. In the sentence above, it's the legislators' work. Therefore, the writer is using the word *their* correctly.

If the words *they're* and *their* don't make sense in the sentence, then the correct word is almost always *there*. The word *there* can be used in many different ways, so it's easy to remember to use it when *they're* and *their* don't work. Now test these methods with the following sentences:

Their going to have a hard time passing these laws.

Enforcement officials will have there hands full.

They're are many issues to consider when discussing car safety.

In the first sentence, asking the question "Whose going is it?" doesn't make sense. Thus the word *their* is wrong. However, when replaced with the conjunction *they're* (or *they are*), the sentence works. Thus the correct word for the first sentence should be *they're*.

In the second sentence, ask this question: "Whose hands are full?" The answer (*enforcement officials*) is correct in the sentence. Therefore, the word *their* should replace *there* in this sentence.

In the third sentence, changing the word *they're* to "they are" ("They are are many issues") doesn't make sense. Ask this question: "Whose are is it?" This makes even less sense, since neither of the words *they're* or *their* makes sense. Therefore, the correct word must be *there*.

Who's vs. Whose

Who's is a contraction of "who is" while the word *whose* indicates possession. Look at the following sentence:

Who's job is it to protect America's drivers?

The easiest way to check for correct usage is to replace the word *who's* with "who is" and see if the sentence makes sense:

Who is job is it to protect America's drivers?

By changing the contraction to "Who is" the sentence no longer makes sense. Therefore, the correct word must be *whose*.

Your vs. You're

The word *your* indicates possession, while *you're* is a contraction for "you are." Look at the following example:

Your going to have to write your congressman if you want to see action.

Again, the easiest way to check correct usage is to replace the word *Your* with "You are" and see if the sentence still makes sense.

You are going to have to write your congressman if you want to see action.

By replacing Your with "You are," the sentence still makes sense. Thus, in this case, the writer should have used "You're."

Its vs. It's

Its is a word that indicates possession, while the word *it's* is a contraction of "it is." Once again, the easiest way to check for correct usage is to replace the word with "it is" and see if the sentence makes sense. Look at the following sentence:

It's going to take a lot of work to pass this law.

Replacing *it's* with "it is" results in this: "It is going to take a lot of work to pass this law." This makes sense, so the contraction (*it's*) is correct. Now look at another example:

The car company will have to redesign it's vehicles.

Replacing *it's* with "it is" results in this: "The car company will have to redesign it is vehicles." This sentence doesn't make sense, so the contraction (*it's*) is incorrect.

Than vs. Then

Than is used in sentences that involve comparisons, while *then* is used to indicate an order of events. Consider the following sentence:

Japan has more traffic fatalities than the US.

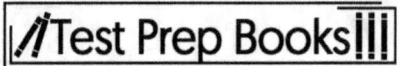

Reading and Writing Section

The use of the word *than* is correct because it compares Japan to the US. Now look at another example:

> Laws must be passed, and then we'll see a change in behavior.

Here the use of the word *then* is correct because one thing happens after the other.

Affect vs. Effect

Affect is a verb that means to change something, while *effect* is a noun that indicates such a change. Look at the following sentence:

> There are thousands of people affected by the new law.

This sentence is correct because *affected* is a verb that tells what's happening. Now look at this sentence:

> The law will have a dramatic effect.

This sentence is also correct because *effect* is a noun and the thing that happens.

Note that a noun version of *affect* is occasionally used. It means "emotion" or "desire," usually in a psychological sense.

Two vs. Too vs. To

Two is the number (2). *Too* refers to an amount of something, or it can mean *also*. *To* is used for everything else. Look at the following sentence:

> Two senators still haven't signed the bill.

This is correct because there are *two* (2) senators. Here's another example:

> There are too many questions about this issue.

In this sentence, the word *too* refers to an amount ("too many questions"). Now here's another example:

> Senator Wilson is supporting this legislation, too.

In this sentence, the word *also* can be substituted for the word *too*, so it's also correct. Finally, one last example:

> I look forward to signing this bill into law.

In this sentence, the tests for *two* and *too* don't work. Thus the word *to* fits the bill!

In addition to all of the above, there are other words that writers often misuse. This doesn't happen because the words sound alike, but because the writer is not aware of the proper way to use them.

Logical Comparison

Writers often make comparisons in their writing. However, it's easy to make mistakes in sentences that involve comparisons, and those mistakes are difficult to spot. Try to find the error in the following sentence:

> Senator Wilson's proposed seat belt legislation was similar to Senator Abernathy.

Can't find it? First, ask what two things are actually being compared. It seems like the writer *wants* to compare two different types of legislation, but the sentence actually compares legislation ("Senator Wilson's proposed seat belt legislation") to a person ("Senator Abernathy"). This is a strange and illogical comparison to make.

So how can the writer correct this mistake? The answer is to make sure that the second half of the sentence logically refers back to the first half. The most obvious way to do this is to repeat words:

> Senator Wilson's proposed seat belt legislation was similar to Senator Abernathy's seat belt legislation.

Now the sentence is logically correct, but it's a little wordy and awkward. A better solution is to eliminate the word-for-word repetition by using suitable replacement words:

> Senator Wilson's proposed seat belt legislation was similar to that of Senator Abernathy.

> Senator Wilson's proposed seat belt legislation was similar to the bill offered by Senator Abernathy.

Here's another similar example:

> More lives in the US are saved by seat belts than Japan.

The writer probably means to compare lives saved by seat belts in the US to lives saved by seat belts in Japan. Unfortunately, the sentence's meaning is garbled by an illogical comparison, and instead refers to US lives saved *by Japan* rather than *in Japan.* To resolve this issue, first repeat the words and phrases needed to make an identical comparison:

> More lives in the US are saved by seat belts than lives in Japan are saved by seat belts.

Then, use a replacement word to clean up the repetitive text:

> More lives in the US are saved by seat belts than in Japan.

Punctuation

On the test there may be a sentence where all the words are correct, but the writer uses *punctuation* incorrectly. It probably won't be something as simple as a missing period or question mark. Instead it could be one of the commonly misunderstood punctuation marks.

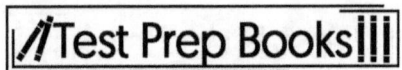

Colons

Colons can be used in the following situations and examples:

- To introduce lists
  - Carmakers have three choices: improve seat belt design, pay financial penalties, or go out of business.
- To introduce new ideas
  - There is only one person who can champion this legislation: Senator Wilson.
- To separate titles and subtitles
  - Show Some Restraint: The History of Seat Belts

Semicolons

Semicolons can be used in the following situations:

- To separate two related independent clauses
  - The proposed bill was voted down; opponents were concerned about the tax implications.

  Note: These are known as *independent clauses* because each one stands on its own as a complete sentence. Semicolons *cannot* be used to separate an independent clause from a dependent clause, nor to separate two dependent clauses.

- To separate complex items in a list
  - Joining Senator Wilson onstage were Jim Robinson, head of the NHTSA; Kristin Gabber, a consumer advocate; and Milton Webster, an accident survivor.

  Note: While items in a list are usually separated by commas, readers can easily get confused if the list items themselves contain internal commas.

Hyphens vs. Dashes

Hyphens (-) and *dashes* (–) are not the same. *Hyphens* are shorter, and they help combine or clarify words in certain situations like:

- Creating an adjective: *safety-conscious*
- Creating compound numbers: *fifty-nine*
- Avoiding confusion with another word: *re-sent* vs. *resent*
- Avoiding awkward letter combinations: *semi-intellectual* vs. *semiintellectual*

Dashes are longer and show an interruption in the flow of the sentence. In this context, they can be used much the same way as commas or parentheses:

- The legislation—which was supported by 80% of Americans—did not pass.

Reading and Writing Section

Commas
Commas are used in many different situations. Here are some of the most misunderstood examples:

- Separating simple items in a list.
    - The legislation had the support of Republicans, Democrats, and Independents.
- Separating adjectives that modify the same noun.
    - The weak, meaningless platitudes had no effect on the listeners.
- Separating independent and dependent clauses.
    - After passing the bill, the lawmakers celebrated.

        Note: "After passing the bill" is a *dependent clause* because it's not a complete sentence on its own.

- Separating quotations from introductory text.
    - Senator Wilson asked, "How can we get this bill passed?"
- Showing interruption in the flow of a sentence. In this context, commas can be used in the same way as semicolons or parentheses.
    - The legislation, which was supported by 80% of Americans, did not pass.

        Note: Commas cannot be used if the clause or phrase in question is essential to the meaning of the sentence.

During the test, it may be hard to remember all the rules for comma usage. Read the sentence and listen to its ebb and flow. If a particular answer looks, sounds, or feels wrong for some reason, there's probably a good reason for it. Look at another option instead.

Apostrophes
Apostrophes are often misused. For the purpose of the test, there are three things to know about using apostrophes:

- Use apostrophes to show possession
    - Senator Wilson's bill just passed committee.
- Use apostrophes in contractions to replace eliminated letters
    - Does not → Doesn't

Note: It's common to see acronyms made plural using apostrophes (RV's, DVD's, TV's), but these are incorrect. Acronyms function as words, so they are pluralized the same way (RVs, DVDs, TVs).

On the test, when an apostrophe-related question is asked, determine if it shows possession or is part of a contraction. If neither answer fits, then the apostrophe probably doesn't belong there.

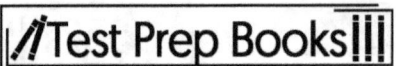

Final Tips

Usage Conventions
On the test, don't overlook simple, obvious writing errors such as these:

- Is the first word in a sentence capitalized?
- Are countries, geographical features, and proper nouns capitalized?
- Conversely, are words capitalized that should *not* be?
- Do sentences end with proper punctuation marks?
- Are commas and quotation marks used appropriately?
- Do contractions include apostrophes?
- Are apostrophes used for plurals? (Almost never!)

Look for Context
Keep in mind that the test may give several choices to replace a writing selection, and all of them may be grammatically correct. In such cases, choose the answer that makes the most sense in the context of the piece. What's the writer trying to say? What's their main idea? Look for the answer that best supports this theme.

Use Your Instincts
With the few notable exceptions above, instinct is often the best guide to spotting writing problems. If something sounds wrong, then it may very well be wrong. The good thing about a test like this is that the problem doesn't have to be labeled as an example of "faulty parallelism" or "improper noun-pronoun agreement." It's enough just to recognize that a problem exists and choose the best solution.

Take a Break
After reading and thinking about all of these aspects of grammar so intensely, the brain may start shutting down. If the words aren't making sense, or reading the same sentence several times still has no meaning, it's time to stop. Take a thirty-second vacation. Forget about grammar, syntax, and writing for half a minute to clear the mind. Take a few deep breaths and think about something to do after the test is over. It's surprising how quickly the brain refreshes itself!

Expression of Ideas

This section of the test is about *how* the information is communicated rather than the subject matter itself. This section is like being an editor helping a writer find the best ways to express their ideas. Things to consider include: how well a topic is developed, how accurately facts are presented, whether the writing flows logically and cohesively, and how effectively the writer uses language. This can seem like a lot to remember, but these concepts are the same ones taught way back in elementary school.

Organization

Good writing is not merely a random collection of sentences. No matter how well written, sentences must relate and coordinate appropriately to one another. If not, the writing seems random, haphazard, and disorganized. Therefore, good writing must be organized (where each sentence fits a larger context and relates to the sentences around it).

Reading and Writing Section

Transitions

The writer should act as a guide, showing the reader how all the sentences fit together. Consider this example:

> Seat belts save more lives than any other automobile safety feature. Many studies show that airbags save lives as well. Not all cars have airbags. Many older cars don't. Air bags aren't entirely reliable. Studies show that in 15% of accidents, airbags don't deploy as designed. Seat belt malfunctions are extremely rare.

There's nothing wrong with any of these sentences individually, but together they're disjointed and difficult to follow. The best way for the writer to communicate information is through the use of *transition words*. Here are examples of transition words and phrases that tie sentences together, enabling a more natural flow:

- To show causality: *as a result*, *therefore*, and *consequently*
- To compare and contrast: *however, but*, and *on the other hand*
- To introduce examples: *for instance, namely*, and *including*
- To show order of importance: *foremost, primarily, secondly*, and *lastly*

The above is not a complete list of transitions. There are many more that can be used; however, most fit into these or similar categories. The important point is that the words should clearly show the relationship between sentences, supporting information, and the main idea.

Here is an update to the previous example using transition words. These changes make it easier to read and bring clarity to the writer's points:

> Seat belts save more lives than any other automobile safety feature. Many studies show that airbags save lives as well. However, not all cars have airbags. For instance, some older cars don't. Furthermore, air bags aren't entirely reliable. For example, studies show that in 15% of accidents, airbags don't deploy as designed. But, on the other hand, seat belt malfunctions are extremely rare.

Also be prepared to analyze whether the writer is using the best transition word or phrase for the situation. Take this sentence for example: "As a result, seat belt malfunctions are extremely rare." This sentence doesn't make sense in the context above because the writer is trying to show the *contrast* between seat belts and airbags, not the causality.

Logical Sequence

Even if the writer includes plenty of information to support their point, the writing is only effective when the information is in a logical order. *Logical sequencing* is really just common sense, but it's also an important writing technique. First, the writer should introduce the main idea, whether for a paragraph, a section, or the entire piece. Second, they should present evidence to support the main idea by using transitional language. This shows the reader how the information relates to the main idea and to the sentences around it. The writer should then take time to interpret the information, making sure necessary connections are obvious to the reader. Finally, the writer can summarize the information in a closing section.

Although most writing follows this pattern, it isn't a set rule. Sometimes writers change the order for effect. For example, the writer can begin with a surprising piece of supporting information to grab the reader's attention, and then transition to the main idea. Thus, if a passage doesn't follow the logical order, don't immediately assume it's wrong. However, most writing usually settles into a logical sequence after a nontraditional beginning.

Focus

Good writing stays *focused* and on topic. During the test, determine the main idea for each passage and then look for times when the writer strays from the point they're trying to make. Let's go back to the seat belt example. If the writer suddenly begins talking about how well airbags, crumple zones, or other safety features work to save lives, they might be losing focus from the topic of "safety belts."

Focus can also refer to individual sentences. Sometimes the writer does address the main topic, but in a confusing way. For example:

> Thanks to seat belt usage, survival in serious car accidents has shown a consistently steady increase since the development of the retractable seat belt in the 1950s.

This statement is definitely on topic, but it's not easy to follow. A simpler, more focused version of this sentence might look like this:

> Seat belts have consistently prevented car fatalities since the 1950s.

Providing *adequate information* is another aspect of focused writing. Statements like "seat belts are important" and "many people drive cars" are true, but they're so general that they don't contribute much to the writer's case. When reading a passage, watch for these kinds of unfocused statements.

Introductions and Conclusions

Examining the writer's strategies for introductions and conclusions puts the reader in the right mindset to interpret the rest of the passage. Look for methods the writer might use for introductions such as:

- Stating the main point immediately, followed by outlining how the rest of the piece supports this claim.

- Establishing important, smaller pieces of the main idea first, and then grouping these points into a case for the main idea.

- Opening with a quotation, anecdote, question, seeming paradox, or other piece of interesting information, and then using it to lead to the main point.

Whatever method the writer chooses, the introduction should make their intention clear, establish their voice as a credible one, and encourage a person to continue reading.

Conclusions tend to follow a similar pattern. In them, the writer restates their main idea a final time, often after summarizing the smaller pieces of that idea. If the introduction uses a quote or anecdote to grab the reader's attention, the conclusion often makes reference to it again. Whatever way the writer chooses to arrange the conclusion, the final restatement of the main idea should be clear and simple for the reader to interpret.

Finally, conclusions shouldn't introduce any new information.

Precision

People often think of *precision* in terms of math, but precise word choice is another key to successful writing. Since language itself is imprecise, it's important for the writer to find the exact word or words to convey the full, intended meaning of a given situation. For example:

> The number of deaths has gone down since seat belt laws started.

There are several problems with this sentence. First, the word *deaths* is too general. From the context, it's assumed that the writer is referring only to *deaths* caused by car accidents. However, without clarification, the sentence lacks impact and is probably untrue. The phrase "gone down" might be accurate, but a more precise word could provide more information and greater accuracy. Did the numbers show a slow and steady decrease of highway fatalities or a sudden drop? If the latter is true, the writer is missing a chance to make their point more dramatically. Instead of "gone down" they could substitute *plummeted*, *fallen drastically*, or *rapidly diminished* to bring the information to life. Also, the phrase "seat belt laws" is unclear. Does it refer to laws requiring cars to include seat belts or to laws requiring drivers and passengers to use them? Finally, *started* is not a strong verb. Words like *enacted* or *adopted* are more direct and make the content more real. When put together, these changes create a far more powerful sentence:

> The number of highway fatalities has plummeted since laws requiring seat belt usage were enacted.

However, it's important to note that precise word choice can sometimes be taken too far. If the writer of the sentence above takes precision to an extreme, it might result in the following:

> The incidence of high-speed, automobile accident related fatalities has decreased 75% and continued to remain at historical lows since the initial set of federal legislations requiring seat belt use were enacted in 1992.

This sentence is extremely precise, but it takes so long to achieve that precision that it suffers from a lack of clarity. Precise writing is about finding the right balance between information and flow. This is also an issue of *conciseness* (discussed in the next section).

The last thing to consider with precision is a word choice that's not only unclear or uninteresting, but also confusing or misleading. For example:

> The number of highway fatalities has become hugely lower since laws requiring seat belt use were enacted.

In this case, the reader might be confused by the word *hugely*. Huge means large, but here the writer uses *hugely* to describe something small. Though most readers can decipher this, doing so disconnects them from the flow of the writing and makes the writer's point less effective.

On the test, there can be questions asking for alternatives to the writer's word choice. In answering these questions, always consider the context and look for a balance between precision and flow.

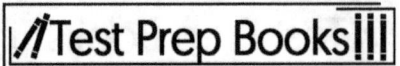

Conciseness

"Less is more" is a good rule to follow when writing a sentence. Unfortunately, writers often include extra words and phrases that seem necessary at the time, but add nothing to the main idea. This confuses the reader and creates unnecessary repetition. Writing that lacks *conciseness* is usually guilty of excessive wordiness and redundant phrases. Here's an example containing both of these issues:

> When legislators decided to begin creating legislation making it mandatory for automobile drivers and passengers to make use of seat belts while in cars, a large number of them made those laws for reasons that were political reasons.

There are several empty or "fluff" words here that take up too much space. These can be eliminated while still maintaining the writer's meaning. For example:

- "decided to begin" could be shortened to "began"
- "making it mandatory for" could be shortened to "requiring"
- "make use of" could be shortened to "use"
- "a large number" could be shortened to "many"

In addition, there are several examples of redundancy that can be eliminated:

- "legislators decided to begin creating legislation" and "made those laws"
- "automobile drivers and passengers" and "while in cars"
- "reasons that were political reasons"

These changes are incorporated as follows:

> When legislators began requiring drivers and passengers to use seat belts, many of them did so for political reasons.

If asked to identify a redundant phrase on the test, look for words that are close together with the same (or similar) meanings.

Proposition

The *proposition* (also called the *claim* since it can be true or false) is a clear statement of the point or idea the writer is trying to make. The length or format of a proposition can vary, but it often takes the form of a *topic sentence*. A good topic sentence is:

- Clear: does not weave a complicated web of words for the reader to decode or unwrap

- Concise: presents only the information needed to make the claim and doesn't clutter up the statement with unnecessary details

- Precise: clarifies the exact point the writer wants to make and doesn't use broad, overreaching statements

Look at the following example:

> The civil rights movement, from its genesis in the Emancipation Proclamation to its current struggles with de facto discrimination, has changed the face of the United States more than any other factor in its history.

Is the statement clear? Yes, the statement is fairly clear, although other words can be substituted for "genesis" and "de facto" to make it easier to understand.

Is the statement concise? No, the statement is not concise. Details about the Emancipation Proclamation and the current state of the movement are unnecessary for a topic sentence. Those details should be saved for the body of the text.

Is the statement precise? No, the statement is not precise. What exactly does the writer mean by "changed the face of the United States"? The writer should be more specific about the effects of the movement. Also, suggesting that something has a greater impact than anything else in US history is far too ambitious a statement to make.

A better version might look like this:

> The civil rights movement has greatly increased the career opportunities available for Black Americans.

The unnecessary language and details are removed, and the claim can now be measured and supported.

Support

Once the main idea or proposition is stated, the writer attempts to prove or *support* the claim with text evidence and supporting details.

Take for example the sentence, "Seat belts save lives." Though most people can't argue with this statement, its impact on the reader is much greater when supported by additional content. The writer can support this idea by:

- Providing statistics on the rate of highway fatalities alongside statistics for estimated seat belt usage.

- Explaining the science behind a car accident and what happens to a passenger who doesn't use a seat belt.

- Offering anecdotal evidence or true stories from reliable sources on how seat belts prevent fatal injuries in car crashes.

However, using only one form of supporting evidence is not nearly as effective as using a variety to support a claim. Presenting only a list of statistics can be boring to the reader, but providing a true story that's both interesting and humanizing helps. In addition, one example isn't always enough to prove the writer's larger point, so combining it with other examples is extremely effective for the writing. Thus, when reading a passage, don't just look for a single form of supporting evidence.

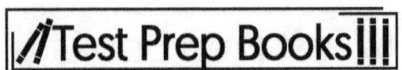

Another key aspect of supporting evidence is a *reliable source*. Does the writer include the source of the information? If so, is the source well known and trustworthy? Is there a potential for bias? For example, a seat belt study done by a seat belt manufacturer may have its own agenda to promote.

Effective Language Use

Language can be analyzed in a variety of ways. But one of the primary ways is its effectiveness in communicating and especially convincing others.

Rhetoric is a literary technique used to make the writing (or speaking) more effective or persuasive. Rhetoric makes use of other effective language devices such as irony, metaphors, allusion, and repetition. An example of the rhetorical use of repetition would be: "Let go, I say, let go!!!".

Figures of Speech

A *figure of speech* (sometimes called an *idiom*) is a rhetorical device. It's a phrase that's not intended to be taken literally.

When the writer uses a figure of speech, their intention must be clear if it's to be used effectively. Some phrases can be interpreted in a number of ways, causing confusion for the reader. In the PSAT Writing and Language Test, questions may ask for an alternative to a problematic word or phrase. Look for clues to the writer's true intention to determine the best replacement. Likewise, some figures of speech may seem out of place in a more formal piece of writing. To show this, here is the previous seat belt example but with one slight change:

> Seat belts save more lives than any other automobile safety feature. Many studies show that airbags save lives as well. However, not all cars have airbags. For instance, some older cars don't. In addition, air bags aren't entirely reliable. For example, studies show that in 15% of accidents, airbags don't deploy as designed. But, on the other hand, seat belt malfunctions happen once in a blue moon.

Most people know that "once in a blue moon" refers to something that rarely happens. However, because the rest of the paragraph is straightforward and direct, using this figurative phrase distracts the reader. In this example, the earlier version is much more effective.

Now it's important to take a moment and review the meaning of the word *literally*. This is because it's one of the most misunderstood and misused words in the English language. *Literally* means that something is exactly what it says it is, and there can be no interpretation or exaggeration. Unfortunately, *literally* is often used for emphasis as in the following example:

> This morning, I literally couldn't get out of bed.

This sentence meant to say that the person was extremely tired and wasn't able to get up. However, the sentence can't *literally* be true unless that person was tied down to the bed, paralyzed, or affected by a strange situation that the writer (most likely) didn't intend. Here's another example:

> I literally died laughing.

The writer tried to say that something was very funny. However, unless they're writing this from beyond the grave, it can't *literally* be true.

Rhetorical Fallacies

A *rhetorical fallacy* is an argument that doesn't make sense. It usually involves distracting the reader from the issue at hand in some way. There are many kinds of rhetorical fallacies. Here are just a few, along with examples of each:

- *Ad Hominem*: Makes an irrelevant attack against the person making the claim, rather than addressing the claim itself.

    o Senator Wilson opposed the new seat belt legislation, but should we really listen to someone who's been divorced four times?

- *Exaggeration*: Represents an idea or person in an obviously excessive manner.

    o Senator Wilson opposed the new seat belt legislation. Maybe she thinks if more people die in car accidents, it will help with overpopulation.

- *Stereotyping (or Categorical Claim)*: Claims that all people of a certain group are the same in some way.

    o Senator Wilson still opposes the new seat belt legislation. You know women can never admit when they're wrong.

When examining a possible rhetorical fallacy, carefully consider the point the writer is trying to make and if the argument directly relates to that point. If something feels wrong, there's a good chance that a fallacy is at play. The PSAT Writing and Language Test doesn't expect the fallacy to be named using specific terms like those above. However, questions can include identifying why something is a fallacy or suggesting a sounder argument.

Style, Tone, and Mood

Style, *tone*, and *mood* are often thought to be the same thing. Though they're closely related, there are important differences to keep in mind. The easiest way to do this is to remember that style "creates and affects" tone and mood. More specifically, style is *how the writer uses words* to create the desired tone and mood for their writing.

Style

Style can include any number of technical writing choices, and some may have to be analyzed on the test. A few examples of style choices include:

- Sentence Construction: When presenting facts, does the writer use shorter sentences to create a quicker sense of the supporting evidence, or do they use longer sentences to elaborate and explain the information?

- Technical Language: Does the writer use jargon to demonstrate their expertise in the subject, or do they use ordinary language to help the reader understand things in simple terms?

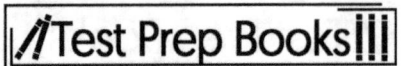

- Formal Language: Does the writer refrain from using contractions such as *won't* or *can't* to create a more formal tone, or do they use a colloquial, conversational style to connect to the reader?

- Formatting: Does the writer use a series of shorter paragraphs to help the reader follow a line of argument, or do they use longer paragraphs to examine an issue in great detail and demonstrate their knowledge of the topic?

On the test, examine the writer's style and how their writing choices affect the way the passage comes across.

Tone

Tone refers to the writer's attitude toward the subject matter. Tone conveys how the writer feels about characters, situations, events, ideas, etc. Nonfiction writing is sometimes thought to have no tone at all, but this is incorrect.

A lot of nonfiction writing has a neutral tone, which is an extremely important tone for the writer to take. A neutral tone demonstrates that the writer is presenting a topic impartially and letting the information speak for itself. On the other hand, nonfiction writing can be just as effective and appropriate if the tone isn't neutral. For instance, consider this example:

Seat belts save more lives than any other automobile safety feature. Many studies show that airbags save lives as well; however, not all cars have airbags. For instance, some older cars don't. Furthermore, air bags aren't entirely reliable. For example, studies show that in 15% of accidents, airbags don't deploy as designed; but, on the other hand, seat belt malfunctions are extremely rare. The number of highway fatalities has plummeted since laws requiring seat belt usage were enacted.

In this passage, the writer mostly chooses to retain a neutral tone when presenting information. If the writer would instead include their own personal experience of losing a friend or family member in a car accident, the tone would change dramatically. The tone would no longer be neutral. Now it would show that the writer has a personal stake in the content, allowing them to interpret the information in a different way. When analyzing tone, consider what the writer is trying to achieve in the passage, and how they *create* the tone using style.

Mood

Mood refers to the feelings and atmosphere that the writer's words create for the reader. Like tone, many nonfiction pieces can have a neutral mood. To return to the previous example, if the writer would choose to include information about a person they know being killed in a car accident, the passage would suddenly carry an emotional component that is absent in the previous examples. Depending on how they present the information, the writer can create a sad, angry, or even hopeful mood. When analyzing the mood, consider what the writer wants to accomplish and whether the best choice was made to achieve that end.

Consistency

Whatever style, tone, and mood the writer uses, good writing should remain *consistent* throughout. If the writer chooses to include the tragic, personal experience above, it would affect the style, tone, and mood of the entire piece. It would seem out of place for such an example to be used in the middle of a neutral, measured, and analytical piece. To adjust the rest of the piece, the writer needs to make additional choices to remain consistent. For example, the writer might decide to use the word *tragedy* in place of the more neutral *fatality*, or they could describe a series of car-related deaths as an *epidemic*. Adverbs and adjectives such as *devastating* or *horribly* could be included to maintain this consistent attitude toward the content. When analyzing writing, look for sudden shifts in style, tone, and mood, and consider whether the writer would be wiser to maintain the prevailing strategy.

Syntax

Syntax is the order of words in a sentence. While most of the writing on the test has proper syntax, there may be questions on ways to vary the syntax for effectiveness. One of the easiest writing mistakes to spot is *repetitive sentence structure*. For example:

> Seat belts are important. They save lives. People don't like to use them. We have to pass seat belt laws. Then more people will wear seat belts. More lives will be saved.

What's the first thing that comes to mind when reading this example? The short, choppy, and repetitive sentences! In fact, most people notice this syntax issue more than the content itself. By combining some sentences and changing the syntax of others, the writer can create a more effective writing passage:

> Seat belts are important because they save lives. Since people don't like to use seat belts, though, more laws requiring their usage need to be passed. Only then will more people wear them and only then will more lives be saved.

Many rhetorical devices can be used to vary syntax (more than can possibly be named here). These often have intimidating names like *anadiplosis*, *metastasis*, and *pareptosis*. The test questions don't ask for definitions of these tricky techniques, but they can ask how the writer plays with the words and what effect that has on the writing. For example, *anadiplosis* is when the last word (or phrase) from a sentence is used to begin the next sentence:

> Cars are driven by people. People cause accidents. Accidents cost taxpayers money.

The test doesn't ask for this technique by name, but be prepared to recognize what the writer is doing and why they're using the technique in this situation. In this example, the writer is probably using *anadiplosis* to demonstrate causation.

Practice Quiz

The next question is based on the following passage:

Wolfgang Mozart, born in 1756 in Salzburg, Austria, was a prodigious composer and musician of the Classical era who remains respected centuries later. His remarkable talent and prolific output continue to be celebrated for their undeniable influence on Western classical music.

1. As used in the text, what does the word *prodigious* most nearly mean?
    a. Ordinary
    b. Large
    c. Grotesque
    d. Exceptional

The next question is based on the following passage:

A shipwreck has recently been discovered at the bottom of Lake Superior during a search for two different ships. The wreckage dates back to 1879 and was identified as a tugboat known as the Satellite. Verifiable history regarding the Satellite is scarce, but there were allegedly no fatalities. There are 550 other shipwrecks in Lake Superior, the majority of which have not been found _____ the best efforts of divers and sonar technology. The hunt to find these long-lost ships will continue.

2. Which choice completes the text with the most logical and precise word or phrase?
    a. without
    b. despite
    c. helping
    d. including

The next question is based on the following passage:

The Importance of Being Earnest is a comedy written by Oscar Wilde. The work was written in order to mock Victorian society through satire. Lady Bracknell, a respectable Victorian woman, is a critical component of this mockery. This can be consistently seen in the text through her clever observations.

3. Which quotation from Lady Bracknell would be the most effective evidence to include in support of this claim?
    a. "Never speak disrespectfully of Society, Algernon. Only people who can't get into it do that."
    b. "To speak frankly, I am not in favor of long engagements. They give people the opportunity of finding out each other's character before marriage, which I think is never advisable."
    c. "35 is a very attractive age. London society is full of women of the very highest birth who have, of their own free choice, remained 35 for years."
    d. "To lose one parent, Mr. Worthing, may be regarded as a misfortune; to lose both looks like carelessness."

Reading and Writing Section

The next question is based on the following passage:

Salesperson	Week 1	Week 2	Week 3
Josie	67	41	98
Nathan	51	59	76
Pierre	44	65	56

A company hosts an annual contest where all salespeople have the opportunity to earn a bonus based on their sales over the course of 3 weeks. Josie, Nathan, and Pierre are three contestants who chose to take part in the competition. Josie won the competition for having the most sales. There was also a secondary prize for the contestant who showed the most consistent progress from week to week.

4. Which choice most effectively uses data from the table to make a correct, factual statement?
   a. Josie won the secondary prize because she consistently increased the number of sales from week to week.
   b. Nathan won the secondary prize because he consistently increased the number of sales from week to week.
   c. Pierre won the secondary prize because he consistently increased the number of sales from week to week.
   d. None of the contestants showed consistent progress in their sales, so that prize will not be awarded to anybody.

The next question is based on the following passage from Jacob's Room *by Virginia Woolf:*

The bareness of Mrs. Pearce's front room was fully displayed at ten o'clock at night when a powerful oil lamp stood on the middle of the table. The harsh light fell on the garden, cut straight across the lawn, _____. Mrs. Flanders had left her sewing on the table. There were her large reels of white cotton and her steel spectacles, her needle-case, and her brown wool wound round an old postcard. A daddy-long-legs shot from corner to corner and hit the lamp globe. The wind blew straight dashes of rain across the window, which flashed silver as they passed through the light. A single leaf tapped hurriedly, persistently, upon the glass.

5. Which choice completes the text so that it conforms to the conventions of Standard English?
   a. lit up a child's bucket, and a purple aster flower and reached the hedge
   b. lit up a child's bucket and a purple aster flower and reached the hedge
   c. lit up a child's bucket and a purple aster flower, and reached the hedge
   d. lit up a child's bucket, a purple aster flower, and reached the hedge

Answer Explanations

1. D: Choice *D* is the correct answer because the context clues tell us that Mozart is respected and incredibly talented. Therefore, *prodigious* can be reasonably said to mean *exceptional*. Choice *A* is incorrect because Mozart's talent is described as remarkable in the text, so to say he was *ordinary* would be a contradiction. Choice *B* is incorrect because, although *prodigious* can mean *large* in size, in this case, it is being used to describe a great amount of talent. Choice *C* is incorrect because *grotesque* is used to describe something that is unappealing or repulsive. This does not apply to Mozart in this context.

2. B: Choice *B* is the correct answer because it is the word that works best in the context of the text. The text states that divers have looked for shipwrecks, but most have not been found. In this context, it is appropriate to say that the shipwrecks have not been found *despite* the best efforts of the divers. Choice *A* is incorrect because the text says that the ships have not been found even with the best efforts. The word *without* does not work in that context. Choice *C* is incorrect because the word *helping* does not make sense within the structure of this sentence. Choice *D* is incorrect because *including* is the wrong preposition for this context.

3. C: Choice *C* is the correct answer because it mocks Victorian society's expectations for youthfulness. The quote satirically points out that women often feel the need to lie about their age and say that they are younger than they really are. Choice *A* is incorrect because it is poking fun at classism. Choice *B* is incorrect because it is discussing marital engagements and not youthfulness. Choice *D* is incorrect because it is discussing the loss of one's parents, which is unrelated to society's views on youthfulness.

4. B: Choice *B* is the correct answer because it matches the information shown in the chart. Nathan's sales consistently went up each week. Choice *A* is incorrect because Josie's sales went down in week 2. Choice *C* is incorrect because Pierre's sales went down in week 3. Choice *D* is incorrect because Nathan's sales consistently went up.

5. C: The proper use of commas can be found in Choice *C*. The "harsh light" lit up both a child's bucket and a purple aster flower, so the two object need to be grouped together within the same element of the list. Then, a comma is needed after *flower* before the last element, "reached the hedge." Choice *A* puts an unnecessary comma after *bucket*, Choice *B* does not have the needed comma after *flower*, and Choice *D* adds an unnecessary comma and removes *and* after *bucket*.

Math Section

Algebra

Creating, Solving, or Interpreting a Linear Expression or Equation in One Variable

Linear expressions and equations are concise mathematical statements that can be written to model a variety of scenarios. Questions found pertaining to this topic will contain one variable only. A variable is an unknown quantity, usually denoted by a letter ($x, n, p,$ etc.). In the case of linear expressions and equations, the power of the variable (its exponent) is 1. A variable without a visible exponent is raised to the first power.

Writing Linear Expressions and Equations

A linear expression is a statement about an unknown quantity expressed in mathematical symbols. The statement "five times a number added to forty" can be expressed as $5x + 40$. A linear equation is a statement in which two expressions (at least one containing a variable) are equal to each other. The statement "five times a number added to forty is equal to ten" can be expressed as:

$$5x + 40 = 10$$

Real-world scenarios can also be expressed mathematically. Consider the following:

> Bob had $20 and Tom had $4. After selling 4 ice cream cones to Bob, Tom has as much money as Bob.

The cost of an ice cream cone is an unknown quantity and can be represented by a variable. The amount of money Bob has after his purchase is four times the cost of an ice cream cone subtracted from his original $20. The amount of money Tom has after his sale is four times the cost of an ice cream cone added to his original $4. This can be expressed as:

$$20 - 4x = 4x + 4$$

x represents the cost of an ice cream cone.

When expressing a verbal or written statement mathematically, it is key to understand words or phrases that can be represented with symbols. The following are examples:

Symbol	Phrase
$+$	added to, increased by, sum of, more than
$-$	decreased by, difference between, less than, take away
x	multiplied by, 3 (4, 5 ...) times as large, product of
$\div$	divided by, quotient of, half (third, etc.) of
$=$	is, the same as, results in, as much as
$x, t, n,$ etc.	a number, unknown quantity, value of

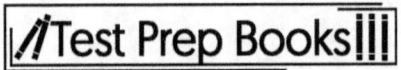

Math Section

Evaluating and Simplifying Algebraic Expressions

Given an algebraic expression, students may be asked to evaluate for given values of variable(s). In doing so, students will arrive at a numerical value as an answer. For example:

$$\text{Evaluate } a - 2b + ab \text{ for } a = 3 \text{ and } b = -1.$$

To evaluate an expression, the given values should be substituted for the variables and simplified using the order of operations. In this case:

$$(3) - 2(-1) + (3)(-1)$$

Parentheses are used when substituting.

Given an algebraic expression, students may be asked to simplify the expression. For example:

$$\text{Simplify } 5x^2 - 10x + 2 - 8x^2 + x - 1.$$

Simplifying algebraic expressions requires combining like terms. A term is a number, variable, or product of a number and variables separated by addition and subtraction. The terms in the above expression are: $5x^2, -10x, 2, -8x^2, x,$ and -1. Like terms have the same variables raised to the same powers (exponents). To combine like terms, the coefficients (numerical factor of the term including sign) are added, while the variables and their powers are kept the same. The example above simplifies to:

$$-3x^2 - 9x + 1$$

Solving Linear Equations

When asked to solve a linear equation, it requires determining a numerical value for the unknown variable. Given a linear equation involving addition, subtraction, multiplication, and division, isolation of the variable is done by working backward. Addition and subtraction are inverse operations, as are multiplication and division; therefore, they can be used to cancel each other out.

The first steps to solving linear equations are to distribute if necessary and combine any like terms that are on the same side of the equation. Sides of an equation are separated by an = sign. Next, the equation should be manipulated to get the variable on one side. Whatever is done to one side of an equation, must be done to the other side to remain equal. Then, the variable should be isolated by using inverse operations to undo the order of operations backward. Undo addition and subtraction, then undo multiplication and division.

Creating, Solving, or Interpreting Linear Inequalities in One Variable

Linear inequalities and linear equations are both comparisons of two algebraic expressions. However, unlike equations in which the expressions are equal to each other, linear inequalities compare expressions that are unequal. Linear equations typically have one value for the variable that makes the statement true. Linear inequalities generally have an infinite number of values that make the statement true. Exceptions to these last two statements are covered in Section 6.

Writing Linear Inequalities

Linear inequalities are a concise mathematical way to express the relationship between unequal values. More specifically, they describe in what way the values are unequal. A value could be greater than (>); less than (<); greater than or equal to (≥); or less than or equal to (≤) another value. The statement "five times a number added to forty is more than sixty-five" can be expressed as:

$$5x + 40 > 65$$

Common words and phrases that express inequalities are:

Symbol	Phrase
<	is under, is below, smaller than, beneath
>	is above, is over, bigger than, exceeds
≤	no more than, at most, maximum
≥	no less than, at least, minimum

Solving Linear Inequalities

When solving a linear inequality, the solution is the set of all numbers that makes the statement true. The inequality $x + 2 \geq 6$ has a solution set of 4 and every number greater than 4 (4.0001, 5, 12, 107, etc.). Adding 2 to 4 or any number greater than 4 would result in a value that is greater than or equal to 6. Therefore, $x \geq 4$ would be the solution set.

Solution sets for linear inequalities often will be displayed using a number line. If a value is included in the set (≥ or ≤), there is a shaded dot placed on that value and an arrow extending in the direction of the solutions. For a variable > or ≥ a number, the arrow would point right on the number line (the direction where the numbers increase); and if a variable is < or ≤ a number, the arrow would point left (where the numbers decrease). If the value is not included in the set (> or <), an open circle on that value would be used with an arrow in the appropriate direction.

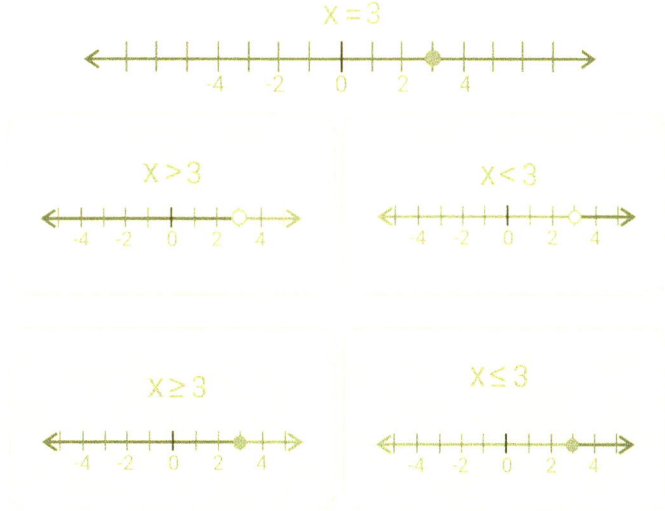

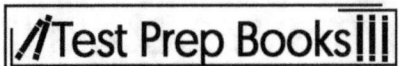

Students may be asked to write a linear inequality given a graph of its solution set. To do so, they should identify whether the value is included (shaded dot or open circle) and the direction in which the arrow is pointing.

In order to algebraically solve a linear inequality, the same steps should be followed as in solving a linear equation (see section on *Solving Linear Equations*). The inequality symbol stays the same for all operations EXCEPT when multiplying or dividing by a negative number. If multiplying or dividing by a negative number while solving an inequality, the relationship reverses (the sign flips). Multiplying or dividing by a positive does not change the relationship, so the sign stays the same. In other words, > switches to < and vice versa. An example is shown below.

Solve $-2(x + 4) \leq 22$ for the value of x.

First, distribute -2 to the binomial by multiplying:

$$-2x - 8 \leq 22$$

Next, add 8 to both sides to isolate the variable:

$$-2x \leq 30$$

Divide both sides by -2 to solve for x:

$$x \geq -15$$

Building a Linear Function that Models a Linear Relationship Between Two Quantities

Linear relationships between two quantities can be expressed in two ways: function notation or as a linear equation with two variables. The relationship is referred to as linear because its graph is represented by a line. For a relationship to be linear, both variables must be raised to the first power only.

Function/Linear Equation Notation

A relation is a set of input and output values that can be written as ordered pairs. A function is a relation in which each input is paired with exactly one output. The domain of a function consists of all inputs, and the range consists of all outputs. Graphing the ordered pairs of a linear function produces a straight line. An example of a function would be:

$$f(x) = 4x + 4$$

read "f of x is equal to four times x plus four." In this example, the input would be x and the output would be $f(x)$. Ordered pairs would be represented as $(x, f(x))$. To find the output for an input value of 3, 3 would be substituted for x into the function as follows: $f(3) = 4(3) + 4$, resulting in $f(3) = 16$. Therefore, the ordered pair:

$$(3, f(3)) = (3, 16)$$

Math Section

Note $f(x)$ is a function of x denoted by f. Functions of x could be named $g(x)$, read "g of x"; $p(x)$, read "p of x"; etc.

A linear function could also be written in the form of an equation with two variables. Typically, the variable x represents the inputs and the variable y represents the outputs. The variable x is considered the independent variable and y the dependent variable. The above function would be written as:

$$y = 4x + 4$$

Ordered pairs are written in the form (x, y).

Writing Linear Equations in Two Variables
When writing linear equations in two variables, the process depends on the information given. Questions will typically provide the slope of the line and its y-intercept, an ordered pair and the slope, or two ordered pairs.

Given the Slope and Y-Intercept
Linear equations are commonly written in slope-intercept form, $y = mx + b$, where m represents the slope of the line and b represents the y-intercept. The slope is the rate of change between the variables, usually expressed as a whole number or fraction. The y-intercept is the value of y when $x = 0$ (the point where the line intercepts the y-axis on a graph). Given the slope and y-intercept of a line, the values are substituted for m and b into the equation. A line with a slope of $\frac{1}{2}$ and y-intercept of -2 would have an equation:

$$y = \frac{1}{2}x - 2$$

Given an Ordered Pair and the Slope
The point-slope form of a line:

$$y - y_1 = m(x - x_1)$$

is used to write an equation when given an ordered pair (point on the equation's graph) for the function and its rate of change (slope of the line). The values for the slope, m, and the point (x_1, y_1) are substituted into the point-slope form to obtain the equation of the line. A line with a slope of 3 and an ordered pair $(4, -2)$ would have an equation:

$$y - (-2) = 3(x - 4)$$

If a question specifies that the equation be written in slope-intercept form, the equation should be manipulated to isolate y:

Solve: $y - (-2) = 3(x - 4)$

Distribute: $y + 2 = 3x - 12$

Subtract 2 from both sides: $y = 3x - 14$

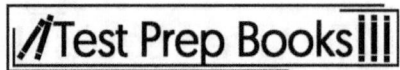

Math Section

Given Two Ordered Pairs

Given two ordered pairs for a function, (x_1, y_1) and (x_2, y_2), it is possible to determine the rate of change between the variables (slope of the line). To calculate the slope of the line, m, the values for the ordered pairs should be substituted into the formula:

$$m = \frac{y_2 - y_1}{x_2 - x_1}$$

The expression is substituted to obtain a whole number or fraction for the slope. Once the slope is calculated, the slope and either of the ordered pairs should be substituted into the point-slope form to obtain the equation of the line.

Creating, Solving, and Interpreting Systems of Linear Inequalities in Two Variables

Expressing Linear Inequalities in Two Variables

A linear inequality in two variables is a statement expressing an unequal relationship between those two variables. Typically written in slope-intercept form, the variable y can be greater than; less than; greater than or equal to; or less than or equal to a linear expression including the variable x. Examples include:

$$y > 3x$$

$$y \leq \frac{1}{2}x - 3$$

Questions may instruct students to model real world scenarios such as:

> You work part-time cutting lawns for $15 each and cleaning houses for $25 each. Your goal is to make more than $90 this week. Write an inequality to represent the possible pairs of lawns and houses needed to reach your goal.

This scenario can be expressed as:

$$15x + 25y > 90$$

where x is the number of lawns cut and y is the number of houses cleaned.

Graphing Solution Sets for Linear Inequalities in Two Variables

A graph of the solution set for a linear inequality shows the ordered pairs that make the statement true. The graph consists of a boundary line dividing the coordinate plane and shading on one side of the boundary. The boundary line should be graphed just as a linear equation would be graphed (see section on *Understanding Connections Between Algebraic and Graphical Representations*). If the inequality symbol is $>$ or $<$, a dashed line can be used to indicate that the line is not part of the solution set.

If the inequality symbol is $\geq$ or $\leq$, a solid line can be used to indicate that the boundary line is included in the solution set. An ordered pair (x, y) on either side of the line should be chosen to test in the inequality statement. If substituting the values for x and y results in a true statement ($15(3) + 25(2) > 90$), that ordered pair and all others on that side of the boundary line are part of the solution set. To indicate this, that region of the graph should be shaded. If substituting the ordered pair results in a false statement, the ordered pair and all others on that side are not part of the solution set.

Therefore, the other region of the graph contains the solutions and should be shaded.

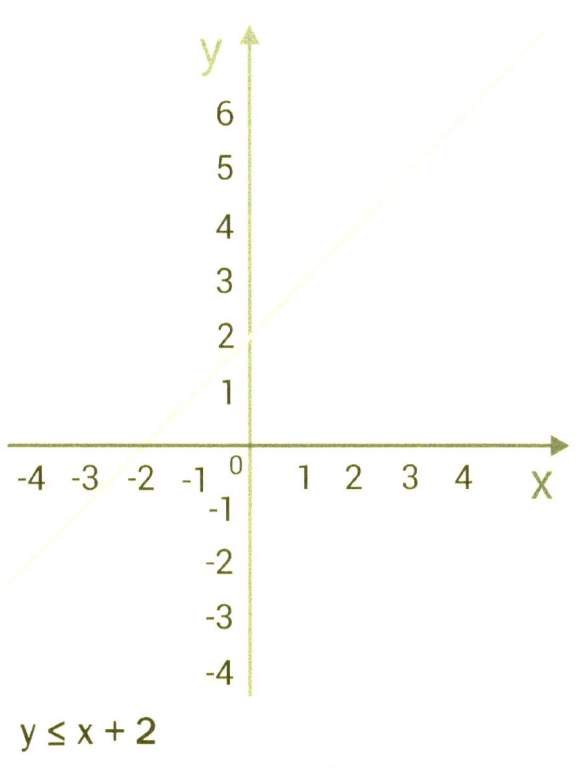

$y \leq x + 2$

A question may simply ask whether a given ordered pair is a solution to a given inequality. To determine this, the values should be substituted for the ordered pair into the inequality. If the result is a true statement, the ordered pair is a solution; if the result is a false statement, the ordered pair is not a solution.

Expressing Systems of Linear Inequalities in Two Variables

A system of linear inequalities consists of two linear inequalities making comparisons between two variables. Students may be given a scenario and asked to express it as a system of inequalities:

> A consumer study calls for at least 60 adult participants. It cannot use more than 25 men. Express these constraints as a system of inequalities.

This can be modeled by the system:

$$x + y \geq 60$$

$$x \leq 25$$

where x represents the number of men and y represents the number of women. A solution to the system is an ordered pair that makes both inequalities true when substituting the values for x and y.

Graphing Solution Sets for Systems of Linear Inequalities in Two Variables

The solution set for a system of inequalities is the region of a graph consisting of ordered pairs that make both inequalities true. To graph the solution set, each linear inequality should first be graphed with appropriate shading. The region of the graph should be identified where the shading for the two inequalities overlaps. This region contains the solution set for the system.

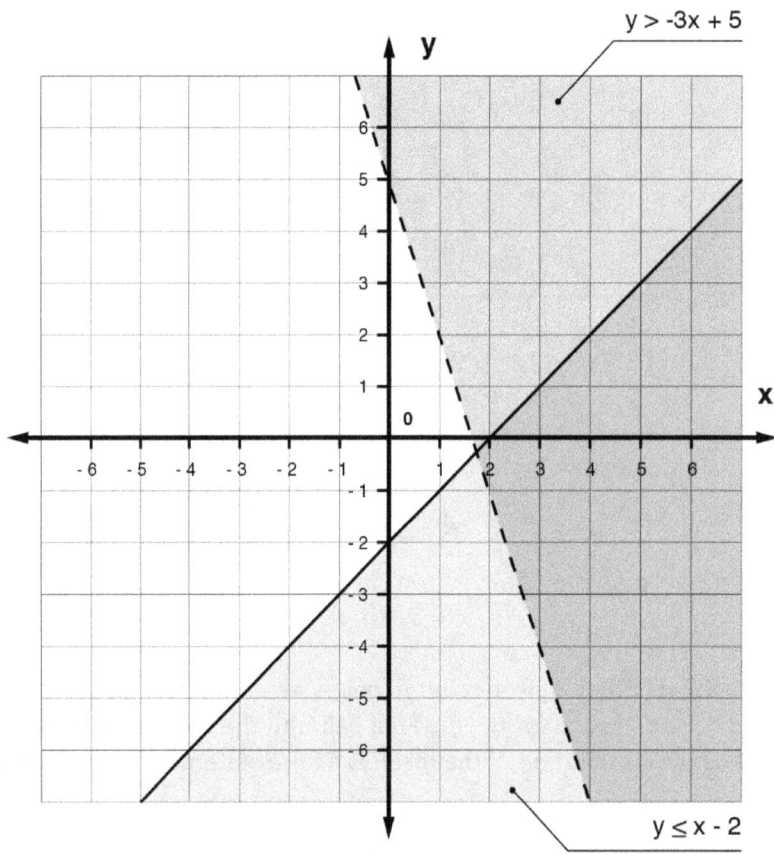

An ordered pair from the region of solutions can be selected to test in the system of inequalities.

Just as with manipulating linear inequalities in one variable, if dividing by a negative number in working with a linear inequality in two variables, the relationship reverses and the inequality sign should be flipped.

Creating, Solving, and Interpreting Systems of Two Linear Equations in Two Variables

Expressing Systems of Two Linear Equations in Two Variables

A system of two linear equations in two variables is a set of equations that use the same variables, usually x and y. Here's a sample problem:

Math Section

An Internet provider charges an installation fee and a monthly charge. It advertises that two months of its offering costs $100 and six months costs $200. Find the monthly charge and the installation fee.

The two unknown quantities (variables) are the monthly charge and the installation fee. There are two different statements given relating the variables: two months added to the installation fee is $100; and six months added to the installation fee is $200. Using the variable x as the monthly charge and y as the installation fee, the statements can be written as the following:

$$2x + y = 100$$

$$6x + y = 200$$

These two equations taken together form a system modeling the given scenario.

Solutions of a System of Two Linear Equations in Two Variables

A solution for a system of equations is an ordered pair that makes both equations true. One method for solving a system of equations is to graph both lines on a coordinate plane (see section on *Understanding Connections Between Algebraic and Graphical Representations*). If the lines intersect, the point of intersection is the solution to the system. Every point on a line represents an ordered pair that makes its equation true. The ordered pair represented by this point of intersection lies on both lines and therefore makes both equations true. This ordered pair should be checked by substituting its values into both of the original equations of the system. Note that given a system of equations and an ordered pair, the ordered pair can be determined to be a solution or not by checking it in both equations.

If, when graphed, the lines representing the equations of a system do not intersect, then the two lines are parallel to each other or they are the same exact line. Parallel lines extend in the same direction without ever meeting. A system consisting of parallel lines has no solution. If the equations for a system represent the same exact line, then every point on the line is a solution to the system. In this case, there would be an infinite number of solutions. A system consisting of intersecting lines is referred to as independent; a system consisting of parallel lines is referred to as inconsistent; and a system consisting of coinciding lines is referred to as dependent.

Parallel Lines	**Intersecting Lines**	**Coincident Lines**
Inconsistent	Independent	Dependent

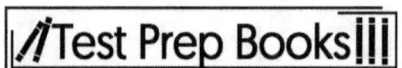

Math Section

Algebraically Solving Linear Equations (or Inequalities) in One Variable

Linear equations in one variable and linear inequalities in one variable can be solved following similar processes. Although they typically have one solution, a linear equation can have no solution or can have a solution set of all real numbers. Solution sets for linear inequalities typically consist of an infinite number of values either greater or less than a given value (where the given value may or may not be included in the set). However, a linear inequality can have no solution or can have a solution set consisting of all real numbers.

Linear Equations in One Variable – Special Cases

Solving a linear equation produces a value for the variable that makes the algebraic statement true. If there is no value for the variable that would make the statement true, there is no solution to the equation. Here's a sample equation:

$$x + 3 = x - 1$$

There is no value for x in which adding 3 to the value would produce the same result as subtracting 1 from that value. Conversely, if any value for the variable would make a true statement, the equation has an infinite number of solutions. Here's another sample equation:

$$3x + 6 = 3(x + 2)$$

Any real number substituted for x would result in a true statement (both sides of the equation are equal).

By manipulating equations similar to the two above, the variable of the equation will cancel out completely. If the constants that are left express a true statement (ex., $6 = 6$), then all real numbers are solutions to the equation. If the constants left express a false statement (ex., $3 = -1$), then there is no solution to the equation.

A question on this material may present a linear equation with an unknown value for either a constant or a coefficient of the variable and ask to determine the value that produces an equation with no solution or infinite solutions. For example:

$$3x + 7 = 3x + 10 + n$$

Find the value of n that would create an equation with an infinite number of solutions for the variable x.

To solve this problem, the equation should be manipulated so the variable x will cancel. To do this, $3x$ should be subtracted from both sides, which would leave:

$$7 = 10 + n$$

By subtracting 10 on both sides, it is determined that $n = -3$. Therefore, a value of -3 for n would result in an equation with a solution set of all real numbers.

If the same problem asked for the equation to have no solution, the value of n would be all real numbers except -3.

Math Section

Linear Inequalities in One Variable – Special Cases

A linear inequality can have a solution set consisting of all real numbers or can contain no solution. When solved algebraically, a linear inequality in which the variable cancels out and results in a true statement (ex., $7 \geq 2$) has a solution set of all real numbers. A linear inequality in which the variable cancels out and results in a false statement (ex., $7 \leq 2$) has no solution.

Compound Inequalities

A compound inequality is a pair of inequalities joined by *and* or *or*. Given a compound inequality, to determine its solution set, both inequalities should be solved for the given variable. The solution set for a compound inequality containing *and* consists of all the values for the variable that make both inequalities true. If solving the compound inequality results in:

$$x \geq -2$$

$$x < 3$$

the solution set would consist of all values between -2 and 3, including 3. This may also be written as follows:

$$-2 \leq x < 3$$

Due to the graphs of their solution sets (shown below), compound inequalities such as these are referred to as conjunctions.

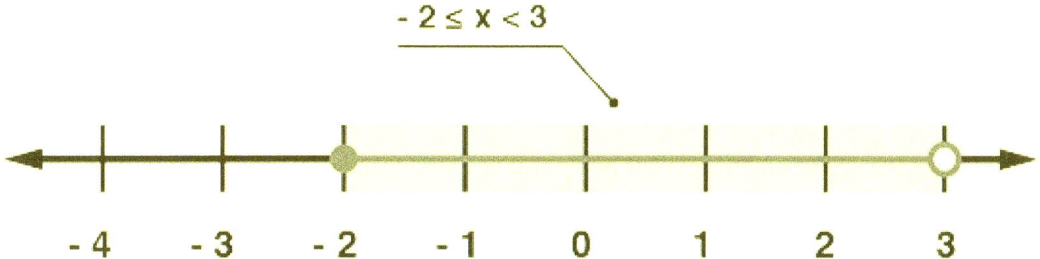

If there are no values that would make both inequalities of a compound inequality containing *and* true, then there is no solution. An example would be $x > 2$ and $x \leq 0$.

The solution set for a compound inequality containing *or* consists of all the values for the variable that make at least one of the inequalities true. The solution set for the compound inequality $x < 3$ or $x \geq 6$

consists of all values less than 3, 6, and all values greater than 6. Due to the graphs of their solution sets (shown below), compound inequalities such as these are referred to as disjunctions.

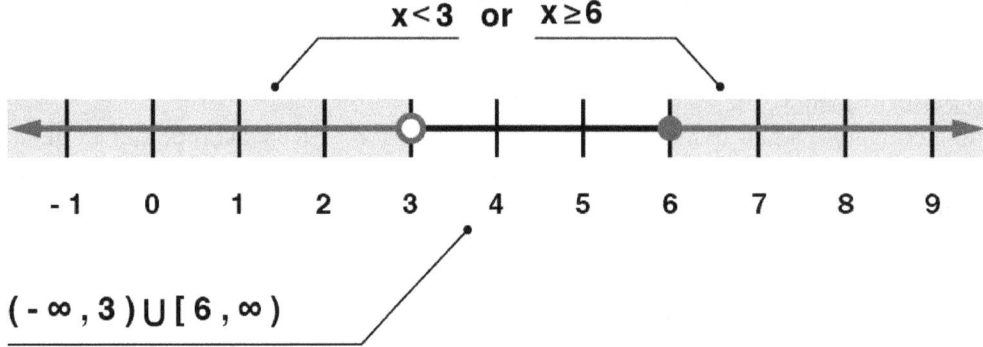

If the two inequalities for a compound inequality containing *or* "overlap," then the solution set contains all real numbers. An example would be $x > 2$ or $x < 7$. Any number would make at least one of these true.

Algebraically Solving Systems of Two Linear Equations in Two Variables

A system of two linear equations in two variables is a set of equations that use the same variables (typically x and y). A solution to the system is an ordered pair that makes both equations true. One method for solving a system is by graphing as explained in an earlier section. This method, however, is not always practical. Students may not have graph paper; or the solution may not consist of integers, making it difficult to identify the exact point of intersection on a graph. There are two methods for solving systems of equations algebraically: substitution and elimination. The method used will depend on the characteristics of the equations in the system.

Solving Systems of Equations with the Substitution Method
If one of the equations in a system has an isolated variable ($x =$ or $y =$) or a variable that can be easily isolated, the substitution method can be used. Here's a sample system:

$$x + 3y = 7$$

$$2x - 4y = 24$$

The first equation can easily be solved for x. By subtracting $3y$ on both sides, the resulting equation is:

$$x = 7 - 3y$$

When one equation is solved for a variable, the expression that it is equal can be substituted into the other equation. For this example, $(7 - 3y)$ would be substituted for x into the second equation as follows:

$$2(7 - 3y) - 4y = 24$$

Solving this equation results in $y = -1$. Once the value for one variable is known, this value should be substituted into either of the original equations to determine the value of the other variable. For the

Math Section

example, -1 would be substituted for y in either of the original equations. Substituting into the first equation results in:

$$x + 3(-1) = 7$$

and solving this equation yields $x = 10$. The solution to a system is an ordered pair, so the solution to the example is written as $(10, -1)$. The solution can be checked by substituting it into both equations of the system to ensure it results in two true statements.

<u>Solving Systems of Equations with the Elimination Method</u>
The elimination method for solving a system of equations involves canceling out (or eliminating) one of the variables. This method is typically used when both equations of a system are written in standard form:

$$(Ax + By = C)$$

An example is:

$$2x + 3y = 12; 5x - y = 13$$

To perform the elimination method, the equations in the system should be arranged vertically to be added together and then one or both of the equations should be multiplied so that one variable will be eliminated when the two are added. Opposites will cancel each other when added together. For example, $8x$ and $-8x$ will cancel each other when added. For the example above, writing the system vertically helps identify that the bottom equation should be multiplied by 3 to eliminate the variable y.

$$2x + 3y = 12 \rightarrow 2x + 3y = 12$$

$$3(5x - y = 13) \rightarrow 15x - 3y = 39$$

Adding the two equations together vertically results in $17x = 51$. Solving yields $x = 3$. Once the value for one variable is known, it can be substituted into either of the original equations to determine the value of the other variable. Once this is obtained, the solution can be written as an ordered pair (x, y) and checked in both equations of the system. In this example, the solution is $(3, 2)$.

<u>Systems of Equations with No Solution or an Infinite Number of Solutions</u>
A system of equations can have one solution, no solution, or an infinite number of solutions. If, while solving a system algebraically, both variables cancel out, then the system has either no solution or has an infinite number of solutions. If the remaining constants result in a true statement (ex., $7 = 7$), then there is an infinite number of solutions. This would indicate coinciding lines. If the remaining constants result in a false statement, then there is no solution to the system. This would indicate parallel lines.

Interpreting Variables and Constants in Expressions for Linear Functions

Linear functions, also written as linear equations in two variables, can be written to model real-world scenarios. Questions on this material will provide information about a scenario and then request a linear equation to represent the scenario. The algebraic process for writing the equation will depend on the given information. The key to writing linear models is to decipher the information given to determine what it represents in the context of a linear equation (variables, slope, ordered pairs, etc.).

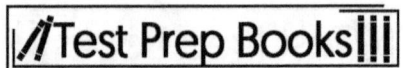

Identifying Variables for Linear Models

The first step to writing a linear model is to identify what the variables represent. A variable represents an unknown quantity, and in the case of a linear equation, a specific relationship exists between the two variables (usually x and y). Within a given scenario, the variables are the two quantities that are changing. The variable x is considered the independent variable and represents the inputs of a function. The variable y is considered the dependent variable and represents the outputs of a function. For example, if a scenario describes distance traveled and time traveled, distance would be represented by y and time represented by x. The distance traveled depends on the time spent traveling (time is independent). If a scenario describes the cost of a cab ride and the distance traveled, the cost would be represented by y and the distance represented by x. The cost of a cab ride depends on the distance traveled.

Identifying the Slope and Y-Intercept for Linear Models

The slope of the graph of a line represents the rate of change between the variables of an equation. In the context of a real-world scenario, the slope will tell the way in which the unknown quantities (variables) change with respect to each other. A scenario involving distance and time might state that someone is traveling at a rate of 45 miles per hour. The slope of the linear model would be 45. A scenario involving the cost of a cab ride and distance traveled might state that the person is charged $3 for each mile. The slope of the linear model would be 3.

The y-intercept of a linear function is the value of y when $x = 0$ (the point where the line intercepts the y-axis on the graph of the equation). It is sometimes helpful to think of this as a "starting point" for a linear function. Suppose for the scenario about the cab ride that the person is told that the cab company charges a flat fee of $5 plus $3 for each mile. Before traveling any distance ($x = 0$), the cost is $5. The y-intercept for the linear model would be 5.

Identifying Ordered Pairs for Linear Models

A linear equation with two variables can be written given a point (ordered pair) and the slope or given two points on a line. An ordered pair gives a set of corresponding values for the two variables (x and y). As an example, for a scenario involving distance and time, it is given that the person traveled 112.5 miles in 2 ½ hours. Knowing that x represents time and y represents distance, this information can be written as the ordered pair (2.5, 112.5).

Understanding Connections Between Algebraic and Graphical Representations

The solution set to a linear equation in two variables can be represented visually by a line graphed on the coordinate plane. Every point on this line represents an ordered pair (x, y), which makes the equation true. The process for graphing a line depends on the form in which its equation is written: slope-intercept form or standard form.

Graphing a Line in Slope-Intercept Form

When an equation is written in slope-intercept form, $y = mx + b$, m represents the slope of the line and b represents the y-intercept. The y-intercept is the value of y when $x = 0$ and the point at which the graph of the line crosses the y-axis. The slope is the rate of change between the variables, expressed as a fraction. The fraction expresses the change in y compared to the change in x. If the slope is an integer, it should be written as a fraction with a denominator of 1. For example, 5 would be written as 5/1.

Math Section

To graph a line given an equation in slope-intercept form, the y-intercept should first be plotted. For example, to graph:

$$y = -\frac{2}{3}x + 7$$

the y-intercept of 7 would be plotted on the y-axis (vertical axis) at the point $(0, 7)$. Next, the slope would be used to determine a second point for the line. Note that all that is necessary to graph a line is two points on that line. The slope will indicate how to get from one point on the line to another. The slope expresses vertical change (y) compared to horizontal change (x) and therefore is sometimes referred to as $\frac{rise}{run}$. The numerator indicates the change in the y value (move up for positive integers and move down for negative integers), and the denominator indicates the change in the x-value. For the previous example, using the slope of $-\frac{2}{3}$, from the first point at the y-intercept, the second point should be found by counting down 2 and to the right 3. This point would be located at $(3, 5)$.

If the midpoint of a line is needed, the midpoint formula can be used if the coordinates of the ends of the line segment are known. The midpoint formula is as follows:

$$M = (\frac{x_1 + x_2}{2}, \frac{y_1 + y_2}{2})$$

M is the midpoint and the coordinates of the two points are:

$$(x_1, y_1)$$

$$(x_2, y_2)$$

Graphing a Line in Standard Form
When an equation is written in standard form:

$$Ax + By = C$$

it is easy to identify the x- and y-intercepts for the graph of the line. Just as the y-intercept is the point at which the line intercepts the y-axis, the x-intercept is the point at which the line intercepts the x-axis. At the y-intercept, $x = 0$; and at the x-intercept, $y = 0$. Given an equation in standard form, $x = 0$ should be used to find the y-intercept. Likewise, $y = 0$ should be used to find the x-intercept. For example, to graph $3x + 2y = 6$, 0 for y results in:

$$3x + 2(0) = 6$$

Solving for y yields $x = 2$; therefore, an ordered pair for the line is $(2, 0)$. Substituting 0 for x results in $3(0) + 2y = 6$. Solving for y yields $y = 3$; therefore, an ordered pair for the line is $(0, 3)$. The two ordered pairs (the x- and y-intercepts) can be plotted, and a straight line through them can be constructed.

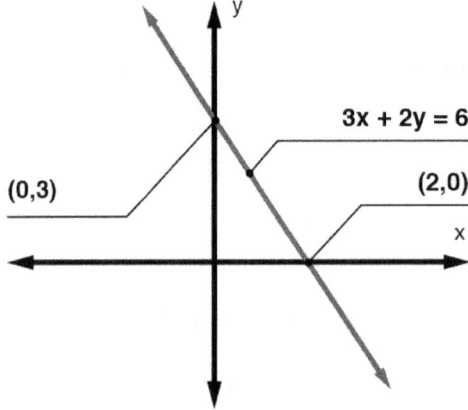

Writing the Equation of a Line Given its Graph

Given the graph of a line, its equation can be written in two ways. If the y-intercept is easily identified (is an integer), it and another point can be used to determine the slope. When determining $\frac{change\ in\ y}{change\ in\ x}$ from one point to another on the graph, the distance for $\frac{rise}{run}$ is being figured. The equation should be written in slope-intercept form, $y = mx + b$, with m representing the slope and b representing the y-intercept.

The equation of a line can also be written by identifying two points on the graph of the line. To do so, the slope is calculated and then the values are substituted for the slope and either of the ordered pairs into the point-slope form of an equation.

Vertical, Horizontal, Parallel, and Perpendicular Lines

For a vertical line, the value of x remains constant (for all ordered pairs (x, y) on the line, the value of x is the same); therefore, the equations for all vertical lines are written in the form $x = number$. For example, a vertical line that crosses the x-axis at -2 would have an equation of $x = -2$. For a horizontal line, the value of y remains constant; therefore, the equations for all horizontal lines are written in the form $y = number$.

Parallel lines extend in the same exact direction without ever meeting. Their equations have the same slopes and different y-intercepts. For example, given a line with an equation of $y = -3x + 2$, a parallel line would have a slope of -3 and a y-intercept of any value other than 2. Perpendicular lines intersect to form a right angle. Their equations have slopes that are opposite reciprocal (the sign is changed and the

Math Section

fraction is flipped; for example, $-\frac{2}{3}$ and $\frac{3}{2}$) and y-intercepts that may or may not be the same. For example, given a line with an equation of $y = \frac{1}{2}x + 7$, a perpendicular line would have a slope of $-\frac{2}{1}$ and any value for its y-intercept.

Advanced Math

Creating a Quadratic or Exponential Function

Quadratic Models

A quadratic function can be written in the standard form:

$$y = ax^2 + bx + c$$

It can be represented by a u-shaped graph called a parabola. For a quadratic function where the value of a is positive, as the inputs increase, the outputs increase until a certain value (maximum of the function) is reached. As inputs increase past the value that corresponds with the maximum output, the relationship reverses, and the outputs decrease. For a quadratic function where a is negative, as the inputs increase, the outputs (1) decrease, (2) reach a maximum, and (3) then increase.

Consider a ball thrown straight up into the air. As time passes, the height of the ball increases until it reaches its maximum height. After reaching the maximum height, as time increases, the height of the ball decreases (it is falling toward the ground). This relationship can be expressed as a quadratic function where time is the input (x), and the height of the ball is the output (y).

Given a scenario that can be modeled by a quadratic function, to write its equation, the following is needed: its vertex and any other ordered pair; or any three ordered pairs for the function. Given three ordered pairs, they should be substituted into the general form

$$(y = ax^2 + bx + c)$$

to create a system of three equations. For example, given the ordered pairs (2, 3), (3, 13), and (4, 29), it yields:

$$3 = a(2)^2 + b(2) + c \rightarrow 4a + 2b + c = 3$$

$$13 = a(3)^2 + b(3) + c \rightarrow 9a + 3b + c = 13$$

$$29 = a(4)^2 + b(4) + c \rightarrow 16a + 4b + c = 29$$

The values for a, b, and c in the system can be found and substituted into the general form to write the equation of the function. In this case, the equation is:

$$y = 3x^2 - 5x + 1$$

Exponential Models

Exponential functions can be written in the form:

$$y = a \times b^x$$

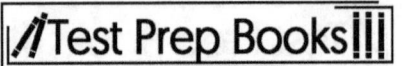

Math Section

Scenarios involving growth and decay can be modeled by exponential functions.

The equation for an exponential function can be written given the y-intercept (a) and the growth rate (b). The y-intercept is the output (y) when the input (x) equals zero. It can be thought of as an "original value" or starting point. The value of b is the rate at which the original value increases ($b > 1$) or decreases ($b < 1$). Suppose someone deposits $1,200 into a bank account that accrues 1% interest per month. The y-intercept, a, would be $1,200, while the growth rate, b, would be 1.01 (100% of the original value + 1% interest). This scenario could be written as the exponential function:

$$y = 1{,}200 \times 1.01^x$$

The x-variable represents the number of months since the deposit and y represents money in the account.

Given a scenario that models an exponential function, the equation can also be written when provided two ordered pairs.

Determining the Most Suitable Form of an Expression

It is possible for algebraic expressions and equations to be written that look completely different, yet are still equivalent. For instance, the expression $4(2x - 3) - 3x + 5$ is equivalent to the expression $5x - 7$. Given two algebraic expressions, it can be determined if they are equivalent by writing them in simplest form. Distribution should be used, if applicable, and like terms should be combined. Given two algebraic equations, it can be determined if they are equivalent by solving each for the same variable. Here are two sample equations to consider:

$$3x - 4y = 7$$

and

$$x + 2 = \frac{4}{3}y + 4\frac{1}{3}$$

To determine if they are equivalent, solving for x is required.

$$3x - 4y = 7 \qquad\qquad x + 2 = \frac{4}{3}y + 4\frac{1}{3}$$

$$3x = 4y + 7 \qquad\qquad x = \frac{4}{3}y + 2\frac{1}{3}$$

$$x = \frac{4}{3}y + \frac{7}{3} \qquad\qquad x = \frac{4}{3}y + 2\frac{1}{3}$$

The equations are equivalent.

Equivalent Forms of Functions

Equations in two variables can often be written in different forms to easily recognize a given trait of the function or its graph. Linear equations written in slope-intercept form allow for recognition of the slope and y-intercept; linear equations written in standard form allow for identification of the x and y-intercepts. Quadratic functions written in standard form allow for identification of the y-intercept and for easy calculation of outputs; quadratic functions written in vertex form allow for identification of the

Math Section

function's minimum or maximum output and its graph's vertex. Polynomial functions written in factored form allow for identification of the zeros of the function.

The method of substituting the same inputs (x-values) into functions to determine if they produce the same outputs can reveal if functions are not equivalent (different outputs). However, corresponding inputs and outputs do not necessarily indicate equivalent functions.

Create Equivalent Expressions Involving Rational Exponents

Converting To and From Radical Form

Algebraic expressions involving radicals ($\sqrt{}$, $\sqrt[3]{}$, etc.) can be written without the radical by using rational (fraction) exponents. For radical expressions, the value under the root symbol is called the radicand, and the type of root determines the index. For example, the expression $\sqrt{6x}$ has a radicand of $6x$ and an index of 2 (it is a square root). If the exponent of the radicand is 1, then:

$$\sqrt[n]{a} = a^{\frac{1}{n}}$$

The n-variable is the index. A number or variable without a power has an implied exponent of 1.

For example:

$$\sqrt{6} = 6^{\frac{1}{2}}$$

and

$$125^{\frac{1}{3}} = \sqrt[3]{125}$$

For any exponent of the radicand:

$$\sqrt[n]{a^m} = \left(\sqrt[n]{a}\right)^m = a^{\frac{m}{n}}$$

For example:

$$64^{\frac{5}{3}} = \sqrt[3]{64^5} \text{ or } \left(\sqrt[3]{64}\right)^5$$

and

$$(xy)^{\frac{2}{3}} = \sqrt[3]{(xy)^2} \text{ or } \left(\sqrt[3]{xy}\right)^2$$

Simplifying Expressions with Rational Exponents

When simplifying expressions with rational exponents, all basic properties for exponents hold true. When multiplying powers of the same base (same value with or without the same exponent), the exponents are added. For example:

$$x^{\frac{2}{7}} \times x^{\frac{3}{14}} = x^{\frac{1}{2}} \left(\frac{2}{7} + \frac{3}{14} = \frac{1}{2}\right)$$

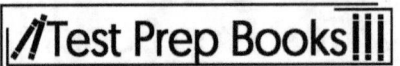

When dividing powers of the same base, the exponents are subtracted. For example:

$$\frac{5^{\frac{2}{3}}}{5^{\frac{1}{2}}} = 5^{\frac{1}{6}} \left(\frac{2}{3} - \frac{1}{2} = \frac{1}{6}\right)$$

When raising a power to a power, the exponents are multiplied. For example:

$$\left(5^{\frac{1}{2}}\right)^4 = 5^2 \left(\frac{1}{2} \times 4 = 2\right)$$

When simplifying expressions with exponents, a number should never be raised to a power or a negative exponent. If a number has an integer exponent, its value should be determined. If the number has a rational exponent, it should be rewritten as a radical and the value determined if possible. A base with a negative exponent moves from the numerator to the denominator of a fraction (or vice versa) and is written with a positive exponent.

For example:

$$x^{-3} = \frac{1}{x^3}$$

and

$$\frac{2}{5x^{-2}} = \frac{2x^2}{5}$$

The exponent of 5 is 1, and therefore the 5 does not move.

Here's a sample expression:

$$(27x^{-9})^{\frac{1}{3}}$$

After the implied exponents are noted, a power should be raised to a power by multiplying exponents, which yields $27^{\frac{1}{3}}x^{-3}$. Next, the negative exponent is eliminated by moving the base and power:

$$\frac{27^{\frac{1}{3}}}{x^3}$$

Then the value of the number is determined to a power by writing it in radical form:

$$\frac{\sqrt[3]{27}}{x^3}$$

Simplifying yields $\frac{3}{x^3}$.

Creating an Equivalent Form of an Algebraic Expression

There are many different ways to write algebraic expressions and equations that are equivalent to each other. Converting expressions from standard form to factored form and vice versa are skills commonly used in advanced mathematics. Standard form of an expression arranges terms with variables powers in descending order (highest exponent to lowest and then constants). Factored form displays an expression as the product of its factors (what can be multiplied to produce the expression).

Converting Standard Form to Factored Form
To factor an expression, a greatest common factor needs to be factored out first. Then, if possible, the remaining expression needs to be factored into the product of binomials. A binomial is an expression with two terms.

Greatest Common Factor
The greatest common factor (GCF) of a monomial (one term) consists of the largest number that divides evenly into all coefficients (number part of a term), and if all terms contain the same variable, the variable with the lowest exponent. The GCF of $3x^4 - 9x^3 + 12x^2$ would be $3x^2$. To write the factored expression, every term needs to be divided by the GCF, then the product of the resulting quotient and the GCF (using parentheses to show multiplication) should be written. For the previous example, the factored expression would be:

$$3x^2(x^2 - 3x + 4)$$

Factoring Ax² + Bx + C When A = 1
To factor a quadratic expression in standard form when the value of a is not equal to 1, the factors that multiply to equal the value of $a \times c$ should be found and then added to equal the value of b. Next, the expression splitting the bx term should be rewritten using those factors. Instead of three terms, there will now be four. Then the first two terms should be factored using GCF, and a common binomial should be factored from the last two terms. The factored form will be: (common binomial) (2 terms out of binomials). In the sample expression $2x^2 + 11x + 12$, the value of $a \times c$ (or 2×12) equals 24.

Two factors that multiply to 24 and added together to yield b (11) are 8 and 3. The bx term ($11x$) can be rewritten by splitting it into the factors:

$$2x^2 + 8x + 3x + 12$$

A GCF from the first two terms can be factored as:

$$2x(x + 4) + 3x + 12$$

A common binomial from the last two terms can then be factored as:

$$2x(x + 4) + 3(x + 4)$$

The factored form can be written as a product of binomials:

$$(x + 4)(2x + 3)$$

Converting Factored Form to Standard Form
To convert an expression from factored form to standard form, the factors are multiplied.

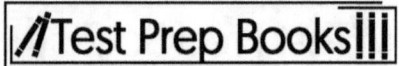

Math Section

Solving a Quadratic Equation

A quadratic equation is one in which the highest exponent of the variable is 2. A quadratic equation can have two, one, or zero real solutions. Depending on its structure, a quadratic equation can be solved by (1) factoring, (2) taking square roots, or (3) using the quadratic formula.

Solving Quadratic Equations by Factoring

To solve a quadratic equation by factoring, the equation should first be manipulated to set the quadratic expression equal to zero. Next, the quadratic expression should be factored using the appropriate method(s). Then each factor should be set equal to zero. If two factors multiply to equal zero, then one or both factors must equal zero. Finally, each equation should be solved. Here's a sample:

$$x^2 - 10 = 3x - 6$$

The expression should be set equal to zero:

$$x^2 - 3x - 4 = 0$$

The expression should be factored:

$$(x - 4)(x + 1) = 0$$

Each factor should be set equal to zero: $x - 4 = 0$; $x + 1 = 0$. Solving yields $x = 4$ or $x = -1$.

Completing the Square

Completing the square is one way to find zeros when factoring is not an option. The following equation cannot be factored:

$$x^2 + 10x - 9 = 0$$

The first step in this method is to move the constant to the right side of the equation, making it:

$$x^2 + 10x = 9$$

Then, the coefficient of x is divided by 2 and squared. This number is then added to both sides of the equation, to make the equation still true. For this example:

$$\left(\frac{10}{2}\right)^2 = 25$$

is added to both sides of the equation to obtain:

$$x^2 + 10x + 25 = 9 + 25$$

This expression simplifies to $x^2 + 10x + 25 = 34$, which can then be factored into:

$$(x + 5)^2 = 34$$

Solving for x then involves taking the square root of both sides and subtracting 5. This leads to two zeros of the function:

$$x = \pm\sqrt{34} - 5$$

Depending on the type of answer the question seeks, a calculator may be used to find exact numbers.

Solving Quadratic Equations by Taking Square Roots

If a quadratic equation does not have a linear term (variable to the first power), it can be solved by taking square roots. This means x^2 needs to be isolated and then the square root of both sides of the equation should be isolated. There will be two solutions because square roots can be positive or negative. ($\sqrt{4} = 2$ or -2 because $2 \times 2 = 4$ and $-2 \times -2 = 4$.) Here's a sample equation:

$$3x^2 - 12 = 0$$

Isolating x^2 yields $x^2 = 4$. The square root of both sides is then solved: $x = 2$ or -2.

The Quadratic Formula

When a quadratic expression cannot be factored or is difficult to factor, the quadratic formula can be used to solve the equation. To do so, the equation must be in the form:

$$ax^2 + bx + c = 0$$

The quadratic formula is:

$$x = \frac{-b \pm \sqrt{b^2 - 4ac}}{2a}$$

(The $\pm$ symbol indicates that two calculations are necessary, one using $+$ and one using $-$.) Here's a sample equation:

$$3x^2 - 2x = 3x + 2$$

First, the quadratic expression should be set equal to zero:

$$3x^2 - 5x - 2 = 0$$

Then the values are substituted for a (3), b (-5), and c (-2) into the formula:

$$x = \frac{-(-5) \pm \sqrt{(-5)^2 - 4(3)(-2)}}{2(3)}$$

Simplification yields:

$$x = \frac{5 \pm \sqrt{49}}{6} \rightarrow x = \frac{5 \pm 7}{6}$$

Calculating two values for x using $+$ and $-$ yields:

$$x = \frac{5 + 7}{6}; x = \frac{5 - 7}{6}$$

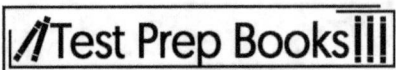

Simplification yields:

$$x = 2 \text{ or } -\frac{1}{3}$$

Just as with any equation, solutions should be checked by substituting the value into the original equation.

Adding, Subtracting, and Multiplying Polynomial Expressions

A polynomial expression is a monomial (one term) or the sum of monomials (more than one term separated by addition or subtraction). A polynomial in standard form consists of terms with variables written in descending exponential order and with any like terms combined.

Adding/Subtracting Polynomials

When adding or subtracting polynomials, each polynomial should be written in parenthesis; the negative sign should be distributed when necessary, and like terms need to be combined. Here's a sample equation: add $3x^3 + 4x - 3$ to $x^3 - 3x^2 + 2x - 2$. The sum is set as follows:

$$(x^3 - 3x^2 + 2x - 2) + (3x^3 + 4x - 3)$$

In front of each set of parentheses is an implied positive 1, which, when distributed, does not change any of the terms. Therefore, the parentheses should be dropped and like terms should be combined:

$$x^3 - 3x^2 + 2x - 2 + 3x^3 + 4x - 3$$

$$4x^3 - 3x^2 + 6x - 5$$

Here's another sample equation: subtract $3x^3 + 4x - 3$ from $x^3 - 3x^2 + 2x - 2$. The difference should be set as follows:

$$(x^3 - 3x^2 + 2x - 2) - (3x^3 + 4x - 3)$$

The implied $+1$ in front of the first set of parentheses will not change those four terms; however, distributing the implied -1 in front of the second set of parentheses will change the sign of each of those three terms:

$$x^3 - 3x^2 + 2x - 2 - 3x^3 - 4x + 3$$

Combining like terms yields:

$$-2x^3 - 3x^2 - 2x + 1$$

Multiplying Polynomials

When multiplying monomials, the coefficients are multiplied, and exponents of the same variable are added. For example:

$$-5x^3y^2z \times 2x^2y^5z^3 = -10x^5y^7z^4$$

Math Section

When multiplying polynomials, the monomials should be distributed and multiplied, then any like terms should be combined and written in standard form. Here's a sample equation:

$$2x^3(3x^2 + 2x - 4)$$

First, $2x^3$ should be multiplied by each of the three terms in parentheses:

$$2x^3 \times 3x^2 + 2x^3 \times 2x + 2x^3 \times -4$$

$$6x^5 + 4x^4 - 8x^3$$

Multiplying binomials will sometimes be taught using the FOIL method (where the products of the first, outside, inside, and last terms are added together). However, it may be easier and more consistent to think of it in terms of distributing. Both terms of the first binomial should be distributed to both terms of the second binomial. For example, the product of binomials $(2x + 3)(x - 4)$ can be calculated by distributing $2x$ and distributing 3:

$$2x \times x + 2x \times -4 + 3 \times x + 3 \times -4$$

$$2x^2 - 8x + 3x - 12$$

Combining like terms yields:

$$2x^2 - 5x - 12$$

The general principle of distributing each term can be applied when multiplying polynomials of any size. To multiply $(x^2 + 3x - 1)(5x^3 - 2x^2 + 2x + 3)$, all three terms should be distributed from the first polynomial to each of the four terms in the second polynomial and then any like terms should be combined. If a problem requires multiplying more than two polynomials, two at a time can be multiplied and combined until all have been multiplied. To multiply $(x + 3)(2x - 1)(x + 5)$, two polynomials should be chosen to multiply together first. Multiplying the last two results in:

$$(2x - 1)(x + 5) = 2x^2 + 9x - 5$$

That product should then be multiplied by the third polynomial:

$$(x + 3)(2x^2 + 9x - 5)$$

The final answer should equal:

$$2x^3 + 15x^2 + 22x - 15$$

Solving an Equation in One Variable

Equations with radicals containing numbers only as the radicand are solved the same way that an equation without a radical would be. For example:

$$3x + \sqrt{81} = 45$$

would be solved using the same steps as if solving:

$$2x + 4 = 12$$

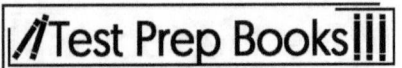

Radical equations are those in which the variable is part of the radicand. For example:

$$\sqrt{5x+1} - 6 = 0$$

and

$$\sqrt{x-3} + 5 = x$$

would be considered radical equations.

Radical Equations

To solve a radical equation, the radical should be isolated and both sides of the equation should be raised to the same power to cancel the radical. Raising both sides to the second power will cancel a square root, raising to the third power will cancel a cube root, etc. To solve $\sqrt{5x+1} - 6 = 0$, the radical should be isolated first:

$$\sqrt{5x+1} = 6$$

Then both sides should be raised to the second power:

$$(\sqrt{5x+1})^2 = (6)^2 \rightarrow 5x + 1 = 36$$

Lastly, the linear equation should be solved: $x = 7$.

Radical Equations with Extraneous Solutions

If a radical equation contains a variable in the radicand and a variable outside of the radicand, it must be checked for extraneous solutions. An extraneous solution is one obtained by following the proper process for solving an equation but does not "check out" when substituted into the original equation. Here's a sample equation:

$$\sqrt{x-3} + 5 = x$$

Isolating the radical yields:

$$\sqrt{x-3} = x - 5$$

Next, both sides should be squared to cancel the radical:

$$(\sqrt{x-3})^2 = (x-5)^2 \rightarrow x - 3 = (x-5)(x-5)$$

The binomials should be multiplied:

$$x - 3 = x^2 - 10x + 25$$

Math Section

The quadratic equation is then solved:

$$0 = x^2 - 11x + 28$$

$$0 = (x - 7)(x - 4)$$

$$x - 7 = 0; x - 4 = 0$$

$$x = 7 \text{ or } x = 4$$

To check for extraneous solutions, each answer can be substituted, one at a time, into the original equation. Substituting 7 for x, results in $7 = 7$. Therefore, 7 is a solution. Substituting 4 for x results in $6 = 4$. This is false; therefore, 4 is an extraneous solution.

Equations with a Variable in the Denominator of a Fraction

For equations with variables in the denominator, if the equation contains two rational expressions (on opposite sides of the equation, or on the same side and equal to zero), it can be solved like a proportion. Here's an equation to consider:

$$\frac{5}{2x - 2} = \frac{15}{x^2 - 1}$$

First, cross-multiplying yields:

$$5(x^2 - 1) = 15(2x - 2)$$

Distributing yields:

$$5x^2 - 5 = 30x - 30$$

In solving the quadratic equation (see section *Solving a Quadratic Equation*), it is determined that $x = 1$ or $x = 5$. Solutions must be checked to see if they are extraneous. Extraneous solutions either produce a false statement when substituted into the original equation or create a rational expression with a denominator of zero (dividing by zero is undefined). Substituting 5 into the original equation produces $\frac{5}{8} = \frac{5}{8}$; therefore, 5 is a solution. Substituting 1 into the original equation results in both denominators equal to zero; therefore, 1 is an extraneous solution.

If an equation contains three or more rational expressions: the least common denominator (LCD) needs to be found for all the expressions, then both sides of the equation should be multiplied by the LCD. The LCD consists of the lowest number that all coefficients divide evenly into and for every variable, the highest power of that variable. Here's a sample equation:

$$\frac{3}{5x} - \frac{4}{3x} = \frac{1}{3}$$

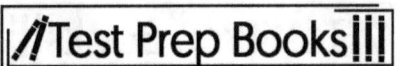

The LCD would be $15x$. Both sides of the equation should be multiplied by $15x$:

$$15x\left(\frac{3}{5x} - \frac{4}{3x}\right) = 15x\left(\frac{1}{3}\right)$$

$$\frac{45x}{5x} - \frac{60x}{3x} = \frac{15x}{3}$$

$$9 - 20 = 5x$$

$$x = -2\frac{1}{5}$$

Any extraneous solutions should be identified.

Solving a System of One Linear Equation and One Quadratic Equation

A system of equations consists of two variables in two equations. A solution to the system is an ordered pair (x, y) that makes both equations true. When displayed graphically, a solution to a system is a point of intersection between the graphs of the equations. When a system consists of one linear equation and one quadratic equation, there may be one, two, or no solutions. If the line and parabola intersect at two points, there are two solutions to the system; if they intersect at one point, there is one solution; if they do not intersect, there is no solution.

One method for solving a system of one linear equation and one quadratic equation is to graph both functions and identify point(s) of intersection. This, however, is not always practical. Graph paper may not be available, or the intersection points may not be easily identified. Solving the system algebraically involves using the substitution method. Consider the following system:

$$y = x^2 + 9x + 11$$

$$y = 2x - 1$$

The equivalent value of y should be substituted from the linear equation $(2x - 1)$ into the quadratic equation.

The resulting equation is:

$$2x - 1 = x^2 + 9x + 11$$

Next, this quadratic equation should be solved using the appropriate method: factoring, taking square roots, or using the quadratic formula (see section *Solving a Quadratic Equation*). Solving this quadratic equation by factoring results in $x = -4$ or $x = -3$. Next, the corresponding y-values should be found by substituting the x-values into the original linear equation:

$$y = 2(-4) - 1$$

$$y = 2(-3) - 1$$

Math Section

The solutions should be written as ordered pairs: $(-4, -9)$ and $(-3, -7)$. Finally, the possible solutions should be checked by substituting each into both of the original equations. In this case, both solutions "check out."

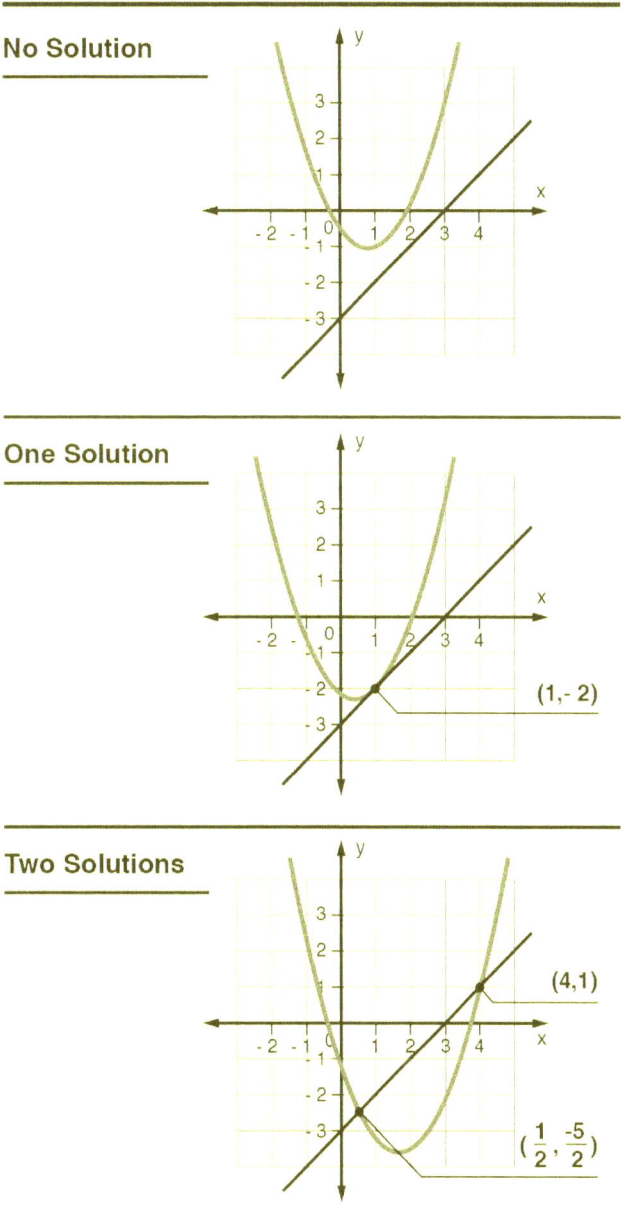

Rewriting Simple Rational Expressions

A rational expression is an algebraic expression including variables that look like a fraction. In simplest form, the numerator and denominator of a rational expression do not have common divisors (factors).

To simplify a rational expression, the numerator and denominator (see Section 4) should be factored; then any common factors in the numerator and denominator should be canceled. To simplify, the numerator and denominator should be written as a product of its factors:

$$\frac{3x^2y}{12xy^3}$$

$$\frac{3 \times x \times x \times y}{2 \times 2 \times 3 \times x \times x \times y \times y \times y}$$

Canceling common factors leaves:

$$\frac{x}{2 \times 2 \times y \times y}$$

Multiplying the remaining factors results in:

$$\frac{x}{4y^2}$$

Here's a rational expression:

$$\frac{x^2 - 1}{x^2 - x - 2}$$

Factoring the numerator and denominator produces:

$$\frac{(x+1)(x-1)}{(x-2)(x+1)}$$

Each binomial in parentheses is a factor and only the exact same binomial would cancel that factor. By canceling factors, the expression is simplified to:

$$\frac{x-1}{x-2}$$

The variable x itself is not a factor. Therefore, they do not cancel each other out.

Multiplying/Dividing Rational Expressions

When multiplying or dividing rational expressions, the basic concepts of operations with fractions are used. To multiply, (1) all numerators and denominators need to be factored, (2) common factors should be canceled between any numerator and any denominator, (3) the remaining factors of the numerator and the remaining factors of the denominator should be multiplied, and (4) the expression should be checked to see whether it can be simplified further.

Math Section

To multiply the following, each numerator and denominator should be written as a product of its factors:

$$\frac{4a^4}{3} \times \frac{6}{5a^2}$$

$$\frac{2 \times 2 \times a \times a \times a \times a}{3} \times \frac{3 \times 2}{5 \times a \times a}$$

After canceling common factors, the remaining expression is:

$$\frac{2 \times 2 \times a \times a}{1} \times \frac{2}{5}$$

A factor of 1 remains if all others are canceled. Multiplying remaining factors produces:

$$\frac{8a^2}{5}$$

To divide rational expressions, the expression should be changed to multiplying by the reciprocal of the divisor (just as with fractions: $\frac{1}{2} \div \frac{3}{4} = \frac{1}{2} \times \frac{4}{3}$); then follow the process for multiplying rational expressions.

Here's a sample expression:

$$\frac{2x}{x^2 - 16} \div \frac{4x^2 + 6x}{x^2 + 6x + 8}$$

First, the division problem should be changed to a multiplication problem:

$$\frac{2x}{x^2 - 16} \times \frac{x^2 + 6x + 8}{4x^2 + 6x}$$

Then, the equation should be factored:

$$\frac{2x}{(x + 4)(x - 4)} \times \frac{(x + 4)(x + 2)}{2x(2x + 3)}$$

Canceling yields:

$$\frac{1}{(x - 4)} \times \frac{(x + 2)}{(2x + 3)}$$

Multiplying the remaining factors produces:

$$\frac{x + 2}{2x^2 - 5x - 12}$$

Adding/Subtracting Rational Expressions

Just as with adding and subtracting fractions, to add or subtract rational expressions, a common denominator is needed. (The numerator is added or subtracted, and the denominator stays the same.) If

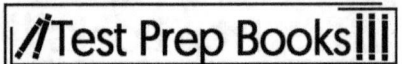

the expressions have like denominators, subtraction should be changed to add the opposite (a -1 is distributed to each term in the numerator of the expression being subtracted); the denominators should be factored and the expressions added; the numerator should then be factored; and the equation should be simplified if possible. Here's a sample expression:

$$\frac{2x^2 + 4x - 3}{x + 3} - \frac{x^2 - 2x - 12}{x + 3}$$

Changing subtraction to add the opposite yields:

$$\frac{2x^2 + 4x - 3}{x + 3} + \frac{-x^2 + 2x + 12}{x + 3}$$

The denominator cannot be factored, so the expression should be added, resulting in:

$$\frac{x^2 + 6x + 9}{x + 3}$$

Simplification is performed by factoring the numerator:

$$\frac{(x + 3)(x + 3)}{(x + 3)}$$

Canceling yields: $\frac{x + 3}{1}$, or simply $x + 3$.

To add or subtract rational expressions with unlike denominators, the denominators must be changed by finding the least common multiple (LCM) of the expressions. To find the LCM, each expression should be factored, and the product should be formed using each factor the greatest number of times it occurs. The LCM of $12xy^2$ and $15x^3y$ would be $60x^3y^2$.

The equation $x^2 + 5x + 4$ factors to $(x + 4)(x + 1)$ and $x^2 + 2x + 1$, which factors to $(x + 1)(x + 1)$. The LCM would be $(x + 4)(x + 1)(x + 1)$.

To add or subtract expressions with unlike denominators: (1) subtraction should be changed to add the opposite; (2) the denominators are factored; (3) an LCM should be determined for the denominators; (4) the numerator and denominator of each expression should be multiplied by the missing factor(s); (5) the expressions that now have like denominators should be added; (6) the numerator should be factored; and (7) simplification should be performed if possible. Here's a sample expression:

$$\frac{x^2 + 6x + 11}{x^2 + 7x + 12} - \frac{2}{x + 3}$$

First, subtraction should be changed to addition:

$$\frac{x^2 + 6x + 11}{x^2 + 7x + 12} + \frac{-2}{x + 3}$$

Math Section

Then, the denominators are factored:

$$\frac{x^2 + 6x + 11}{(x + 4)(x + 3)} + \frac{-2}{x + 3}$$

The LCM of $(x + 4)(x + 3)$ and $(x + 3)$ should be determined, which is $(x + 4)(x + 3)$. The numerator and denominator should be multiplied by the missing factor:

$$\frac{x^2 + 6x + 11}{(x + 4)(x + 3)} + \frac{-2}{x + 3} \times \frac{(x + 4)}{(x + 4)}$$

$$\frac{x^2 + 6x + 11}{(x + 4)(x + 3)} + \frac{-2x - 8}{(x + 4)(x + 3)}$$

The expressions should be added, resulting in:

$$\frac{x^2 + 4x + 3}{(x + 4)(x + 3)}$$

The numerator should be factored:

$$\frac{(x + 3)(x + 1)}{(x + 4)(x + 3)}$$

Simplifying yields:

$$\frac{x + 1}{x + 4}$$

Interpreting Parts of Nonlinear Expressions in Terms of Their Context

When a nonlinear function is used to model a real-life scenario, some aspects of the function may be relevant while others may not. The context of each scenario will dictate what should be used. In general, x- and y-intercepts will be points of interest. A y-intercept is the value of y when x equals zero; and an x-intercept is the value of x when y equals zero. Suppose a nonlinear function models the value of an investment (y) over the course of time (x). It would be relevant to determine the initial value (the y-intercept where time equals zero), as well as any point in time in which the value would be zero (the x-intercept).

Another aspect of a function that is typically desired is the rate of change. This tells how fast the outputs are growing or decaying with respect to given inputs. For more on rates of change regarding quadratic and exponential functions, see the earlier sections on those types of functions. For polynomial functions, the rate of change can be estimated by the highest power of the function. Polynomial functions also include absolute and/or relative minimums and maximums. Functions modeling production or expenses should be considered. Maximum and minimum values would be relevant aspects of these models.

Finally, the domain and range for a function should be considered for relevance. The domain consists of all input values, and the range consists of all output values. For instance, a function could model the volume of a container to be produced in relation to its height. Although the function that models the

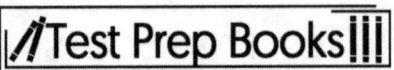

scenario may include negative values for inputs and outputs, these parts of the function would obviously not be relevant.

Understanding the Relationship Between Zeros and Factors of Polynomials

The zeros of a function are the x-intercepts of its graph. They are called zeros because they are the x-values for which $y = 0$.

Finding Zeros
To find the zeros of a polynomial function, it should be written in factored form, then each factor should be set equal to zero and solved. To find the zeros of the function $y = 3x^3 - 3x^2 - 36x$, the polynomial should be factored first. Factoring out a GCF results in:

$$y = 3x(x^2 - x - 12)$$

Then factoring the quadratic function yields:

$$y = 3x(x - 4)(x + 3)$$

Next, each factor should be set equal to zero: $3x = 0; x - 4 = 0; x + 3 = 0$. By solving each equation, it is determined that the function has zeros, or x-intercepts, at 0, 4, and -3.

Writing a Polynomial with Given Zeros
Given zeros for a polynomial function, to write the function, a linear factor corresponding to each zero should be written. The linear factor will be the opposite value of the zero added to x. Then the factors should be multiplied, and the function written in standard form. To write a polynomial with zeros at -2, 3, and 3, three linear factors should be written:

$$y = (x + 2)(x - 3)(x - 3)$$

Then, multiplication is used to convert the equation to standard form, producing:

$$y = x^3 - 4x^2 - 3x + 18$$

Dividing Polynomials by Linear Factors
To determine if a linear binomial is a factor of a polynomial, the polynomial should be divided by the binomial. If there is no remainder (it divides evenly), then the binomial is a factor of the polynomial. To determine if a value is a zero of a function, a binomial can be written from that zero and tested by division. To divide a polynomial by a linear factor, the terms of the dividend should be divided by the linear term of the divisor; the same process as long division of numbers (divide, multiply, subtract, drop down, and repeat) should be followed.

$$\frac{divisor \sqrt{quotient}}{dividend}$$

Remember that when subtracting a binomial, the signs of both terms should be changed. Here's a sample equation: divide $9x^3 - 18x^2 - x + 2$ by $3x + 1$. First, the problem should be set up as long division:

$$3x + 1 \overline{) 9x^3 - 18x^2 - x + 2}$$

Then the first term of the dividend ($9x^3$) should be divided by the linear term of the divisor ($3x$):

$$\begin{array}{r} 3x^2 \\ 3x + 1 \overline{) 9x^3 - 18x^2 - x + 2} \end{array}$$

Next, the divisor should be multiplied by that term of the quotient:

$$\begin{array}{r} 3x^2 - 7x + 2 \\ 3x + 1 \overline{) 9x^3 - 18x^2 - x + 2} \\ -9x^3 - 3x^2 \end{array}$$

Subtraction should come next:

$$\begin{array}{r} 3x^2 - 7x + 2 \\ 3x + 1 \overline{) 9x^3 - 18x^2 - x + 2} \\ \underline{-9x^3 - 3x^2 } \\ -21x^2 \end{array}$$

Now, the next term ($-x$) should be dropped down:

$$\begin{array}{r} 3x^2 - 7x + 2 \\ 3x + 1 \overline{) 9x^3 - 18x^2 - x + 2} \\ \underline{-9x^3 - 3x^2 } \\ -21x^2 - x \end{array}$$

Then the process should be repeated, dividing $-21x^2$ by $3x$:

$$\begin{array}{r} 3x^2 - 7x + 2 \\ 3x + 1 \overline{) 9x^3 - 18x^2 - x + 2} \\ \underline{-9x^3 - 3x^2 } \\ -21x^2 - x \\ \underline{+21x^2 + 7x } \\ 6x \end{array}$$

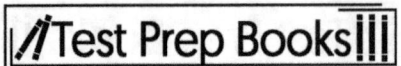

The next term (2) should be dropped and repeated by dividing $6x$ by $3x$:

$$\begin{array}{r}
3x^2 - 7x + 2 \\
3x + 1 \overline{\smash{)}\, 9x^3 - 18x^2 - x + 2} \\
\underline{-9x^3 - 3x^2 } \\
-21x^2 - x \\
\underline{+21x^2 + 7x } \\
6x + 2 \\
\underline{-6x - 2} \\
0
\end{array}$$

There is no remainder; therefore, $3x + 1$ is a factor of:

$$9x^3 - 18x^2 - x + 2$$

By the definition of factors:

$$(3x + 1)(3x^2 - 7x + 2) = 9x^3 - 18x^2 - x + 2$$

The quadratic expression can further be factored to produce:

$$(3x + 1)(3x - 1)(x - 2)$$

Understanding a Nonlinear Relationship Between Two Variables

Questions on this material will assess the ability of test takers to make connections between linear or nonlinear equations and their graphical representations. It will also require interpreting graphs in relation to systems of equations.

Graphs of Polynomial Functions

A polynomial function consists of a monomial or sum of monomials arranged in descending exponential order. The graph of a polynomial function is a smooth continuous curve that extends infinitely on both ends. From the equation of a polynomial function, the following can be determined: (1) the end behavior of the graph—does it rise or fall to the left and to the right; (2) the *y*-intercept and *x*-intercept(s) and whether the graph simply touches or passes through each *x*-intercept; and (3) the largest possible number of turning points, where the curve changes from rising to falling or vice versa. To graph the function, these three aspects of the graph should be determined and extra points between the intercepts should be found if necessary.

End Behavior

The end behavior of the graph of a polynomial function can be determined by the degree of the function (largest exponent) and the leading coefficient (coefficient of the term with the largest exponent). There are four possible scenarios for the end behavior: (1) if the degree is odd and the coefficient is positive, the graph falls to the left and rises to the right; (2) if the degree is odd and the coefficient is negative, the graph rises to the left and falls to the right; (3) if the degree is even and the coefficient is positive, the graph rises to the left and rises to the right, or (4) if the degree is even and the coefficient is negative, the graph falls to the left and falls to the right.

Odd degree polynomials	with a positive leading coefficient	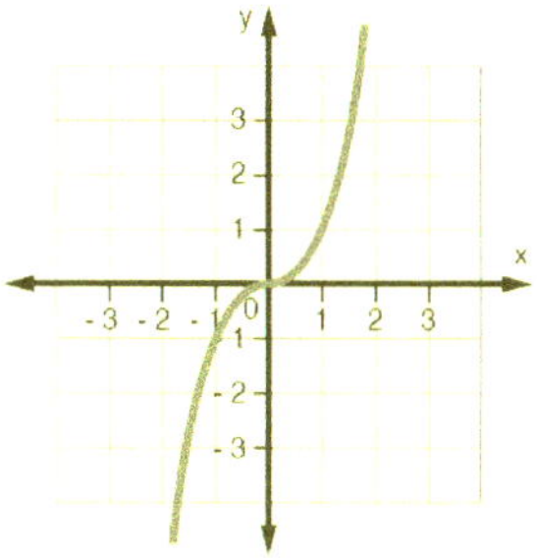	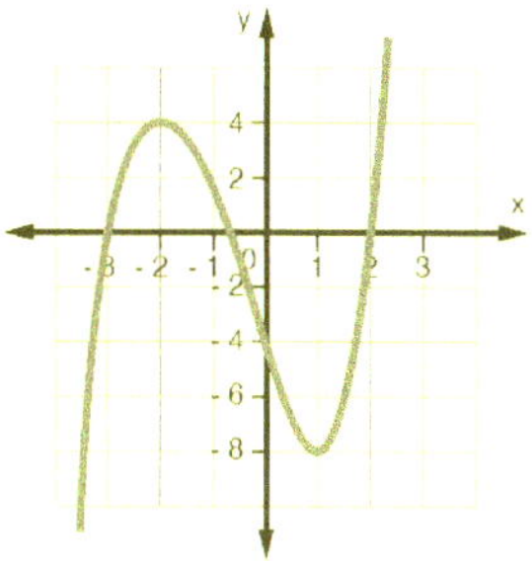
	with a positive leading coefficient	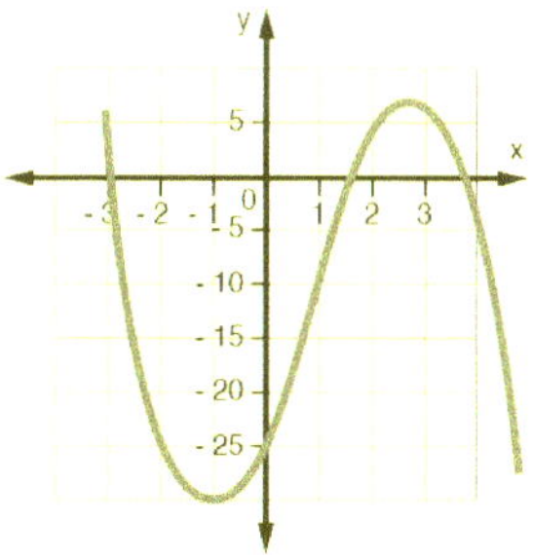	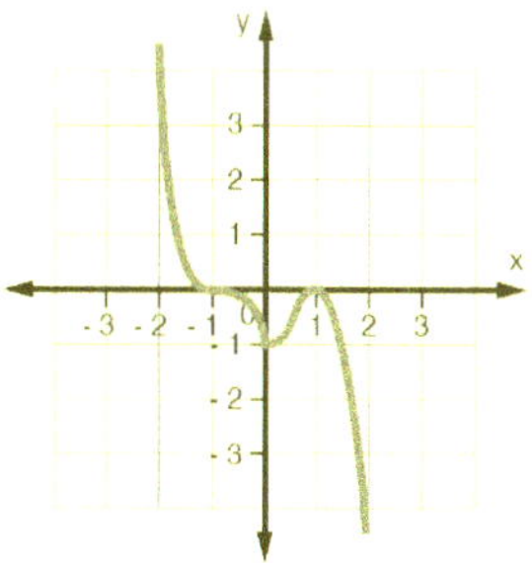
Even degree polynomials	with a positive leading coefficient	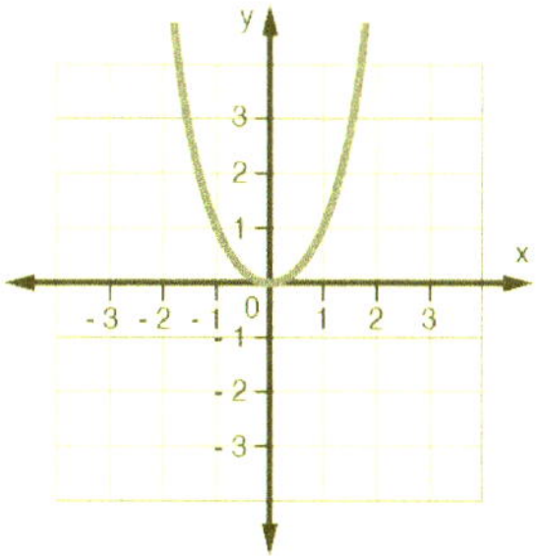	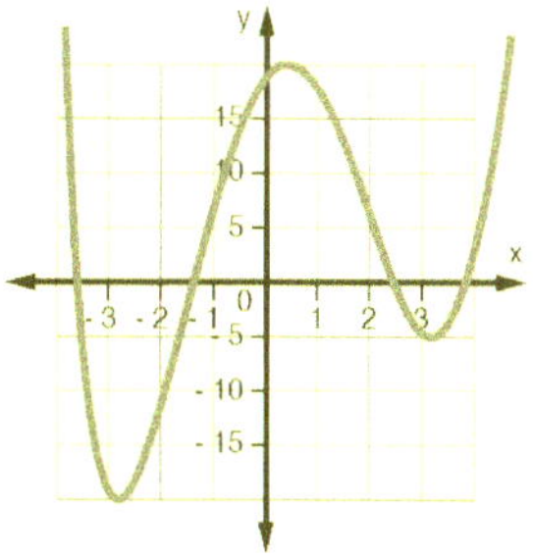
	with a positive leading coefficient	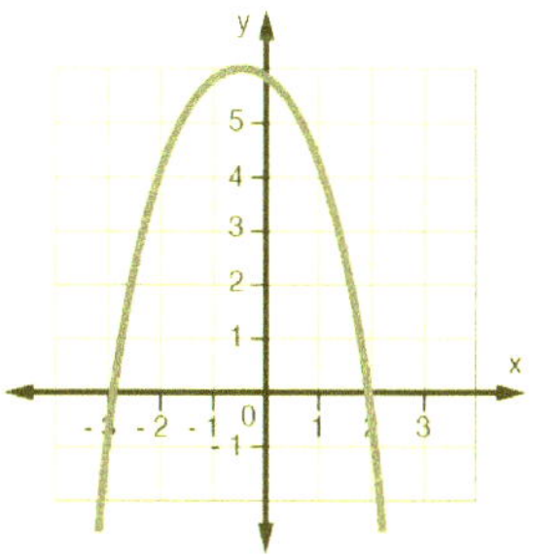	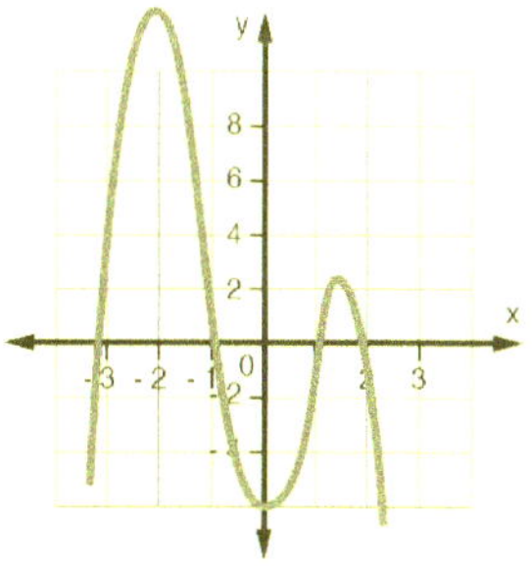

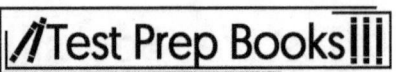

Math Section

X and Y-Intercepts

The y-intercept for any function is the point at which the graph crosses the y-axis. At this point $x = 0$; therefore, to determine the y-intercept, $x = 0$ should be substituted into the function and solved for y. Finding x-intercepts, also called zeros, is covered in a previous section. For a given zero of a function, the graph can either pass through that point or simply touch that point (the graph turns at that zero). This is determined by the multiplicity of that zero. The multiplicity of a zero is the number of times its corresponding factor is multiplied to obtain the function in standard form. For example:

$$y = x^3 - 4x^2 - 3x + 18$$

can be written in factored form as:

$$y = (x + 2)(x - 3)(x - 3)$$

or

$$y = (x + 2)(x - 3)^2$$

The zeros of the function would be -2 and 3. The zero at -2 would have a multiplicity of 1, and the zero at 3 would have a multiplicity of 2. If a zero has an even multiplicity, then the graph touches the x-axis at that zero and turns around. If a zero has an odd multiplicity, then the graph crosses the x-axis at that zero.

Turning Points

The graph of a polynomial function can have, at most, a number of turning points equal to one less than the degree of the function. It is possible to have fewer turning points than this value. For example, the function:

$$y = 3x^5 + 2x^2 - 3x$$

could have no more than four turning points.

Using Function Notation, and Interpreting Statements Using Function Notation.

Function notation is covered in the *Function/Linear Equation Notation* section under *Heart of Algebra*.

Addition, Subtraction, Multiplication and Division of Functions

Functions denoted by $f(x)$, $g(x)$, etc., can be added, subtracted, multiplied, or divided. For example, the function:

$$f(x) = 15x + 100$$

represents the cost to have a catered party at a banquet hall (where x represents the number of guests); and the function $g(x) = 10x$ represents the cost for unlimited drinks at the party. The total cost of a catered party with unlimited drinks can be represented by adding the functions $f(x)$ and $g(x)$. In this case:

$$f(x) + g(x) = (15x + 100) + (10x)$$

Math Section

Therefore:

$$f(x) + g(x) = 25x + 100$$

$(f(x) + g(x))$ can also be written $(f + g)(x))$. To add, subtract, multiply, or divide functions, the values of the functions should be substituted and the rules for operations with polynomials should be followed. It should be noted:

$$(f - g)(x) = f(x) - g(x); (f \times g)(x) = f(x) \times g(x)$$

and

$$\left(\frac{f}{g}\right)(x) = \frac{f(x)}{g(x)}$$

Composition of Functions

A composite function is one in which two functions are combined such that the output from the first function becomes the input for the second function (one function should be applied after another function). The composition of a function written as $(g \circ f)(x)$ or $g(f(x))$ is read "g of f of x." The inner function, $f(x)$, would be evaluated first and the answer would be used as the input of the outer function, $g(x)$. To determine the value of a composite function, the value of the inner function should be substituted for the variable of the outer function.

Here's a sample problem:

A store is offering a 20% discount on all of its merchandise. You have a coupon worth $5 off any item.

The cost of an item with the 20% discount can be modeled by the function:

$$d(x) = 0.8x$$

The cost of an item with the coupon can be modeled by the function $c(x) = x - 5$. A composition of functions to model the cost of an item applying the discount first and then the coupon would be:

$$c(d(x))$$

Replacing $d(x)$ with its value $(0.8x)$ results in $c(0.8x)$. By evaluating the function $c(x)$ with an input of $0.8x$, it is determined that:

$$c(d(x)) = 0.8x - 5$$

To model the cost of an item if the coupon is applied first and then the discount, $d(c(x))$ should be determined. The result would be:

$$d(c(x)) = 0.8x - 4$$

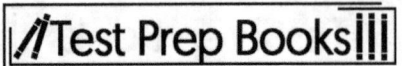

Math Section

Evaluating Functions

If a problem asks to evaluate with operations between functions, the new function should be determined and then the given value should be substituted as the input of the new function. To find $(f \times g)(3)$, given $f(x) = x + 1$ and $g(x) = 2x - 3$, the following should be determined:

$$(f \times g)(x)$$

$$f(x) \times g(x)$$

$$(x + 1)(2x - 3)$$

$$2x^2 - x - 3$$

Therefore:

$$(f \times g)(x) = 2x^2 - x - 3$$

To find $(f \times g)(3)$, the function $(f \times g)(x)$ needs to be evaluated for an input of 3:

$$(f \times g)(3)$$

$$2(3)^2 - (3) - 3 = 12$$

Therefore:

$$(f \times g)(3) = 12$$

Using Structure to Isolate or Identify a Quantity of Interest

Formulas are mathematical expressions that define the value of one quantity given the value of one or more different quantities. A formula or equation expressed in terms of one variable can be manipulated to express the relationship in terms of any other variable. The equation $y = 3x + 2$ is expressed in terms of the variable y. By manipulating the equation, it can be written as:

$$x = \frac{y - 2}{3}$$

This is expressed in terms of the variable x. To manipulate an equation or formula to solve for a variable of interest, how the equation would be solved if all other variables were numbers should be considered. The same steps for solving should be followed, leaving operations in terms of the variables, instead of calculating numerical values.

The formula $P = 2l + 2w$ expresses how to calculate the perimeter of a rectangle given its length and width. To write a formula to calculate the width of a rectangle given its length and perimeter, the previous formula relating the three variables should be used and the variable w should be solved. If P and l were numerical values, this would be a two-step linear equation solved by subtraction and division.

To solve the equation $P = 2l + 2w$ for w, $2l$ should be subtracted from both sides:

$$P - 2l = 2w$$

Math Section

Then, both sides should be divided by 2:

$$\frac{P - 2l}{2} = w$$

or

$$\frac{P}{2} - l = w$$

The distance formula between two points on a coordinate plane can be found using the formula:

$$d = \sqrt{(x_2 - x_1)^2 + (y_2 - y_1)^2}$$

A problem might require determining the x-coordinate of one point (x_2), given its y-coordinate (y_2) and the distance (d) between that point and another given point (x_1, y_1). To do so, the above formula for x_1 should be solved just as a radical equation containing numerical values in place of the other variables.

Both sides should be squared; the quantity should be subtracted $(y_2 - y_1)^2$; the square root of both sides should be taken; x_1 should be subtracted to produce:

$$\sqrt{d^2 - (y_2 - y_1)^2} + x_1 = x_2$$

Problem-Solving and Data Analysis

Using Ratios, Rates, Proportions, and Scale Drawings to Solve Single- and Multistep Problems

Ratios, rates, proportions, and scale drawings are used when comparing two quantities. Questions on this material will include expressing relationships in simplest terms and solving for missing quantities.

Ratios

A ratio is a comparison of two quantities that represent separate groups. For example, if a recipe calls for 2 eggs for every 3 cups of milk, it can be expressed as a ratio. Ratios can be written three ways: (1) with the word "to"; (2) using a colon; or (3) as a fraction. For the previous example, the ratio of eggs to cups of milk can be written as: 2 to 3, 2:3, or $\frac{2}{3}$. When writing ratios, the order is important. The ratio of eggs to cups of milk is not the same as the ratio of cups of milk to eggs, 3:2.

In simplest form, both quantities of a ratio should be written as integers. These should also be reduced just as a fraction would be. For example, 5:10 would reduce to 1:2. Given a ratio where one or both quantities are expressed as a decimal or fraction, both should be multiplied by the same number to produce integers. To write the ratio $\frac{1}{3}$ to 2 in simplest form, both quantities should be multiplied by 3. The resulting ratio is 1 to 6.

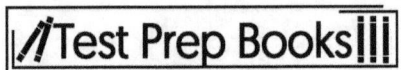

Math Section

When a problem involving ratios gives a comparison between two groups, then: (1) a total should be provided and a part should be requested; or (2) a part should be provided and a total should be requested. Consider the following:

The ratio of boys to girls in the 11th grade is 5:4. If there is a total of 270 11th grade students, how many are girls?

To solve this, the total number of "ratio pieces" first needs to be determined. The total number of 11th grade students is divided into 9 pieces. The ratio of boys to total students is 5:9; and the ratio of girls to total students is 4:9. Knowing the total number of students, the number of girls can be determined by setting up a proportion:

$$\frac{4}{9} = \frac{x}{270}$$

Solving the proportion, it shows that there are 120 11th grade girls.

Rates

A rate is a ratio comparing two quantities expressed in different units. A unit rate is one in which the second is one unit. Rates often include the word *per*. Examples include miles per hour, beats per minute, and price per pound. The word *per* can be represented with a / symbol or abbreviated with the letter "p" and the units abbreviated. For example, miles per hour would be written mi/h. Given a rate that is not in simplest form (second quantity is not one unit), both quantities should be divided by the value of the second quantity. Suppose a patient had 99 heartbeats in 1½ minutes. To determine the heart rate, 1½ should divide both quantities. The result is 66 bpm.

Scale Drawings

Scale drawings are used in designs to model the actual measurements of a real-world object. For example, the blueprint of a house might indicate that it is drawn at a scale of 3 inches to 8 feet. Given one value and asked to determine the width of the house, a proportion should be set up to solve the problem. Given the scale of 3in:8ft and a blueprint width of 1 ft (12 in.), to find the actual width of the building, the proportion:

$$\frac{3}{8} = \frac{12}{x}$$

should be used. This results in an actual width of 32 ft.

Proportions

A proportion is a statement consisting of two equal ratios. Proportions will typically give three of four quantities and require solving for the missing value. The key to solving proportions is to set them up properly. Here's a sample problem:

If 7 gallons of gas costs $14.70, how many gallons can you get for $20?

The information should be written as equal ratios with a variable representing the missing quantity:

$$\left(\frac{\text{gallons}}{\text{cost}} = \frac{\text{gallons}}{\text{cost}}\right) : \frac{7}{14.70} = \frac{x}{20}$$

To solve, cross multiplication (multiplying the numerator of the first ratio by the denominator of the second and vice versa) is used, and the products are set equal to each other. Cross-multiplying results in:

$$(7)(20) = (14.7)(x)$$

Solving the equation for x, it can be determined that 9.5 gallons of gas can be purchased for $20.

Indirect Proportions

The proportions described above are referred to as direct proportions or direct variation. For direct proportions, as one quantity increases, the other quantity also increases. For indirect proportions (also referred to as indirect variations, inverse proportions, or inverse variations), as one quantity increases, the other decreases. Direct proportions can be written:

$$\frac{y_1}{x_1} = \frac{y_2}{x_2}$$

Conversely, indirect proportions are written:

$$y_1 x_1 = y_2 x_2$$

Here's a sample problem:

It takes 3 carpenters 10 days to build the frame of a house. How long should it take 5 carpenters to build the same frame?

In this scenario, as one quantity increases (number of carpenters), the other decreases (number of days building); therefore, this is an inverse proportion. To solve, the products of the two variables (in this scenario, the total work performed) are set equal to each other:

$$(y_1 x_1 = y_2 x_2)$$

Using y to represent carpenters and x to represent days, the resulting equation is:

$$(3)(10) = (5)(x_2)$$

Solving for x_2, it is determined that it should take 5 carpenters 6 days to build the frame of the house.

Solving Single- and Multistep Problems Involving Percentages

The word percent means "per hundred." When dealing with percentages, it may be helpful to think of the number as a value in hundredths. For example, 15% can be expressed as "fifteen hundredths" and written as $\frac{15}{100}$ or .15.

Converting from Decimals and Fractions to Percentages

To convert a decimal to a percent, a number is multiplied by 100. To write .25 as a percent, the equation $.25 \times 100$ yields 25%. To convert a fraction to a percent, the fraction is converted to a decimal and then multiplied by 100. To convert $\frac{3}{5}$ to a decimal, the numerator (3) is divided by the denominator (5). This results in .6, which is then multiplied by 100 to get 60%.

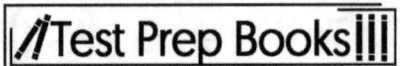

Math Section

To convert a percent to a decimal, the number is divided by 100. For example, 150% is equal to 1.5 $\left(\frac{150}{100}\right)$. To convert a percent to a fraction, the percent sign is deleted, and the value is written as the numerator with a denominator of 100. For example:

$$2\% = \frac{2}{100}$$

Fractions should be reduced:

$$\frac{2}{100} = \frac{1}{50}$$

Percent Problems

Material on percentages can include questions such as: What is 15% of 25? What percent of 45 is 3? Five is $\frac{1}{2}$% of what number? To solve these problems, the information should be rewritten as an equation where the following helpful steps are completed: (1) "what" is represented by a variable (x); (2) "is" is represented by an = sign; and (3) "of" is represented by multiplication. Any values expressed as a percent should be written as a decimal; and if the question is asking for a percent, the answer should be converted accordingly. Here are three sample problems based on the information above:

What is 15% of 25?
$x = .15 \times 25$
$x = 3.75$

What percent of 45 is 3?
$x \times 45 = 3$
$x = 0.0\overline{6}$
$x = 6.\overline{6}\%$

Five is $\frac{1}{2}$% of what number?
$5 = .005 \times x$
$x = 1,000$

Percent Increase/Decrease

Problems dealing with percentages may involve an original value, a change in that value, and a percentage change. A problem will provide two pieces of information and ask to find the third. To do so, this formula is used:

$$\frac{change}{original\ value} \times 100 = percent\ change$$

Here's a sample problem:

Attendance at a baseball stadium has dropped 16% from last year. Last year's average attendance was 40,000. What is this year's average attendance?

Using the formula and information, the change is unknown (x), the original value is 40,000, and the percent change is 16%. The formula can be written as:

$$\frac{x}{40,000} \times 100 = 16$$

When solving for x, it is determined the change was 6,400. The problem asked for this year's average attendance, so to calculate, the change (6,400) is subtracted from last year's attendance (40,000) to determine this year's average attendance is 33,600.

Math Section

Percent More Than/Less Than

Percentage problems may give a value and what percent that given value is more than or less than an original unknown value. Here's a sample problem:

A store advertises that all its merchandise has been reduced by 25%. The new price of a pair of shoes is $60. What was the original price?

This problem can be solved by writing a proportion. Two ratios should be written comparing the cost and the percent of the original cost. The new cost is 75% of the original cost (100% - 25%), and the original cost is 100% of the original cost. The unknown original cost can be represented by x. The proportion would be set up as:

$$\frac{60}{75} = \frac{x}{100}$$

Solving the proportion, it is determined the original cost was $80.

Solving Single- and Multistep Problems

Unit Rates

A rate is a ratio in which two terms are in different units. When rates are expressed as a quantity of one, they are considered unit rates. To determine a unit rate, the first quantity is divided by the second. Knowing a unit rate makes calculations easier than simply having a rate. Suppose someone bought a 3 lbs bag of onions for $1.77. To calculate the price of 5lbs of onions, a proportion could be set up as follows:

$$\frac{3}{1.77} = \frac{5}{x}$$

However, knowing the unit rate, multiplying the value of pounds of onions by the unit price is another way to find the solution: (The unit price would be calculated $\frac{\$1.77}{3 \text{ lbs}} = \frac{\$0.59}{\text{lb}}$ or $0.59 per pound.)

$$5 \text{ lbs} \times \frac{\$.59}{\text{lb}} = \$2.95 \text{ (The "lbs" units cancel out.)}$$

Unit Conversion

Unit conversions apply to many real-world scenarios, including cooking, measurement, construction, and currency. Problems on this material can be solved similarly to those involving unit rates. Given the conversion rate, it can be written as a fraction (ratio) and multiplied by a quantity in one unit to convert it to the corresponding unit. For example, someone might want to know how many minutes are in 3½ hours. The conversion rate of 60 minutes to 1 hour can be written as:

$$\frac{60 \text{ min}}{1 \text{ h}}$$

Multiplying the quantity by the conversion rate results in:

$$3\frac{1}{2} \text{ h} \times \frac{60 \text{ min}}{1 \text{ h}} = 210 \text{ min}$$

The "h" unit is canceled. To convert a quantity in minutes to hours, the fraction for the conversion rate would be flipped (to cancel the "min" unit). To convert 195 minutes to hours, the equation:

$$195 \text{ min} \times \frac{1 \text{ h}}{60 \text{ min}}$$

would be used. The result is $\frac{195 \text{ h}}{60}$, which reduces to $3\frac{1}{4}$ hours.

Converting units may require more than one multiplication. The key is to set up the conversion rates so that units cancel out each other and the desired unit is left. Suppose someone wants to convert 3.25 yards to inches, given that 1 yd = 3 ft and 12 in = 1 ft. To calculate, the equation:

$$3.25 \text{ yd} \times \frac{3 \text{ ft}}{1 \text{ yd}} \times \frac{12 \text{ in}}{1 \text{ ft}}$$

would be used. The "yd" and "ft" units will cancel, resulting in 117 inches.

Using Linear, Quadratic, or Exponential Models

Scatterplots can be used to determine whether a correlation exists between two variables. The horizontal (x) axis represents the independent variable and the vertical (y) axis represents the dependent variable. If when graphed, the points model a linear, quadratic, or exponential relationship, then a correlation is said to exist. If so, a line of best-fit or curve of best-fit can be drawn through the points, with the points relatively close on either side. Writing the equation for the line or curve allows for predicting values for the variables. Suppose a scatterplot displays the value of an investment as a function of years after investing. By writing an equation for the line or curve and substituting a value for one variable into the equation, the corresponding value for the other variable can be calculated.

Linear Models
If the points of a scatterplot model a linear relationship, a line of best-fit is drawn through the points. If the line of best-fit has a positive slope (y-values increase as x-values increase), then the variables have a positive correlation. If the line of best-fit has a negative slope (y-values decrease as x-values increase), then a negative correlation exists. A positive or negative correlation can also be categorized as strong or weak, depending on how closely the points are grouped around the line of best-fit.

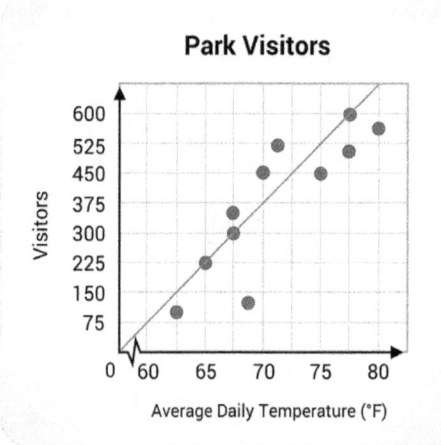

Math Section

Given a line of best-fit, its equation can be written by identifying: the slope and y-intercept; a point and the slope; or two points on the line.

Quadratic Models

A quadratic function can be written in the form:

$$y = ax^2 + bx + c$$

The u-shaped graph of a quadratic function is called a parabola. The graph can either open up or open down (upside down u). The graph is symmetric about a vertical line, called the axis of symmetry. Corresponding points on the parabola are directly across from each other (same y-value) and are the same distance from the axis of symmetry (on either side). The axis of symmetry intersects the parabola at its vertex. The y-value of the vertex represents the minimum or maximum value of the function. If the graph opens up, the value of a in its equation is positive, and the vertex represents the minimum of the function. If the graph opens down, the value of a in its equation is negative, and the vertex represents the maximum of the function.

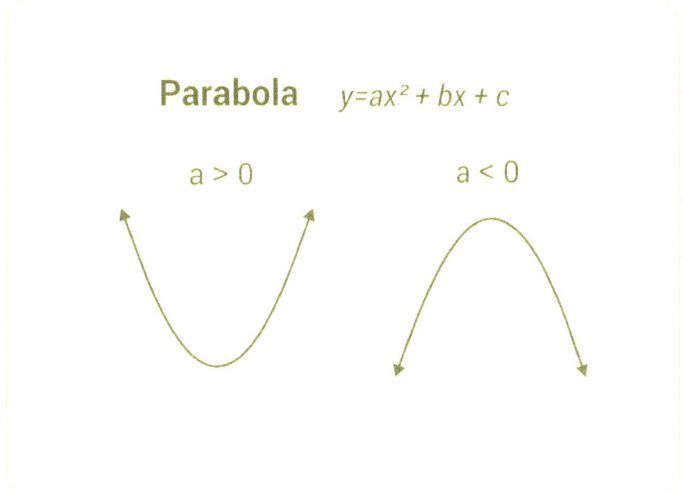

Given a curve of best-fit that models a quadratic relationship, the equation of the parabola can be written by identifying the vertex of the parabola and another point on the graph. The values for the vertex (h, k) and the point (x, y) should be substituted into the vertex form of a quadratic function:

$$y = a(x - h)^2 + k$$

to determine the value of a. To write the equation of a quadratic function with a vertex of $(4, 7)$ and containing the point $(8, 3)$, the values for $h, k, x,$ and y should be substituted into the vertex form of a quadratic function, resulting in:

$$3 = a(8 - 4)^2 + 7$$

Solving for a, yields $a = -\frac{1}{4}$. Therefore, the equation of the function can be written as:

$$y = -\frac{1}{4}(x-4)^2 + 7$$

The vertex form can be manipulated in order to write the quadratic function in standard form.

Exponential Models

An exponential curve can be used as a curve of best-fit for a scatterplot. The general form for an exponential function is:

$$y = ab^x$$

where b must be a positive number and cannot equal 1. When the value of b is greater than 1, the function models exponential growth (as x increases, y increases). When the value of b is less than 1, the function models exponential decay (as x increases, y decreases). If a is positive, the graph consists of points above the x-axis; if a is negative, the graph consists of points below the x-axis.

An asymptote is a line that a graph approaches.

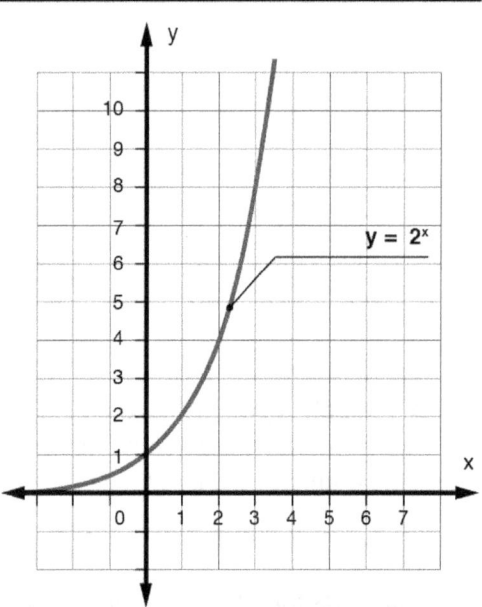

Given a curve of best-fit modeling an exponential function, its equation can be written by identifying two points on the curve. To write the equation of an exponential function containing the ordered pairs $(2, 2)$ and $(3, 4)$, the ordered pair $(2, 2)$ should be substituted in the general form and solved for a:

$$2 = a \times b^2 \rightarrow a = \frac{2}{b^2}$$

Math Section

The ordered pair $(3, 4)$ and $\frac{2}{b^2}$ should be substituted in the general form and solved for b

$$4 = \frac{2}{b^2} \times b^3 \rightarrow b = 2$$

Then, 2 should be substituted for b in the equation for a and then solved for a:

$$a = \frac{2}{2^2} \rightarrow a = \frac{1}{2}$$

Knowing the values of a and b, the equation can be written as:

$$y = \frac{1}{2} \times 2^x$$

Investigating Key Features of a Graph

Material on graphing relationships between two variables may include linear, quadratic, and exponential functions. Graphing linear functions is covered in a previous section.

Graphing Quadratic Functions

The standard form of a quadratic function is:

$$y = ax^2 + bx + c$$

The graph of a quadratic function is a u-shaped (or upside down u) curve, called a parabola, which is symmetric about a vertical line (axis of symmetry). To graph a parabola, its vertex (high or low point for the curve) and at least two points on each side of the axis of symmetry need to be determined.

Given a quadratic function in standard form, the axis of symmetry for its graph is the line:

$$x = -\frac{b}{2a}$$

The vertex for the parabola has an x-coordinate of $-\frac{b}{2a}$. To find the y-coordinate for the vertex, the calculated x-coordinate needs to be substituted. To complete the graph, two different x-values need to be selected and substituted into the quadratic function to obtain the corresponding y-values. This will give two points on the parabola. These two points and the axis of symmetry are used to determine the two points corresponding to these. The corresponding points are the same distance from the axis of symmetry (on the other side) and contain the same y-coordinate.

Plotting the vertex and four other points on the parabola allows for constructing the curve.

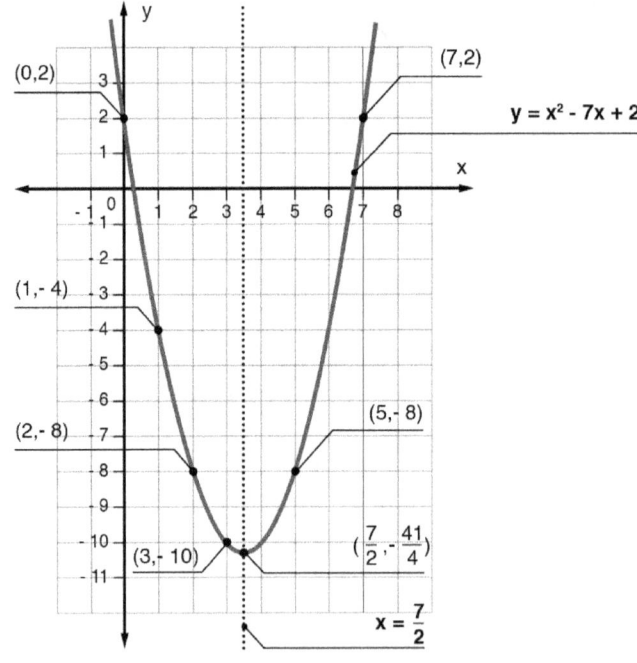

Graphing Exponential Functions
Exponential functions have a general form of:

$$y = a \times b^x$$

The graph of an exponential function is a curve that slopes upward or downward from left to right. The graph approaches a line, called an asymptote, as x or y increases or decreases. To graph the curve for an exponential function, x-values are selected and then substituted into the function to obtain the corresponding y-values. A general rule of thumb is to select three negative values, zero, and three positive values. Plotting the seven points on the graph for an exponential function should allow for constructing a smooth curve through them.

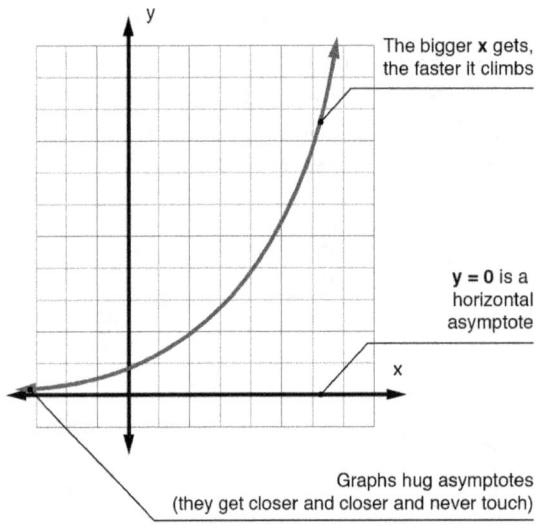

Math Section

Comparing Linear Growth with Exponential Growth

Both linear and exponential equations can model a relationship of growth or decay between two variables. If the dependent variable (y) increases as the independent variable (x) increases, the relationship is referred to as growth. If y decreases as x increases, the relationship is referred to as decay.

Linear Growth and Decay
A linear function can be written in the form:

$$y = mx + b$$

where x represents the inputs, y represents the outputs, b represents the y-intercept for the graph, and m represents the slope of the line. The y-intercept is the value of y when $x = 0$ and can be thought of as the "starting point." The slope is the rate of change between the variables x and y. A positive slope represents growth; a negative slope represents decay. Given a table of values for inputs (x) and outputs (y), a linear function would model the relationship if: x and y change at a constant rate per unit interval—for every two inputs a given distance apart, the distance between their corresponding outputs is constant. Here are some sample ordered pairs:

x	0	1	2	3
y	-7	-4	-1	2

For every 1 unit increase in x, y increases by 3 units. Therefore, the change is constant and thus represents linear growth.

Given a scenario involving growth or decay, determining if there is a constant rate of change between inputs (x) and outputs (y) will identify if a linear model is appropriate. A scenario involving distance and time might state that someone is traveling at a rate of 45 miles per hour. For every hour traveled (input), the distance traveled (output) increases by 45 miles. This is a constant rate of change.

The process for writing the equation to represent a linear model is covered in the section *Writing Linear Equations in Two Variables*.

Exponential Growth and Decay
An exponential function can be written in the form:

$$y = a \times b^x$$

The x- variable represents the inputs, y represents the outputs, a represents the y-intercept for the graph, and b represents the growth rate. The y-intercept is the value of y when $x = 0$ and can be thought of as the "starting point." If b is greater than 1, the function describes exponential growth; and if b is less than 1, the function describes exponential decay. Given a table of values for inputs (x) and outputs (y), an exponential function would model the relationship if the variables change by a common ratio over given intervals—for every two inputs a given distance apart, the quotients of their corresponding outputs is constant. Here are some sample ordered pairs:

x	0	1	2	3
y	3	6	12	24

For every 1 unit increase in x, the quotient of the corresponding y-values equals 2 (e.g., $\frac{6}{3}, \frac{12}{6}, \frac{24}{12}$). Therefore, the table represents exponential growth.

Given a scenario describing an exponential function, the growth or decay is expressed using multiplication. Words such as "doubling" and "halving" will often be used. A problem might indicate that the value of an investment triples every year or that every decade the population of an insect is halved. These indicate exponential growth and decay.

The process for writing the equation to represent an exponential model is covered in a previous section.

Using Two-Way Tables

Categorical data consists of numerical values found by dividing the entire set into subsets based on variables that represent categories. An example would be the survey results of high school seniors, specifying gender and asking whether they consume alcohol. The data can be arranged in a two-way frequency table (also called a contingency table).

Two-Way Frequency/Contingency Tables
A contingency table presents the frequency tables of both variables simultaneously, as shown below. The levels of one variable constitute the rows of the table, and the levels of the other constitute the columns. The margins consist of the sum of cell frequencies for each row and each column (marginal frequencies). The lower right corner value is the sum of marginal frequencies for the rows or the sum of the marginal frequencies for the columns. Both are equal to the total sample size.

	Drink Alcohol	Do Not Drink Alcohol	Total
Male	63	51	114
Female	37	68	105
Total	100	119	219

Conditional Frequencies
To calculate a conditional relative frequency, the cell frequency is divided by the marginal frequency for the desired outcome given the conditional category. For instance, using the table to determine the relative frequency that a female drinks, the number of females who drink (desired outcome) is divided by the total number of females (conditional category). The conditional relative frequency would equal $\frac{37}{105}$, which equals .35. If a problem asks for a conditional probability, the answer would be expressed as a fraction in simplest form. If asked for a percent, multiply the decimal by 100.

Association of Variables
An association between the variables exists if the conditional relative frequencies are different depending on condition. If the conditional relative frequencies are close to equal, then the variables are independent. For our example, 55% of senior males and 35% of senior females drink alcohol. The

difference between frequencies across conditions (male or female) is enough to conclude that an association exists between the variables.

Making Inferences about Population Parameters Based on Sample Data

Statistical inference, based in probability theory, makes calculated assumptions about an entire population based on data from a sample set from that population.

Population Parameters
A population is the entire set of people or things of interest. Suppose a study is intended to determine the number of hours of sleep per night for college females in the US. The population would consist of EVERY college female in the country. A sample is a subset of the population that may be used for the study. It would not be practical to survey every female college student, so a sample might consist of 100 students per school from 20 different colleges in the country. From the results of the survey, a sample statistic can be calculated. A sample statistic is a numerical characteristic of the sample data, including mean and variance. A sample statistic can be used to estimate a corresponding population parameter. A population parameter is a numerical characteristic of the entire population. Suppose the sample data had a mean (average) of 5.5. This sample statistic can be used as an estimate of the population parameter (average hours of sleep for every college female in the US).

Confidence Intervals
A population parameter is usually unknown and therefore is estimated using a sample statistic. This estimate may be highly accurate or relatively inaccurate based on errors in sampling. A confidence interval indicates a range of values likely to include the true population parameter. These are constructed at a given confidence level, such as 95%. This means that if the same population is sampled repeatedly, the true population parameter would occur within the interval for 95% of the samples.

Measurement Error
The accuracy of a population parameter based on a sample statistic may also be affected by measurement error, which is the difference between a quantity's true value and its measured value. Measurement error can be divided into random error and systematic error. An example of random error for the previous scenario would be a student reporting 8 hours of sleep when she actually sleeps 7 hours per night. Systematic errors are those attributed to the measurement system. Suppose the sleep survey gave response options of 2, 4, 6, 8, or 10 hours. This would lead to systematic measurement error.

Using Statistics

Descriptive statistics are used to gain an understanding of properties of a data set. This entails examining the center, spread, and shape of the sample data.

Center
The center of the sample set can be represented by its mean, median, or mode. The mean is the average of the data set, calculated by adding the data values and dividing by the sample size. The median is the value of the data point in the middle when the sample is arranged in numerical order. If the sample has an even number of data points, the mean of the two middle values is the median. The mode is the value that appears most often in a data set. It is possible to have multiple modes (if different values repeat equally as often) or no mode (if no value repeats).

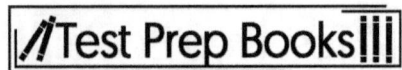

Spread

Methods for determining the spread of the sample include calculating the range and standard deviation for the data. The range is calculated by subtracting the lowest value from the highest value in the set. The standard deviation of the sample can be calculated using the formula:

$$\sigma = \sqrt{\frac{\sum(x - \bar{x})^2}{n - 1}}$$

where $\bar{x}$ = sample mean and n = sample size.

Shape

The shape of the sample when displayed as a histogram or frequency distribution plot helps to determine if the sample is normally distributed (bell-shaped curve), symmetrical, or has measures of skewness (lack of symmetry) or kurtosis. Kurtosis is a measure of whether the data are heavy-tailed (high number of outliers) or light-tailed (low number of outliers).

Evaluating Reports

The presentation of statistics can be manipulated to produce a desired outcome. Here's a statement to consider: "Four out of five dentists recommend our toothpaste." Who are the five dentists? This statement is very different from the statement: "Four out of every five dentists recommend our toothpaste." Whether intentional or unintentional, statistics can be misleading. Statistical reports should be examined to verify the validity and significance of the results. The context of the numerical values allows for deciphering the meaning, intent, and significance of the survey or study. Questions on this material will require students to use critical thinking skills to justify or reject results and conclusions.

When analyzing a report, who conducted the study and their intent should be considered. Was it performed by a neutral party or by a person or group with a vested interest? A study on health risks of smoking performed by a health insurance company would have a much different intent than one performed by a cigarette company. The sampling method and the data collection method should be considered too. Was it a true random sample of the population or was one subgroup over- or underrepresented? The sleep study scenario from the previous section is one example. If all 20 schools included in the study were state colleges, the results may be biased due to a lack of private school participants. Also, the measurement system used to obtain the data should be noted. Was the system accurate and precise or was it a flawed system? If possible responses were limited for the sleep study to 2, 4, 6, 8, or 10, it could be argued that the measurement system was flawed.

Every scenario involving statistical reports will be different. The key is to examine all aspects of the study before determining whether to accept or reject the results and corresponding conclusions.

Geometry and Trigonometry

Volume Formulas

Volume is the capacity of a three-dimensional shape. Volume is useful in determining the space within a certain three-dimensional object. Volume can be calculated for a cube, rectangular prism, cylinder, pyramid, cone, and sphere. By knowing specific dimensions of the objects, the volume of the object is computed with these figures. The units for the volumes of solids can include cubic centimeters, cubic meters, cubic inches, and cubic feet.

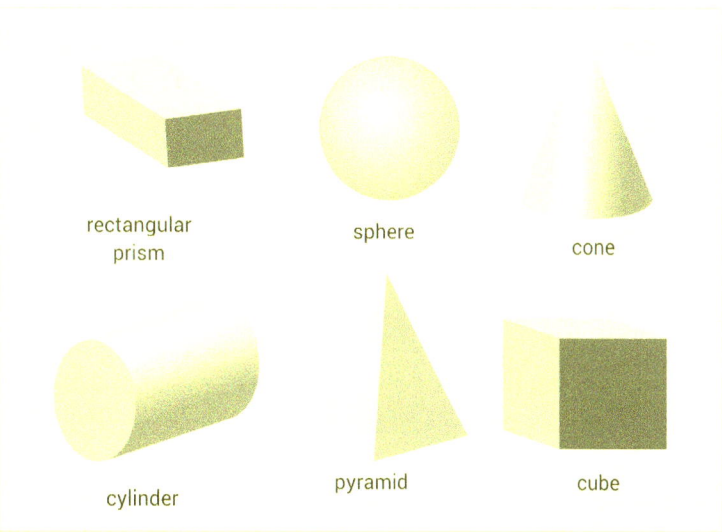

Cube

The cube is the simplest figure for which volume can be determined because all dimensions in a cube are equal. In the following example, the length, width, and height of the cube are all represented by the variable a because these measurements are equal lengths.

The volume of any rectangular, three-dimensional object is found by multiplying its length by its width by its height. In the case of a cube, the length, width, and height are all equal lengths, represented by the variable a. Therefore, the equation used to calculate the volume is $(a \times a \times a)$ or a^3. In a real-world example of this situation, if the length of a side of the cube is 3 centimeters, the volume is calculated by utilizing the formula:

$$(3 \times 3 \times 3) = 27 \text{ cm}^3$$

Rectangular Prism

The dimensions of a rectangular prism are not necessarily equal as those of a cube. Therefore, the formula for a rectangular prism recognizes that the dimensions vary and use different variables to represent these lengths. The length, width, and height of a rectangular prism can be represented with the variables a, b, and c.

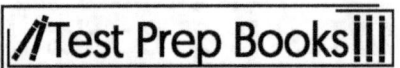

The equation used to calculate volume is length times width times height. In a real-world application of this situation, if $a = 2$ cm, $b = 3$ cm, and $c = 4$ cm, the volume is calculated by utilizing the formula:

$$2 \times 3 \times 4 = 24 \text{ cm}^3$$

Cylinder

Discovering a cylinder's volume requires the measurement of the cylinder's base, length of the radius, and height. The height of the cylinder can be represented with variable h, and the radius can be represented with variable r.

The formula to find the volume of a cylinder is $\pi r^2 h$. Notice that πr^2 is the formula for the area of a circle. This is because the base of the cylinder is a circle. To calculate the volume of a cylinder, the slices of circles needed to build the entire height of the cylinder are added together. For example, if the radius is 5 feet and the height of the cylinder is 10 feet, the cylinder's volume is calculated by using the following equation:

$$\pi 5^2 \times 10$$

Substituting 3.14 for π, the volume is 785 ft³.

Pyramid

To calculate the volume of a pyramid, the area of the base of the pyramid is multiplied by the pyramid's height and by $\frac{1}{3}$. The area of the base of the pyramid is found by multiplying the base length by the base width.

Therefore, the formula to calculate a pyramid's volume is:

$$(L \times W \times H) \div 3$$

Cone

The formula to calculate the volume of a circular cone is similar to the formula for the volume of a pyramid. The primary difference in determining the area of a cone is that a circle serves as the base of a cone. Therefore, the area of a circle is used for the cone's base.

The variable r represents the radius, and the variable h represents the height of the cone. The formula used to calculate the volume of a cone is:

$$\frac{1}{3}\pi r^2 h$$

Essentially, the area of the base of the cone is multiplied by the cone's height. In a real-life example where the radius of a cone is 2 meters and the height of a cone is 5 meters, the volume of the cone is calculated by utilizing the formula:

$$\frac{1}{3}\pi 2^2 \times 5 = 21$$

After substituting 3.14 for π, the volume is 21 m³.

Math Section

Sphere

The volume of a sphere uses π due to its circular shape.

The length of the radius, r, is the only variable needed to determine the sphere's volume. The formula to calculate the volume of a sphere is $\frac{4}{3}\pi r^3$. Therefore, if the radius of a sphere is 8 centimeters, the volume of the sphere is calculated by utilizing the formula:

$$\frac{4}{3}\pi(8)^3 = 2,144 \text{ cm}^3$$

Right Triangles: Pythagorean Theorem and Trigonometric Ratio

The value of a missing side of a right triangle may be determined two ways. The first way is to apply the Pythagorean Theorem, and the second way is to apply Trigonometric Ratios. The Pythagorean Theorem states that for every right triangle, the square of the length of the hypotenuse is equal to the sum of the squares of the lengths of the remaining two sides. The hypotenuse is the longest side of a right triangle and is also the side opposite the right angle.

According to the diagram $a^2 + b^2 = c^2$ where c represents the hypotenuse, and a and b represent the lengths of the remaining two sides of the right triangle.

The Pythagorean Theorem may be applied a multitude of ways. For example, a person wishes to build a garden in the shape of a rectangle, having the dimensions of 5 feet by 8 feet. The garden's design includes a diagonal board to separate various types of plants. The Pythagorean Theorem can be used to determine the length of the diagonal board.

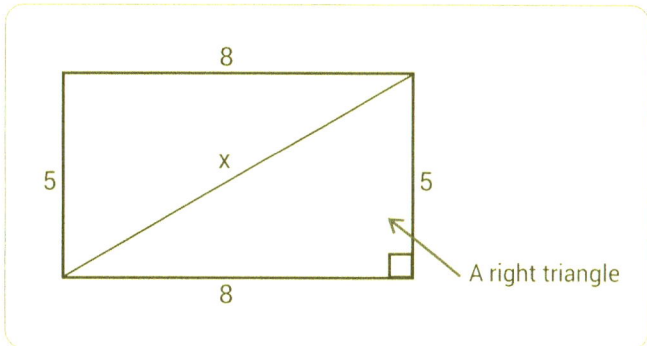

Given that side $a = 5$, side $b = 8$, and side c is unknown, use the following equation:

$$a^2 + b^2 = c^2$$

$$5^2 + 8^2 = c^2$$

$$25 + 64 = c^2$$

$$c = \sqrt{89}$$

$$c = 9.43$$

To solve for unknown sides of a right triangle using trigonometric ratios, the sine, cosine, and tangent are required.

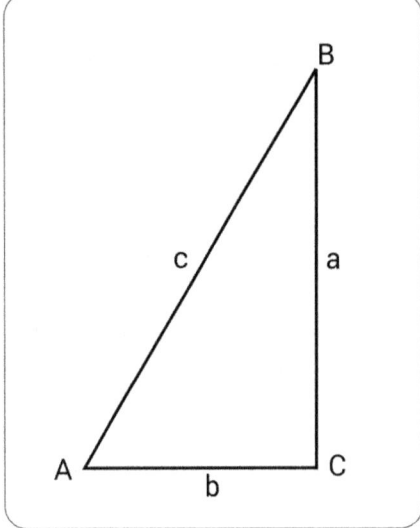

In the image above, angles are denoted by capital letters, and sides are denoted by lowercase letters. When examining angle A, b is the adjacent side, a is the opposite side, and c is the hypotenuse side. The various ratios of the lengths of the sides of the right triangle are used to find the sine, cosine, and tangent of angle A.

Thus:

$$\sin(A) = \frac{opposite}{hypotenuse}$$

$$\cos(A) = \frac{adjacent}{hypotenuse}$$

$$\tan(A) = \frac{opposite}{adjacent}$$

After substituting variables for the sides of the right triangle, $sin(A) = \frac{a}{c}$, $cos(A) = \frac{b}{c}$, and $tan(A) = \frac{a}{b}$.

Math Section

As a real-world example, the height of a tree can be discovered by using the information above. Surveying equipment can determine the tree's angle of inclination is 55.3 degrees, and the distance from the tree is 10 feet.

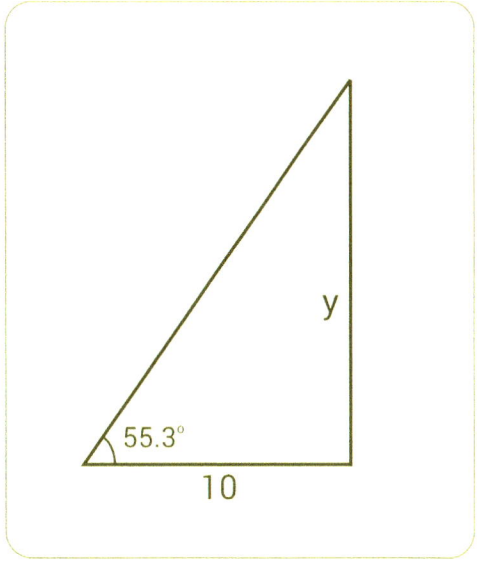

To find the height of the tree, substitute the known values into the trigonometric ratio of tangent:

$$\tan(55.3) = \frac{y}{10}$$

$$10 \times \tan(55.3) = y$$

$$10 \times 1.44418 = y$$

$$y = 14.4418$$

Operations with Complex Numbers

Complex numbers are numbers that have a real component and an imaginary component. An example of a complex number is $3 + 4i$. The real part of this complex number is 3, and the imaginary part of this complex number is $4i$. It is important to note that the imaginary number i is $\sqrt{-1}$. Complex numbers can be added, subtracted, multiplied, and divided.

Adding complex numbers together is similar to adding like terms. If given two complex numbers, students should first add the real components together and then add the imaginary components together. In this way, i is treated like a variable because it is only added or subtracted with other terms that contain i.

For example, if asked to simplify:

$$(2 + 4i) + (3 - 5i)$$

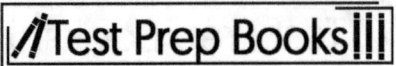

students should first add the real components together and then add the imaginary components together:

$$(2 + 4i) + (3 - 5i)$$

$$(2 + 3) + (4i + -5i) = 5 - i$$

In addition, if asked to subtract two complex numbers, students should first subtract the real components and then subtract the imaginary components: $(3 + 4i) - (1 + 2i)$ simplifies to:

$$(3 - 1) + (4i - 2i) = 2 + 2i$$

The examples below demonstrate how the imaginary number i is treated when it is raised to a power:

$$i^1 = i$$

$$i^2 = -1$$

$$i^3 = i \times -1 = -i$$

$$i^4 = -1 \times -1 = 1$$

To multiply complex numbers, students should use the FOIL distribution method and combine like terms. FOIL stands for first, outer, inner, and last. For example, when given two expressions of:

$$(2 + 4i)(3 + 2i)$$

the student multiplies the first term in each expression (2×3) to get 6. Next, the student multiplies the two outer terms together ($2 \times 2i$) to get $4i$. The student multiplies the two inner terms together ($4i \times 3$) to get $12i$. Then the student multiplies the last term of each expression together ($4i \times 2i$) to get $8i^2$. If using the values described above, $8i^2$ can be further simplified to -8 (since $i^2 = -1$). As a final step, the student combines like terms:

$$6 + 4i + 12i + -8 = -2 + 16i$$

To find the conjugate of a complex number, the sign is changed between the two terms in the denominator. For example, given the complex number $4 + 2i$, the student should change the operation sign in the middle of the two terms from addition to subtraction. Therefore, the complex conjugate becomes $4 - 2i$.

To divide complex numbers, the student should multiply by the conjugate of the complex number. The next step is to use the FOIL method in both the numerator and the denominator with the conjugate. For example, when given:

$$\frac{2 + 2i}{3 + i}$$

the conjugate of the denominator should be found first. The conjugate of $(3 + i)$ is $(3 - i)$, because the addition sign is changed to a subtraction sign. Given the new expression:

$$\frac{2 + 2i}{3 + i} \times \frac{3 - i}{3 - i}$$

Math Section

the student multiplies the two expressions in the numerator using the FOIL distribution method and the two expressions in the denominator using the FOIL distribution method. The numerator simplifies to:

$$(6 - 2i + 6i + -2i^2) = 8 + 4i$$

The denominator simplifies to:

$$(9 - 3i + 3i \pm i^2) = 10$$

As a final step, the student combines like terms: $\frac{8+4i}{10}$, which simplifies to $\frac{4+2i}{5}$.

Degrees and Radians

Degrees are used to express the size of an angle. A complete circle is represented by 360°, and a half circle is represented by 180°. In addition, a right angle fills one quarter of a circle and is represented by 90°.

Radians are another way to denote angles in terms of π, rather than degrees. A complete circle is represented by 2π radians. The formula used to convert degrees to radians is:

$$Radians = \frac{degrees \times \pi}{180}$$

For example, to convert 270 degrees to radians:

$$Radians = \frac{270 \times \pi}{180} = 4.71$$

The *arc of a circle* is the distance between two points on the circle. The length of the arc of a circle in terms of *degrees* is easily determined if the value of the central angle is known. The length of the arc is simply the value of the central angle. In this example, the length of the arc of the circle in degrees is 75°.

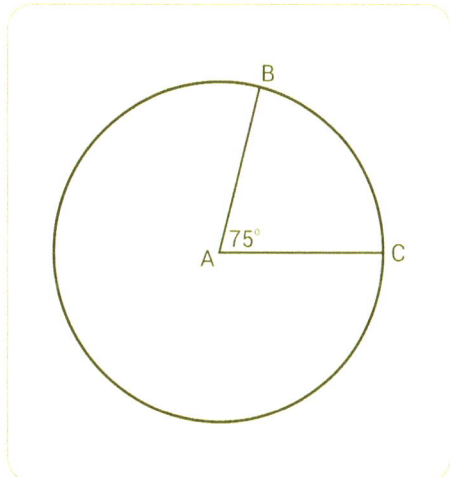

To determine the length of the arc of a circle in distance, the values for both the central angle and the radius must be known. This formula is:

$$\frac{\text{central angle}}{360°} = \frac{\text{arc length}}{2\pi r}$$

The equation is simplified by cross-multiplying to solve for the arc length.

In the following example, to solve for arc length, substitute the values of the central angle (75°) and the radius (10 inches) into the equation above.

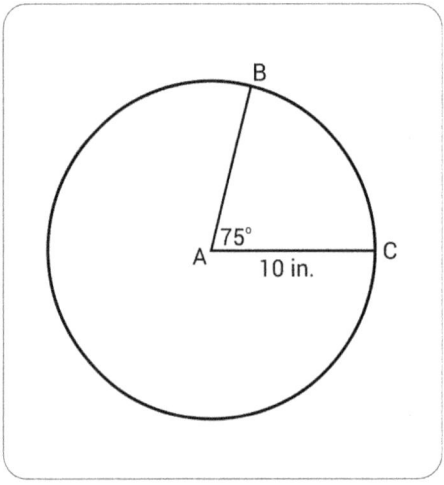

$$\frac{75°}{360°} = \frac{\text{arc length}}{2(3.14)(10\text{in.})}$$

To solve the equation, first cross-multiply: $4710 = 360(\text{arc length})$. Next, divide each side of the equation by 360. The result of the formula is that the arc length is 13.1 (rounded). Please note that arc length is often referred to as s.

As a special technological note for trigonometric functions, when finding the trigonometric function or an angle on the calculator, make a note using degrees or radians to get the correct value. Whether computing the sine of $\frac{\pi}{6}$ or computing the sine of 30°, the answer should come out to $\frac{1}{2}$. However, there is usually a "Mode" function on the calculator to select either radian or degree.

Circles

The equation used to find the area of a circle is $A = \pi r^2$. For example, if a circle has a radius of 5 centimeters, the area is computed by substituting 5 for the radius: $(5)^2$. Using this reasoning, to find half of the area of a circle, the formula is $A = 0.5\pi r^2$. Similarly, to find the quarter of an area of a circle, the formula is $A = 0.25\pi r^2$. To find any fractional area of a circle, a student can use the formula $A = \frac{C}{360}\pi r^2$, where C is the number of degrees of the central angle of the sector. The area of a circle can also be found by using the arc length rather than the degree of the sector. This formula is $A = rs^2$, where s is the arc length and r is the radius of the circle.

A chord is a line that connects two points on a circle's circumference. If the radius and the value of the angle subtended at the center by the chord is known, the formula to find the chord length is:

$$C = 2 \times radius \times \sin\frac{angle}{2}$$

Remember that this formula is based on half the length of the chord, so the radius is doubled to determine the full length of the chord.

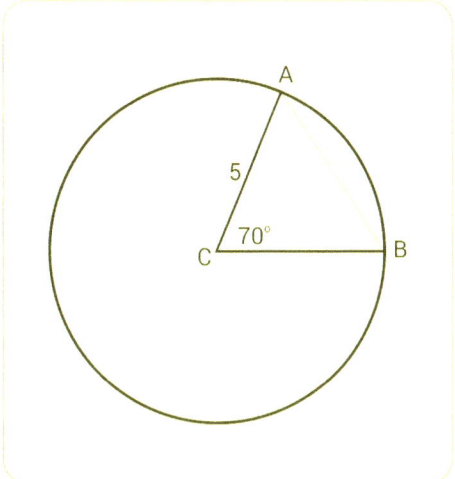

For example, the radius in the diagram above is 5 and the angle is 70 degrees. To find the chord length, plug in the values for the radius and angle to obtain the answer of 5.7.

$$5 \times \sin\frac{70}{2} = 2.87 \times 2 = 5.7$$

Chords that intersect each other at a point within a circle are related. The intersecting chord theorem states that when two chords intersect, each is cut into two portions or segments. The products of the two segments of each respective chord are equal to one another.

Other related concepts for circles include the diameter and circumference. *Circumference* is the distance around a circle. The formula for circumference is $C = 2\pi r$. The *diameter* of a circle is the distance across a circle through its center point. The formula for circumference can also be thought of as $C = d\pi$ where d is the circle's diameter, since the diameter of a circle is $2r$.

Similarity, Congruence, and Triangles

Triangles are similar if they have the same shape, the same angle measurements, and their sides are proportional to one another. Triangles are congruent if the angles of the triangles are equal in measurement and the sides of the triangles are equal in measurement.

There are five ways to show that a triangle is congruent.

- SSS (Side-Side-Side Postulate): When all three corresponding sides are equal in length, then the two triangles are congruent.

- SAS (Side-Angle-Side Postulate): If a pair of corresponding sides and the angle in between those two sides are equal, then the two triangles are congruent.

- ASA (Angle-Side-Angle Postulate): If a pair of corresponding angles are equal and the side within those angles are equal, then the two triangles are equal.

- AAS (Angle-Angle-Side Postulate): When a pair of corresponding angles for two triangles and a non-included side are equal, then the two triangles are congruent.

- HL (Hypotenuse-Leg Theorem): If two right triangles have the same hypotenuse length, and one of the other sides are also the same length, then the two triangles are congruent.

If two triangles are discovered to be similar or congruent, this information can assist in determining unknown parts of triangles, such as missing angles and sides.

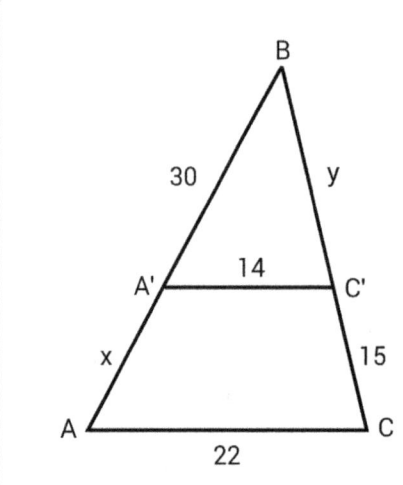

In the triangle shown above, AC and $A'C'$ are parallel lines. Therefore, BA is a transversal that intersects the two parallel lines. The corresponding angles $BA'C'$ and BAC are congruent. In a similar way, BC is also a transversal. Therefore, angle $BC'A'$ and BCA are congruent. If two triangles have two congruent angles, the triangles are similar. If the triangles are similar, their corresponding sides are proportional.

Therefore, the following equation is established:

$$\frac{30+x}{30} = \frac{22}{14} = \frac{y+15}{y}$$

$$\frac{30+x}{30} = \frac{22}{14}$$

$$x = 17.1$$

$$\frac{22}{14} = \frac{y+15}{y}$$

$$y = 26.25$$

Math Section

The example below involves the question of congruent triangles. The first step is to examine whether the triangles are congruent. If the triangles are congruent, then the measure of a missing angle can be found.

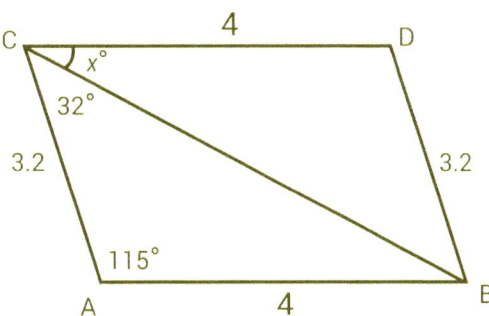

The above diagram provides values for angle measurements and side lengths in triangles CAB and CDB. Note that side CA is 3.2 and side DB is 3.2. Side CD is 4 and side AB is 4. Furthermore, line CB is congruent to itself by the reflexive property. Therefore, the two triangles are congruent by SSS (Side-Side-Side). Because the two triangles are congruent, all of the corresponding parts of the triangles are also congruent. Therefore, angle x is congruent to the inside of the angle for which a measurement is not provided in Triangle CAB. Thus:

$$115° + 32° = 147°$$

A triangle measures 180°, therefore:

$$180° - 147° = 33°$$

$Angle\ x = 33°$, because the two triangles are reversed.

Complementary Angle Theorem

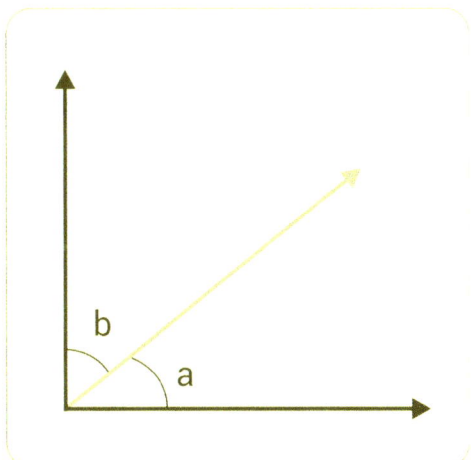

Two angles are complementary if the sum of the two angles equals 90°.

In the above diagram:

$$Angle\ a + Angle\ b = 90°$$

Therefore, the two angles are complementary. Certain trigonometric rules are also associated with complementary angles.

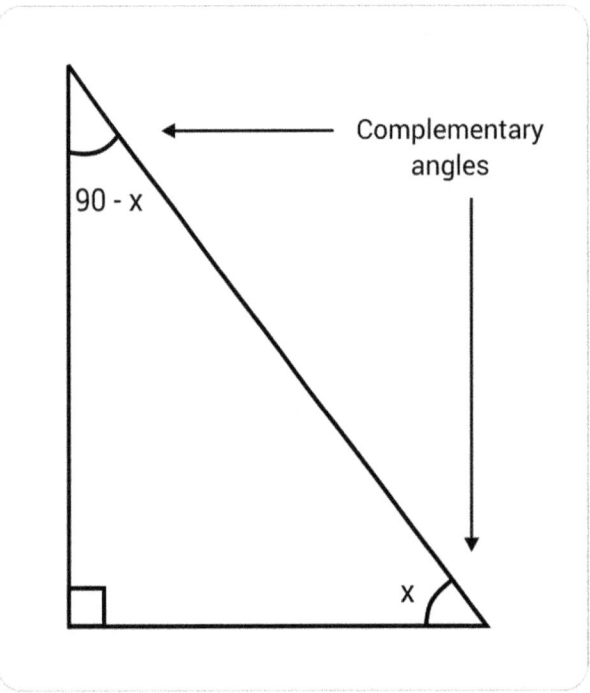

In the diagram above of a right triangle, if Angle A and Angle C are determined to be complementary angles, then certain relationships can be stated between the trigonometry of those angles.

$$sin(90° - x) = cos\ x$$

$$cos(90° - x) = sin\ x$$

For example, the sine of 80 degrees equals the cosine of $(90° - 80°)$, which is the $cos(10°)$.

This is true because the sine of an angle in a right triangle is equal to the cosine of its complement. Sine is known as the conjunction of cosine, and cosine is known as the conjunction of sine.

Examples:

1. $cos\ 5° = sin\ x°$?
2. $sin(90° - x) = ?$

For problem number 1, the student should remember that:

$$sin(90° - x) = cos\ x$$

Math Section

$Cos\ 5°$ would be the same as $sin(90 − 5)°$. Therefore:

$$cos\ 5° = sin\ 85°$$

For problem number 2, the student would use the same fact that:

$$sin(90° − x)° = \cos x$$

An *acute angle* is an angle that is less than 90°. If Angle A and Angle B are acute angles of a right triangle, then $\sin A = \cos B$. Therefore, the sine of any acute angle in a right triangle is equal to the cosine of its complement, and the cosine of any acute angle is equal to the sine of its complement.

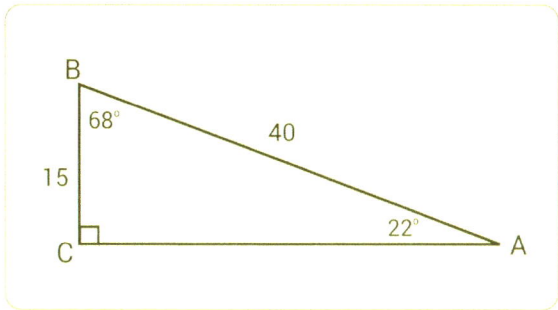

The example above is a right triangle. If only the value of angle BAC (which is 22°) was provided, the student would be able to figure out the value for angle CBA (68°) by knowing that a triangle is made up of:

$$180°(180° − 90° − 22° = 68°)$$

From the information given about acute angles on the previous page, the following statement is true:

$\sin(angle\ BAC) = \frac{15}{40}$, which is equivalent to the $\cos(angle\ CBA) = \frac{15}{40}$

Circles on the Coordinate Plane

If a circle is placed on the coordinate plane with the center of the circle at the origin $(0,0)$, then point (x, y) is a point on the circle. Furthermore, the line extending from the center to point (x, y) is the radius, or r. By applying the Pythagorean Theorem $(a^2 + b^2 = c^2)$ it can be stated that:

$$x^2 + y^2 = r^2$$

However, the center of the circle does not always need to be on the origin of the coordinate plane.

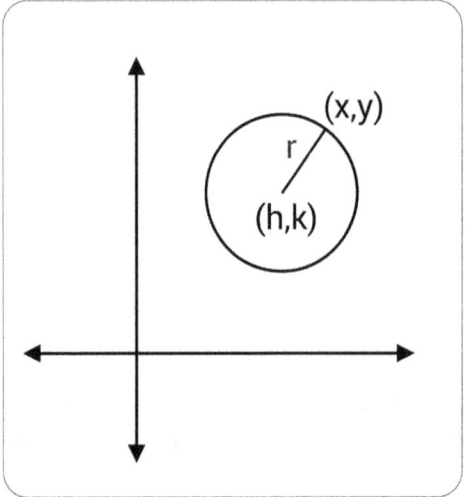

In the diagram above, the center of the circle is noted by (h, k). By applying the distance formula, the equation becomes:

$$r = \sqrt{(x - h)^2 + (y - k)^2}$$

When squaring both sides of the equation, the result is the standard form of a circle with the center (h, k) and radius r. Namely, $r^2 = (x - h)^2 + (y - k)^2$ where r equal radius and center equals (h, k). The following examples may be solved by using this information:

Example: Graph the equation:

$$-x^2 + y^2 = 25$$

To graph this equation, first note that the center of the circle is $(0, 0)$. The radius is the positive square root of 25 or 5.

Example: Find the equation for the circle below.

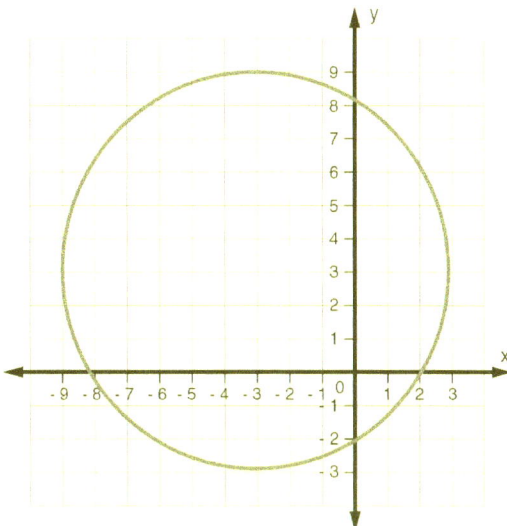

To find the equation for the circle, note that its center is not zero. Therefore, to find the circle's center, draw vertical and horizontal diameters to examine where they intersect. The center is located at point: $(-3, 3)$. Next, count the number of spaces from the center to the outside of the circle. This number is 6. Therefore, 6 is the radius. Finally, plug in the numbers that are known into the standard equation for a circle:

$$36 = (x - (-3))^2 + (y - 3)^2$$

or

$$36 = (x + 3)^2 + (y - 3)^2$$

It is possible to determine whether a point lies on a circle or not within the coordinate plane. For example, a circle has a center of $(2, -5)$, and a radius of 6 centimeters. The first step is to apply the equation of a circle, which is $r^2 = (x - h)^2 + (y - k)^2$ where r equals radius and the center equals (h, k). Next, substitute the numbers for the center point and the number for the radius. This action simplifies the equation to:

$$36 = (x - 2)^2 + (y + 5)^2$$

Note that the radius of 6 was squared to get 36.

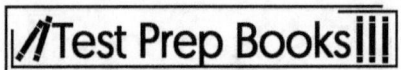

To prove that the point $(2, 1)$ lies on the circle, apply the equation of the circle that was just used and input the values of $(2, 1)$ for x and y in the equation.

$$36 = (x - 2)^2 + (y + 5)^2$$

$$36 = (2 - 2)^2 + (1 + 5)^2$$

$$36 = (0)^2 + (6)^2$$

$$36 = 36$$

Because the left side of the equation equals the right side of the equation, point $(2, 1)$ lies on the given circle.

Practice Quiz

1. Which of the following is a factor of both $x^2 + 4x + 4$ and $x^2 - x - 6$?
   a. $x - 3$
   b. $x + 2$
   c. $x - 2$
   d. $x + 3$

2. How could the following function be rewritten to identify the zeros?

$$y = 3x^3 + 3x^2 - 18x$$

   a. $y = 3x(x + 3)(x - 2)$
   b. $y = x(x - 2)(x + 3)$
   c. $y = 3x(x - 3)(x + 2)$
   d. $y = (x + 3)(x - 2)$

3. A statistician recorded the average weekly number of hours of practice, x, and score, y, on a round of 18 holes at a golf tournament for 100 golfers last weekend. From his research, the corresponding line of best fit was $y = -5.15x + 119.02$. Using this line, what is the corresponding prediction for a golfer that practices 11 hours per week?
   a. 57
   b. 100
   c. 85
   d. 62

4. A local candy store reports that of the 100 customers that bought lollypops, 35 of them bought cherry. What is the probability of selecting 2 customers simultaneously at random that both purchased a cherry lollypop?
   a. $\frac{119}{990}$
   b. $\frac{35}{100}$
   c. $\frac{49}{400}$
   d. $\frac{69}{99}$

5. A data set is comprised of the following values: 30, 33, 33, 26, 27, 32, 33, 35, 29, 27. Which of the following has the greatest value?
   a. Mean
   b. Median
   c. Mode
   d. Range

Answer Explanations

1. B: To factor $x^2 + 4x + 4$, the numbers needed are those that add to 4 and multiply to 4. Therefore, both numbers must be 2, and the expression factors to:

$$x^2 + 4x + 4 = (x + 2)^2$$

Similarly, the second expression factors to:

$$x^2 - x - 6 = (x - 3)(x + 2)$$

Therefore, they have $x + 2$ in common.

2. A: The function can be factored to identify the zeros. First, the term $3x$ is factored out to the front because each term contains $3x$. Then, the quadratic is factored into $(x + 3)(x - 2)$.

3. D: Substitute 11 into the function for x since that is the variable that represents the number of hours practiced weekly. $y = -5.15(11) + 119.02 = 62.37$. This rounds to 62.

4. A: The probability of choosing two customers simultaneously is the same as choosing one and then choosing a second without putting the first back into the pool of customers. This means that the probability of choosing a customer who bought cherry is $\frac{35}{100}$. Then without placing them back in the pool, it would be $\frac{34}{99}$.

So, the probability of choosing 2 customers simultaneously that both bought cherry would be:

$$\frac{35}{100} \times \frac{34}{99}$$

$$\frac{1,190}{9,900}$$

$$\frac{119}{990}$$

5. C: Each value can be calculated so that they can be compared to find which one is the greatest. The mean is equal to:

$$\frac{26 + 27 + 27 + 29 + 30 + 32 + 33 + 33 + 33 + 35}{10} = 30.5$$

The median is equal to:

$$\frac{30 + 32}{2} = 31$$

The mode is equal to 33 because that number occurs 3 times in the data set. The range is equal to:

$$35 - 26 = 9$$

Therefore, the mode is the greatest value of the answer choices.

Practice Test #1

Reading and Writing 1

The next question is based on the following passage:

> At times history and fate meet at a single time in a single place to shape a turning point in man's unending search for freedom. So it was at Lexington and Concord. So it was a century ago at Appomattox. So it was last week in Selma, Alabama. There, long-suffering men and women peacefully protested the denial of their rights as Americans. Many were brutally assaulted. One good man, a man of God, was killed.
>
> Excerpt from Lyndon Johnson's "Address to Joint Session of Congress," March 15, 1965

1. What was being protested in Selma?
    a. The search for freedom
    b. Suppression of rights
    c. A brutal assault
    d. A murder

The next question is based on the following passage:

> While studying at Triton, Hampton joined and became a leader of the National Association for the Advancement of Colored People (NAACP). <u>As a result of his leadership, the NAACP gained more than 500 members.</u> Hampton worked relentlessly to establish recreational facilities in the Maywood neighborhood and improve the educational resources provided to the impoverished black community.

2. Which of the following statements, if true, would further validate the selected sentence?
    a. Several of these new members went on to earn scholarships.
    b. With this increase in numbers, Hampton was awarded a medal for his contribution to the NAACP.
    c. This increase in membership was unprecedented in the NAACP's history.
    d. The NAACP has been growing steadily every year.

The next question is based on the following passage:

> The final expression of the opinion of the people with us is through free and honest elections, with valid choices on basic issues and candidates. The secret ballot is an essential to free elections but you must have a choice before you. I have heard my husband say many times that a people need never lose their freedom if they kept their right to a secret ballot and if they used that secret ballot to the full. Basic decisions of our society are made through the expressed will of the people. That is why when we see these liberties threatened, instead of falling apart, our nation becomes unified and our

democracies come together as a unified group in spite of our varied backgrounds and many racial strains.

Excerpt from Eleanor Roosevelt's "The Struggle for Human Rights," September 28, 1948

3. Why does Roosevelt assert that a "secret" ballot is important?
   a. Public voting was too raucous an event.
   b. It decreases the chance for bribery.
   c. Privacy secures freedom of choice.
   d. It ensures physical safety.

The next question is based on the following graph:

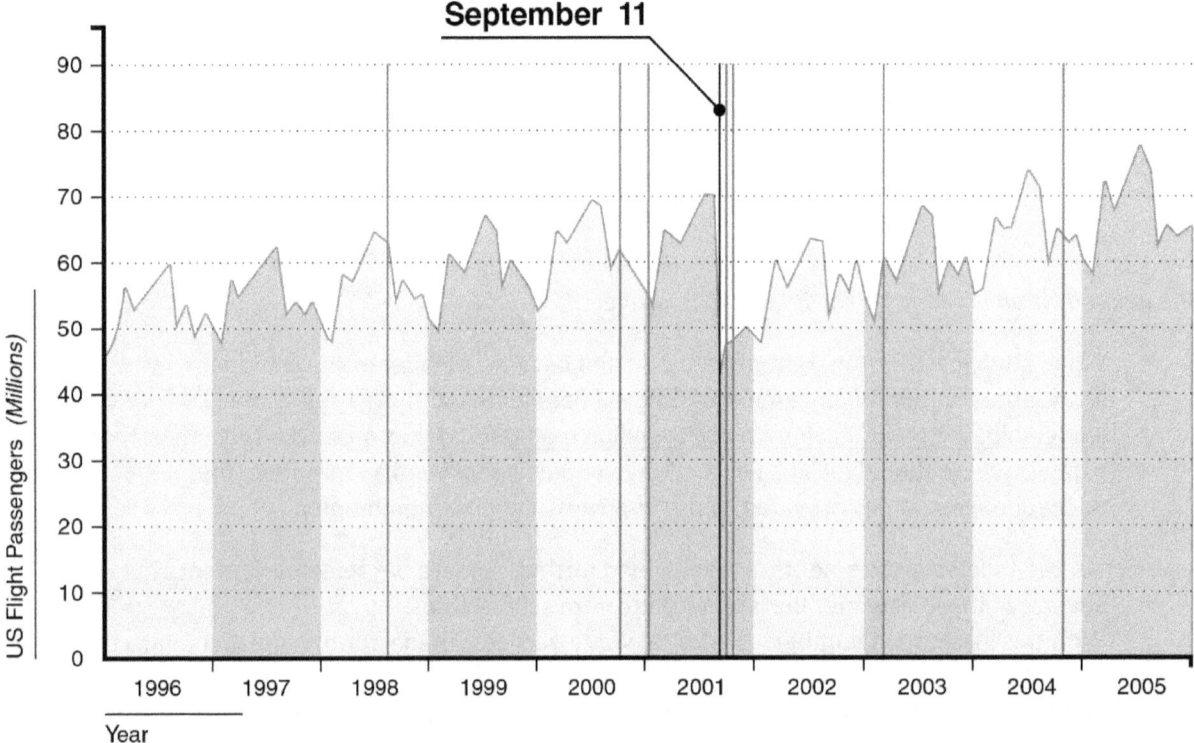

4. Which statement about September 11 is best supported by the graph above?
   a. As canceled flights were rescheduled, air travel became backed up and chaotic for quite some time.
   b. Over 500 flights had to turn back or be redirected to other countries.
   c. Canada alone received 226 flights and thousands of stranded passengers.
   d. In the first few months following the attacks, there was a significant decrease in passengers boarding flights.

Practice Test #1

5. Which of the following would be the best choice for the underlined portion of the sentences below?

All discoveries associated with dinosaurs are based on physical remains. To gauge behavioral characteristics, scientists cross-examine these finds with living animals that seem similar in order to gain understanding.

a. NO CHANGE
b. finds with living animals to explore potential similarities.
c. finds with living animals to gain understanding of similarities.
d. finds with living animals that seem similar, in order, to gain understanding.

The next question is based on the following passage:

Everyone has heard the idea of the end justifying the means; that would be Weston's philosophy. Weston is willing to cross any line, commit any act no matter how heinous, to achieve success in his goal. Ransom is repulsed by this fact, seeing total evil in Weston's plan. To do an evil act in order to gain a result that's supposedly good would ultimately warp the final act. This opposing viewpoints immediately distinguishes Ransom as the hero. In the conflict with Un-man, Ransom remains true to his moral principles as someone who refuses to be compromised by power. Instead, Ransom makes it clear that by allowing such processes as murder and lying dictate how one attains a positive outcome, the righteous goal becomes corrupted. The good end would not be truly good, but rather it would become a twisted end that conceals corrupt deeds.

Based on an excerpt from *Perelandra* by C.S. Lewis

6. Which of the following would be the best choice for the underlined portion of the sentence below?

Instead, Ransom makes it clear that by allowing such processes as murder and lying dictate how one attains a positive outcome, the righteous goal becomes corrupted.

a. NO CHANGE
b. the goal becomes corrupted and no longer righteous.
c. the righteous goal becomes, corrupted.
d. the goal becomes corrupted, when once it was righteous.

7. Which of the following would be the best choice for the underlined portion of the sentences below?

Looking deeper into the myth of Prometheus sheds light not only on the character of Frankenstein but also poses a psychological dilemma to the audience. Prometheus is the titan who gave fire to mankind. However, more than just fire he gave people knowledge and power.

a. NO CHANGE
b. However, more than just fire he gave people, knowledge, and power.
c. However, more than just fire, he gave people knowledge and power.
d. In addition to fire, Prometheus gave people knowledge and power.

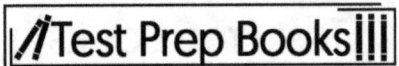

The next question is based on the following passage:

> The RV was a great purchase for our family and brought us all closer together. Every morning we would wake up, eat breakfast, and break camp. We laughed at our own comical attempts to back The Beast into spaces that seemed impossibly small. <u>We rejoiced as "hackers."</u> When things inevitably went wrong and we couldn't solve the problems on our own, we discovered the incredible helpfulness and friendliness of the RV community.

8. Which is the best version of the underlined portion of the paragraph above?
    a. NO CHANGE
    b. To a nagging problem of technology, we rejoiced as "hackers."
    c. We rejoiced when we figured out how to "hack" a solution during a difficult situation.
    d. To "hack" our way to a solution, we had to rejoice.

The next question is based on the following passage:

> In May 2015, the United States Bureau of Labor Statistics (BLS) reported that the median annual salary of aircraft engineers was $107,830. <u>However,</u> employment opportunities for aircraft engineers are projected to decrease by 2 percent by 2024.

9. Which of the following would be the best choice for the underlined portion above?
    a. NO CHANGE
    b. Similarly,
    c. In other words,
    d. Accordingly,

The next question is based on the following passage:

> Present George W. Bush announced a War on Terror. He desired to bring bin Laden and al-Qaeda to justice and prevent future terrorist networks from gaining strength. The War in Afghanistan began in October of 2001 when the United States and British forces bombed al-Qaeda camps. <u>The Taliban, a group of fundamentalist Muslims who protected Osama bin Laden, was overthrown on December 9, 2001. However, the war continued in order to defeat insurgency campaigns in neighboring countries.</u> Ten years later, the United State Navy SEALS killed Osama bin Laden in Pakistan. During 2014, the United States declared the end of its involvement in the War on Terror in Afghanistan.

10. Which of the following would be the best choice for the underlined sentences above?
    a. NO CHANGE
    b. The Taliban was overthrown on December 9, 2001. They were a group of fundamentalist Muslims who protected Osama bin Laden. However, the war continued in order to defeat insurgency campaigns in neighboring countries.
    c. The Taliban, a group of fundamentalist Muslims who protected Osama bin Laden, on December 9, 2001 was overthrown. However, the war continued in order to defeat insurgency campaigns in neighboring countries.
    d. Osama bin Laden's fundamentalist Muslims who protected him were called the Taliban and overthrown on December 9, 2001. Yet the war continued in order to defeat the insurgency campaigns in neighboring countries.

Practice Test #1

The next question is based on the following passage:

> These wounds are still very deep. They have never been healed. Looking for a way out of this crisis, our people have turned to the Federal Government and found it isolated from the mainstream of our Nation's life. Washington, D.C. has become an island. The gap between our citizens and our Government has never been so wide. The people are looking for honest answers, not easy answers; clear leadership, not false claims and evasiveness and politics as usual.

Excerpt from "The Crisis of Confidence" by Jimmy Carter

11. What does Carter mean, metaphorically, when he says that "Washington, D.C. has become an island"?
    a. Members of Congress are relaxing on vacation while the people suffer.
    b. The government is using limited resources unwisely.
    c. The White House is an oasis for Americans in need.
    d. The government has isolated itself from its citizens.

The next question is based on the following passage:

> A lane was forthwith opened through the crowd of spectators. Preceded by the beadle, and attended by an irregular procession of stern-browed men and unkindly visaged women, Hester Prynne set forth towards the place appointed for her punishment. A crowd of eager and curious schoolboys, understanding little of the matter in hand, except that it gave them a half-holiday, ran before her progress, turning their heads continually to stare into her face, and at the winking baby in her arms, and at the ignominious letter on her breast. It was no great distance, in those days, from the prison-door to the marketplace. Measured by the prisoner's experience, however, it might be reckoned a journey of some length; for, haughty as her demeanor was, she perchance underwent an agony from every footstep of those that thronged to see her, as if her heart had been flung into the street for them all to spurn and trample upon.

Excerpt from *The Scarlet Letter*, Nathaniel Hawthorne, 1878

12. Based on the passage, what might Hester Prynne have felt on her walk from the prison to the marketplace?
    a. Anger
    b. Fear
    c. Agony
    d. Pride

13. What edit to the underlined portion is needed to correct the following sentence?

    Students have to <u>read between the lines, identify bias, and determine</u> who they can trust in the milieu of ads, data, and texts presented to them.

    a. NO CHANGE
    b. read between the lines, identify bias, and determining
    c. read between the lines, identifying bias, and determining
    d. reads between the lines, identifies bias, and determines

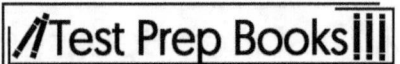

14. Which of the following would be the best choice for the underlined portion of the sentence below?

   In natural selection, animals must adapt to their environments increase their chance of survival.

   a. NO CHANGE
   b. animals must adapt to their environments to increase their chance of survival.
   c. animals must adapt to their environments, increase their chance of survival.
   d. animals must adapt to their environments, increasing their chance of survival.

15. Which of the following would be the best choice for the underlined portion of the sentences below?

   I'm not alone when I say that it's hard to pay attention sometimes. I can't count how many times I've sat in a classroom, lecture, speech, or workshop and been bored to tears or rather sleep.

   a. NO CHANGE
   b. been bored to, tears, or rather sleep.
   c. been bored, to tears or rather sleep.
   d. been bored to tears or, rather, sleep.

16. Which of the following would be the best choice for the sentence below?

   Because I wasn't invested in what was going on I wasn't motivated to listen.

   a. NO CHANGE
   b. Because I wasn't invested, in what was going on, I wasn't motivated to listen.
   c. Because I wasn't invested in what was going on. I wasn't motivated to listen.
   d. I wasn't motivated to listen because I wasn't invested in what was going on.

17. Which of the following would be the best choice for the underlined portion of the sentence below?

   What really makes people pay attention? Easy it's interest.

   a. NO CHANGE
   b. Easy it is interest.
   c. Easy its interest.
   d. Easy—it's interest.

18. Which of the following would be the best choice for the underlined sentence below?

   The biggest problem with studying dinosaurs is simply that there are no living dinosaurs to observe.

   a. NO CHANGE
   b. The biggest problem with studying dinosaurs is simple, that there are no living dinosaurs to observe.
   c. The biggest problem with studying dinosaurs is simple, there are no living dinosaurs to observe.
   d. The biggest problem with studying dinosaurs, is simply that there are no living dinosaurs to observe.

19. Which of the following would be the best choice for the underlined portion of the sentence below?

   While it's plausible, even likely that dinosaurs share many traits with modern animals, there is the danger of over-attributing these qualities to a unique, extinct species.

   a. NO CHANGE
   b. plausible, even likely that, dinosaurs share many
   c. plausible, even likely, that dinosaurs share many
   d. plausible even likely that dinosaurs share many

The next question is based on the following passage:

   We were sure that ours was a nation of the ballot, not the bullet, until the murders of John Kennedy and Robert Kennedy and Martin Luther King, Jr. We were taught that our armies were always invincible and our causes were always just, only to suffer the agony of Vietnam. We respected the Presidency as a place of honor until the shock of Watergate.

   We remember when the phrase "sound as a dollar" was an expression of absolute dependability, until ten years of inflation began to shrink our dollar and our savings. We believed that our Nation's resources were limitless until 1973, when we had to face a growing dependence on foreign oil.

   Excerpt from "The Crisis of Confidence" by Jimmy Carter

20. What is the purpose of the paragraphs above?
    a. To point out that previous presidents have made mistakes
    b. To provide examples of why people are losing respect for government and other institutions
    c. To prove that our past is full of tragedy and our future is full of hope
    d. To suggest Americans' expectations are too high

21. What is the meaning of the word *transgression* in the following excerpt?

   "They will see, understand, and forgive. For our gift is greater than our transgression."

   Excerpt from *Anthem* by Ayn Rand

   a. Obedience
   b. Disruption
   c. Confession
   d. Offense

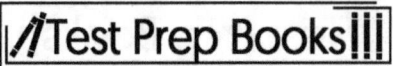

22. What does the underlined word mean in the following sentence?

    "After the bee has traversed a few flowers along the spike and has become well supplied with free pollen, it begins to collect it from its body, head, and forward appendages and to transfer it to the posterior pair of legs."

    a. Strongest
    b. Anterior
    c. Ambulatory
    d. Rear

The next question is based on the following passage:

   ...there is cause for hope and for faith in our democracy in what is happening here tonight. For the cries of pain and the hymns and protests of oppressed people have summoned into convocation all the majesty of this great government—the government of the greatest nation on earth. Our mission is at once the oldest and the most basic of this country: to right wrong, to do justice, to serve man.

   Except from Lyndon Johnson's "Address to Joint Session of Congress," March 15, 1965

23. What does the word "convocation" mean as it is used in the paragraph above?
    a. A vocal duet
    b. A second career
    c. A gathering or assembly
    d. Closure

24. Which organizational style is used in the following passage?

    There are several reasons why the new student café has not been as successful as expected. One factor is that prices are higher than originally advertised, so many students cannot afford to buy food and beverages there. Also, the café closes rather early; as a result, students go out into town to other late-night gathering places rather than meeting friends at the café on campus.

    a. Cause-and-effect order
    b. Compare-and-contrast order
    c. Spatial order
    d. Time order

The next question is based on the following passage:

   Hank is a professional writer. He submits regular columns at two blogs and self-publishes romance novels. Hank recently signed with an agent based in New York. To date, Hank has never made any money off his writing.

25. The strength of the argument depends on which of the following?
    a. Hank's agent works at the biggest firm in New York.
    b. Being a professional writer requires representation by an agent.
    c. Hank's self-published novels and blogs have received generally positive reviews.
    d. Being a professional writer does not require earning money.

Practice Test #1

The next question is based on the following passage:

> David Foster Wallace's *Infinite Jest* is the holy grail of modern literature. It will stand the test of time in its relevance. Every single person who starts reading *Infinite Jest* cannot physically put down the book until completing it.

26. Which of the following is the main point of the passage?
    a. David Foster Wallace's *Infinite Jest* is the holy grail of modern literature.
    b. *Infinite Jest* is a page-turner.
    c. David Foster Wallace wrote *Infinite Jest*.
    d. *Infinite Jest* is a modern classic for good reason, and everybody should read it.

The next question is based on the following passage:

> When researchers and engineers undertake a large-scale scientific project, they may end up making discoveries and developing technologies that have far wider uses than originally intended. This is especially true in NASA, one of the most influential and innovative scientific organizations in America. NASA spinoff technology refers to innovations originally developed for NASA space projects that are now used in a wide range of different commercial fields. Many consumers are unaware that products they are buying are based on NASA research! Spinoff technology proves that it is worthwhile to invest in science research because it could enrich people's lives in unexpected ways.
>
> The first spinoff technology worth mentioning is baby food. In space, where astronauts have limited access to fresh food and fewer options about their daily meals, malnutrition is a serious concern. Consequently, NASA researchers were looking for ways to enhance the nutritional value of astronauts' food. Scientists found that a certain type of algae could be added to food, improving the food's neurological benefits. When experts in the commercial food industry learned of this algae's potential to boost brain health, they were quick to begin their own research. The nutritional substance from algae was developed into a product called life's DHA, which can be found in over 90% of infant food sold in America.

27. Why did NASA scientists research algae?
    a. They already knew algae was healthy for babies.
    b. They were interested in how to grow food in space.
    c. They were looking for ways to add health benefits to food.
    d. They hoped to use it to protect expensive research equipment.

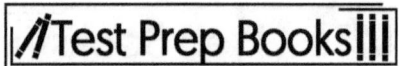

Reading and Writing 2

The next question is based on the following passage:

A flood occurs when an area of land that is normally dry becomes submerged with water. Floods have affected Earth since the beginning of time and are caused by many different factors. <u>Flooding can occur slowly or within seconds and can submerge small regions or extend over vast areas of land.</u> Their impact on society and the environment can be harmful or helpful.

1. Which of the following revisions can be made to the underlined sentence that will still maintain the original meaning while making the sentence more concise?
    a. NO CHANGE
    b. Flooding can either be slow or occur within seconds. It doesn't take long to submerge small regions or extend vast areas of land.
    c. Flooding occurs slowly or rapidly submerging vast areas of land.
    d. Small regions or vast areas of land can be flooded either slowly or within seconds.

2. Which of the following would be the best choice for the underlined portion of the sentence below?

    Ransom must literally <u>show her the right path, to accomplish this, he does this based on the same principle as the "means to an end" argument</u>—that good follows good, and evil follows evil.

    Based on an excerpt from *Perelandra* by C.S. Lewis

    a. NO CHANGE
    b. show her the right path. To accomplish this, he uses the same principle as the "means to an end" argument
    c. show her the right path; to accomplish this he uses the same principle as the "means to an end" argument
    d. show her the right path, to accomplish this, the same principle as the "means to an end" argument is applied

3. Which of the following would be the best choice for the sentence below?

    It is because of these respective media types that ethical and news-related subject matter can sometimes seem different or altered.

    a. NO CHANGE
    b. It is because of these respective media types, that ethical and news-related subject matter, can sometimes seem different or altered.
    c. It is because of these respective media types, that ethical and news-related subject matter can sometimes seem different or altered.
    d. It is because of these respective media types that ethical and news-related subject matter can sometimes seem different. Or altered.

4. Which of the following would be the best choice for the underlined portion of the sentence below?

   Finer details are usually expanded on <u>in written articles, usually people who</u> read newspapers or go online for web articles want more than a quick blurb.

   a. NO CHANGE
   b. in written articles. Usually, people who
   c. in written articles, usually, people who
   d. in written articles usually people who

5. What edit to the underlined portion is needed to correct the following sentence?

   Early in my career, <u>a master's teacher shared this thought with me "Education is the last bastion of civility."</u>

   a. NO CHANGE
   b. a professor shared this thought with me: "Education is the last bastion of civility."
   c. a professor shared this thought with me: "Education is the last bastion of civility".
   d. a professor shared this thought with me. "Education is the last bastion of civility."

The next question is based on the following passage:

   Education provides society with a vehicle for raising its children to be civil, decent human beings with something valuable to contribute to the world. It is really what makes us human and what <u>distinguishes</u> us as <u>civelized</u> <u>creatures</u>.

6. Which word, if any, is misspelled?
   a. None of the underlined words are misspelled.
   b. distinguishes
   c. civelized
   d. creatures

7. What edit to the underlined portion is needed to correct the following sentences?

   <u>All children can learn. Although not all children learn in the same manner.</u> All children learn best, however, when their basic physical needs are met and they feel safe, secure, and loved.

   a. NO CHANGE
   b. All children can learn although not all children learn in the same manner.
   c. All children can learn although, not all children learn in the same manner.
   d. All children can learn, although not all children learn in the same manner.

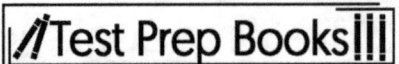

8. What edit to the underlined portion is needed to correct the following sentence?

Teachers have to work harder than ever before to help students identify salient information <u>so to think critically</u> about the information they encounter.

a. NO CHANGE
b. and to think critically
c. but to think critically
d. nor to think critically

The next question is based on the following passage:

Assault is an unlawful and intentional act that causes reasonable <u>apprehension</u> in another individual, either by an imminent threat or by initiating offensive contact. Assaults can vary, encompassing physical strikes, threatening body language, and even provocative language. In the case of the latter, even if a hand has not been laid, it is still considered an assault because of its threatening nature.

9. As it is used in the paragraph above, the word *apprehension* most nearly means:
   a. Pain
   b. Exhaustion
   c. Fear
   d. Honor

The next question is based on the following passage:

Today, the plume hunters who do not dare to raid the guarded <u>rookeries</u> are trying to study out the lines of flight of the birds, to and from their feeding-grounds, and shoot them in transit. Their motto is—"Anything to beat the law, and get the plumes." It is there that the state of Florida should take part in the war.

Excerpt from *Our Vanishing Wildlife* by William T. Hornaday

10. What is the meaning of the word *rookeries* in the text above?
    a. Houses in a slum area
    b. A place where hunters gather to trade tools
    c. A place where wardens go to trade stories
    d. A colony of breeding birds

The next question is based on the following passage:

> Once the job begins, this line of work requires critical thinking, business skills, problem solving, and creativity. This level of <u>expertise</u> allows aircraft engineers to apply mathematical equations and scientific processes to aeronautical and aerospace issues or inventions.

11. What is the meaning of *expertise* in the paragraph above?
    a. Care
    b. Skill
    c. Work
    d. Composition

12. What can the reader infer from the following text?

    > I, Gulliver, would sometimes lie down, and let five or six of them dance on my hand; and at last, the boys and girls would venture to come and play at hide-and-seek in my hair.

    a. The children tortured Gulliver.
    b. Gulliver traveled because he wanted to meet new people.
    c. Gulliver is considerably larger than the children who are playing around him.
    d. Gulliver has a genuine love and enthusiasm for people of all sizes.

The next question is based on the following passage:

> The assassination of Archduke Franz Ferdinand of Austria is often ascribed as the cause of World War I. However, the assassination merely lit the fuse in a combustible situation since many of the world powers were in complicated and convoluted military alliances. For example, England, France, and Russia entered into a mutual defense treaty seven years prior to World War I. Even without Franz Ferdinand's assassination, _____

13. Which of the following most logically completes the passage?
    a. a war between the world powers was extremely likely.
    b. World War I never would have happened.
    c. England, France, and Russia would have started the war.
    d. Austria would have started the war.

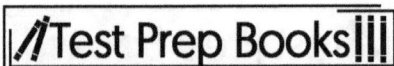

The next question is based on the following passage:

> A famous children's author recently published a historical fiction novel under a pseudonym; however, it did not sell as many copies as her children's books. In her earlier years, she had majored in history and earned a graduate degree in Antebellum American History, which is the time frame of her new novel. Critics praised this newest work far more than the children's series that made her famous. In fact, her new novel was nominated for the prestigious Albert J. Beveridge Award but still isn't selling like her children's books, which fly off the shelves because of her name alone.

14. Which one of the following statements might be accurately inferred based on the above passage?
    a. The famous children's author produced an inferior book under her pseudonym.
    b. The famous children's author is the foremost expert on Antebellum America.
    c. The famous children's author did not receive the bump in publicity for her historical novel that it would have received if it were written under her given name.
    d. People generally prefer to read children's series over historical fiction.

The next question is based on the following passage:

> In 2015, 28 countries, including Estonia, Portugal, Slovenia, and Latvia, scored significantly higher than the United States on standardized high school math tests. In the 1960s, the United States consistently ranked first in the world. Today, the United States spends more than $800 billion on education, which exceeds the next highest country by more than $600 billion. The United States also leads the world in spending per school-aged child by an enormous margin.

15. If the statements above are true, which of the following statements must be correct?
    a. Outspending other countries on education has benefits beyond standardized math tests.
    b. The United States' education system is corrupt and broken.
    c. The standardized math tests are not representative of American academic prowess.
    d. Spending more money does not guarantee success on standardized math tests.

The next question is based on the following passage:

> This dual nature of the electrons presents a conundrum. While humans now have a better understanding of electrons, the fact remains that people cannot entirely perceive how electrons behave without the use of instruments. We can only observe one of the mentioned behaviors, which only provides a partial understanding of the entire function of electrons. Therefore, we're forced to ask ourselves whether the world we observe is objective or if it is subjectively perceived by humans. Or, an alternative question: can humans understand the world only through machines that will allow them to observe natural phenomena?

16. Which of the following best describes how this paragraph is structured?
    a. It offers one solution, questions the solution, and then ends with an alternative solution.
    b. It presents an inquiry, explains the details of that inquiry, and then offers a solution.
    c. It presents a problem, explains the details of that problem, and then ends with more inquiries.
    d. It gives a definition, offers an explanation, and then ends with an inquiry.

Practice Test #1

The next question is based on the timeline of the life of Alexander Graham Bell:

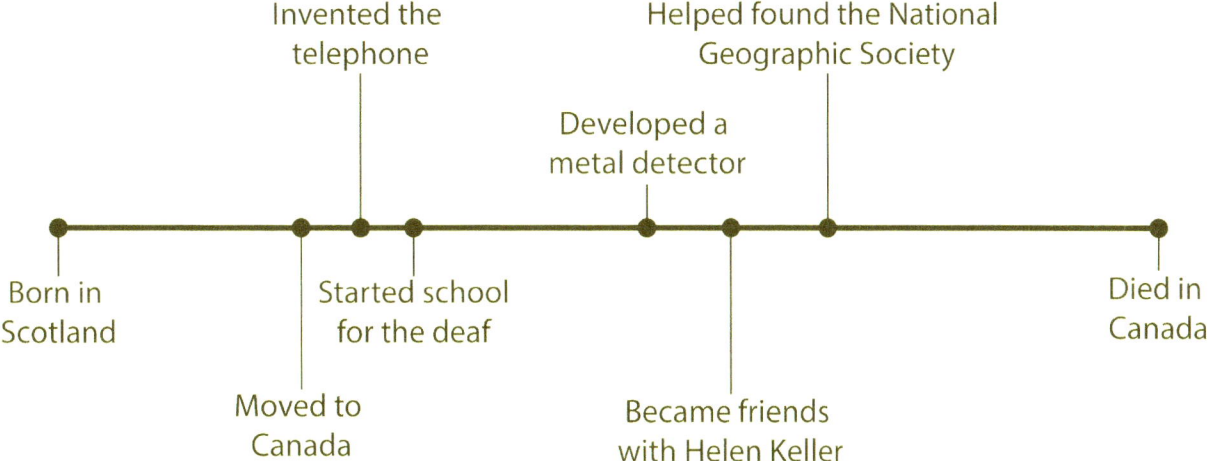

17. Which one of the following statements is accurate based on the timeline?
    a. Bell did nothing significant after he helped found the National Geographic Society.
    b. Bell started a school for the deaf in Canada.
    c. Bell lived in at least two countries.
    d. Developing a metal detector allowed Bell to meet Helen Keller.

The next question is based on the following passage:

> There are two major kinds of cameras on the market right now for amateur photographers. Camera enthusiasts can either purchase a digital single-lens reflex (DSLR) camera or a compact system camera (CSC). The main difference between a DSLR and a CSC is that the DSLR has a full-sized sensor, which means it fits in a much larger body. The CSC uses a mirrorless system, which makes for a lighter, smaller camera. While both take quality pictures, the DSLR generally has better picture quality due to the larger sensor. CSCs still take very good quality pictures and are more convenient to carry than a DSLR. This makes the CSC an ideal choice for the amateur photographer looking to step up from a point-and-shoot camera.

18. What is the main difference between the DSLR and CSC?
    a. The picture quality is better in the DSLR.
    b. The CSC is less expensive than the DSLR.
    c. The DSLR is a better choice for amateur photographers.
    d. The DSLR's larger sensor makes it a bigger camera than the CSC.

The next question is based on the following passage:

> While scientists aren't entirely certain why tornadoes form, they have some clues about the process. Tornadoes are dangerous funnel clouds that occur during a large thunderstorm. When warm, humid air near the ground meets cold, dry air from above, a column of the warm air can be drawn up into the clouds. Winds at different altitudes blowing at different speeds make the column of air rotate. As the spinning column of air picks up speed, a funnel cloud is formed. This funnel cloud moves rapidly and

haphazardly. Rain and hail inside the cloud cause it to touch down, creating a tornado. Tornadoes move in a rapid and unpredictable pattern, making them extremely destructive and dangerous. Scientists continue to study tornadoes to improve radar detection and warning times.

19. The main purpose of this passage is to do which of the following?
    a. Show why tornadoes are dangerous.
    b. Explain how a tornado forms.
    c. Compare thunderstorms to tornadoes.
    d. Explain what to do in the event of a tornado.

The next question is based on the following passage:

Another intriguing example of a spinoff technology can be found in fashion. People who are always dropping their sunglasses may have invested in a pair of sunglasses with scratch-resistant lenses—that is, it's impossible to scratch the glass, even if the glasses are dropped on an abrasive surface. This innovation is incredibly advantageous for people who are clumsy, but most shoppers don't know that this technology was originally developed by NASA. Scientists first created scratch-resistant glass to help protect costly and crucial equipment from getting scratched in space, especially the helmet visors in space suits. However, sunglasses companies later realized that this technology could be profitable for their products, and they licensed the technology from NASA.

20. Why does the author mention space suit helmets?
    a. To give an example of astronaut fashion
    b. To explain where sunglasses got their shape
    c. To explain how astronauts protect their eyes
    d. To give an example of valuable space equipment

The next question is based on the following passage:

[Sherlock Holmes] was still, as ever, deeply attracted by the study of crime, and occupied his immense faculties and extraordinary powers of observation in following out those clues, and clearing up those mysteries which had been abandoned as hopeless by the official police. From time to time I heard some vague account of his doings: of his summons to Odessa in the case of the Trepoff murder, of his clearing up of the singular tragedy of the Atkinson brothers at Trincomalee, and finally of the mission which he had accomplished so delicately and successfully for the reigning family of Holland. Beyond these signs of his activity, however, which I merely shared with all the readers of the daily press, I knew little of my former friend and companion.

Excerpt from The Adventures of Sherlock Holmes by A. Conan Doyle

21. How did the narrator learn of Sherlock Holmes' latest cases?
    a. Reading the newspaper
    b. Reviewing police reports
    c. Talking with Holmes
    d. Watching the cases unfold

The next question is based on the following passage:

> There is a common misconception that NASA only focuses on subjects related to space. However, NASA is responsible for increasing the efficiency of commercial flights that millions of people take part in each day. Many of the tools that pilots and air traffic controllers use have been developed by NASA's ATD (Airspace Technology Demonstration) project team.
>
> Excerpt from "NASA Delivers on Making Gate to Gate Flights More Efficient" by Jim Banke, published on NASA's website

22. Which detail would best help demonstrate the work that NASA has done for flight?
    a. "There's still so much more that can be done, and will need to be done, as demand for safe, sustainable air travel grows and the skies get busier than ever, not only here in the U.S., but around the world."
    b. "To accomplish its many and diverse goals, ATD was divided into three subprojects, each seeking to improve the efficiency of a particular stage of an airliner's flight from departure gate to arrival gate."
    c. "Following early tests of the ground-based component with American Airlines, NASA and Alaska Airlines conducted flight tests of these ATD-3 tools beginning in 2018."
    d. "For example: more than a million gallons of jet fuel were saved by airlines at one airport during a four-year period testing new computer software that greatly reduces surface congestion at busy airports."

23. Which transition word works best within the context of these two sentences?

    My friend's wedding had a theme of a Renaissance fairytale. <u>Therefore</u>, most people will be wearing long, draped skirts and corsets.

    a. NO CHANGE
    b. Similarly
    c. Moreover
    d. Because

The next question is based on the following passage:

> During Pearl Harbor, the Japanese used a variety of different fighter planes, torpedo bombers, and dive bombers to carry out their attack. These planes were <u>exceptionally</u> picked because they could launch from aircraft carriers that were hundreds of miles away. This was a relatively new warfare strategy.

24. Which word choice works best in place of the underlined word in the passage?
    a. NO CHANGE
    b. Specifically
    c. Usually
    d. Unnecessarily

The next question is based on the following passage:

> The diner was a staple part of American culture during the 1950s and 60s. They were a popular hangout spot for teenagers and became iconic for their unique aesthetic. Their importance in building community cannot be <u>understated</u>.

25. Which word choice works best in place of the underlined word in the passage?
    a. NO CHANGE
    b. Overstated
    c. Outdone
    d. Understood

The next question is based on the following passage:

> Turtle shells are composed of two parts. The carapace, which is the top portion of the shell, provides structural support and protection for the turtle's body. The plastron, the bottom of the shell, helps protect the turtle's organs. Both portions of the shell are made of keratin. <u>This is the same material that human nails are made out of</u>.

26. The author is considering deleting the underlined portion of text. Should this sentence be kept or deleted?
    a. Kept, because discussion of human nails is the natural continuation of the text.
    b. Kept, because humans are responsible for the declining turtle population.
    c. Deleted, because human nails are not relevant to the overall topic.
    d. Deleted, because the information is inaccurate.

The next question is based on the following passage:

> It is imperative that scholars of the prestigious university meticulously <u>stick to</u> the grammatical conventions of the English language.

27. Which choice best maintains the tone of the text?
    a. NO CHANGE
    b. obey
    c. agree with
    d. adhere to

Math 1

1. Which of the following inequalities is equivalent to $3 - \frac{1}{2}x \geq 2$?
    a. $x \geq 2$
    b. $x \leq 2$
    c. $x \geq 1$
    d. $x \leq 1$

2. A National Hockey League store in the state of Michigan advertises 50% off all items. Sales tax in Michigan is 6%. How much would a hat originally priced at $32.99 and a jersey originally priced at $64.99 cost during this sale? Round to the nearest penny.
   a. $97.98
   b. $103.86
   c. $51.93
   d. $48.99

3. Which equation best represents the scatter plot below?

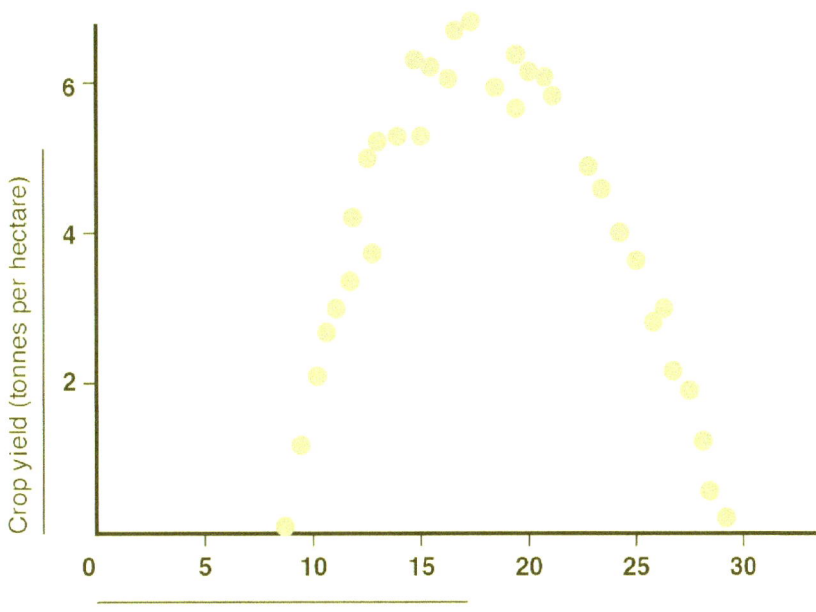

   a. $y = 3x - 4$
   b. $y = 2x^2 + 7x - 9$
   c. $y = (3)(4^x)$
   d. $y = -\frac{1}{14}x^2 + 2x - 8$

4. What is the volume of a cylinder, in terms of π, with a radius of 5 inches and a height of 10 inches?
   a. 250π in^3
   b. 50π in^3
   c. 100π in^3
   d. 200π in^3

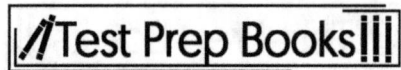

5. What type of function is modeled by the values in the following table?

X	$f(x)$
1	2
2	4
3	8
4	16
5	32

a. Linear
b. Exponential
c. Quadratic
d. Cubic

6. $(2x - 4y)^2$ can be expanded to which of the following?
a. $4x^2 - 16xy + 16y^2$
b. $4x^2 - 8xy + 16y^2$
c. $4x^2 - 16xy - 16y^2$
d. $2x^2 - 8xy + 8y^2$

7. What are the zeros of $f(x) = x^2 + 4$?
a. $x = -4$
b. $x = \pm 2i$
c. $x = \pm 2$
d. $x = \pm 4i$

8. If x is not zero, then $\frac{3}{x} + \frac{5u}{2x} - \frac{u}{4} =$
a. $\frac{12+10u-ux}{4x}$
b. $\frac{3+5u-ux}{x}$
c. $\frac{12x+10u+ux}{4x}$
d. $\frac{12+10u-u}{4x}$

9. Karen gets paid a weekly salary and a commission for every sale that she makes. The table below shows the number of sales and her pay for different weeks.

Sales	2	7	4	8
Pay	$380	$580	$460	$620

Which of the following equations represents Karen's weekly pay?
a. $y = 90x + 200$
b. $y = 90x - 200$
c. $y = 40x + 300$
d. $y = 40x - 300$

10. The square and circle share a center. The circle has a radius of r. What is the area of the shaded region?

a. $r^2 - \pi r^2$
b. $4r^2 - 2\pi r$
c. $(4 - \pi)r^2$
d. $(\pi - 1)r^2$

11. Given the following triangle, what is the length of the missing side? Round the answer to the nearest tenth.

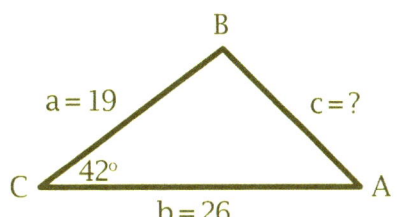

a. 17.0
b. 17.4
c. 18.0
d. 18.4

12. For the following similar triangles, what are the values of x and y (rounded to the nearest tenth)?

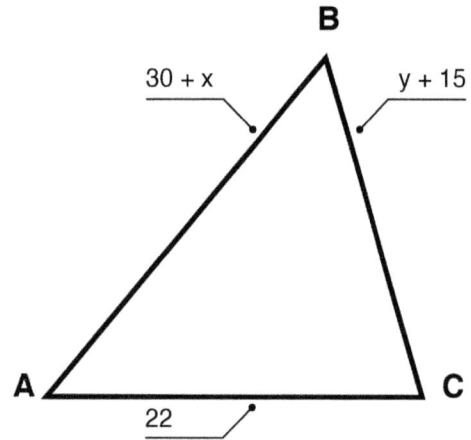
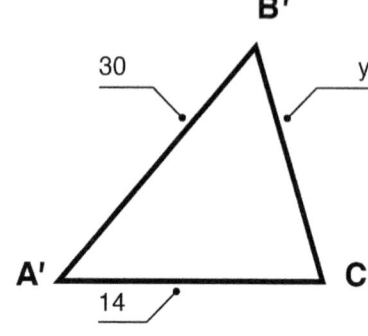

a. $x = 16.5, y = 25.1$
b. $x = 19.5, y = 24.1$
c. $x = 17.1, y = 26.3$
d. $x = 26.3, y = 17.1$

13. At the store, Jan spends $90 on apples and oranges. Apples cost $1 each and oranges cost $2 each. If Jan buys the same number of apples as oranges, how many oranges did she buy?

14. Solve for x given the following two equations:

$$4x + 2y = 8$$

$$10x + 3y = 15$$

a. $x = \dfrac{3}{4}$
b. $x = \dfrac{5}{2}$
c. $x = 4$
d. $x = \dfrac{3}{2}$

15. Solve for x given the following two equations:

$$\dfrac{2}{5}x + 5y = 18$$

$$x - 8y = 4$$

a. $x = 14$
b. $x = 20$
c. $x = 2$
d. $x = 41$

Practice Test #1

16. The graph of which function has an x-intercept of −2?
   a. $y = 2x - 3$
   b. $y = 4x + 2$
   c. $y = x^2 + 5x + 6$
   d. $y = 2x^2 + 3x - 1$

17. Kristen purchases $100 worth of CDs and DVDs. The CDs cost $10 each and the DVDs cost $15 each. If she bought 4 DVDs, how many CDs did she buy?

18. $(4x^2y^4)^{\frac{3}{2}}$ can be simplified to which of the following?
   a. $8x^3y^6$
   b. $4x^{\frac{5}{2}}y$
   c. $4xy$
   d. $32x^{\frac{7}{2}}y^{\frac{11}{2}}$

19. A company invests $50,000 in a building where they can produce saws. If the cost of producing one saw is $40, then which function expresses the total amount of money the company spends on producing saws? The variable y is the money paid, and x is the number of saws produced.
   a. $y = 50,000x + 40$
   b. $y + 40 = x - 50,000$
   c. $y = 40x - 50,000$
   d. $y = 40x + 50,000$

20. Which of the following functions represents the graph below?

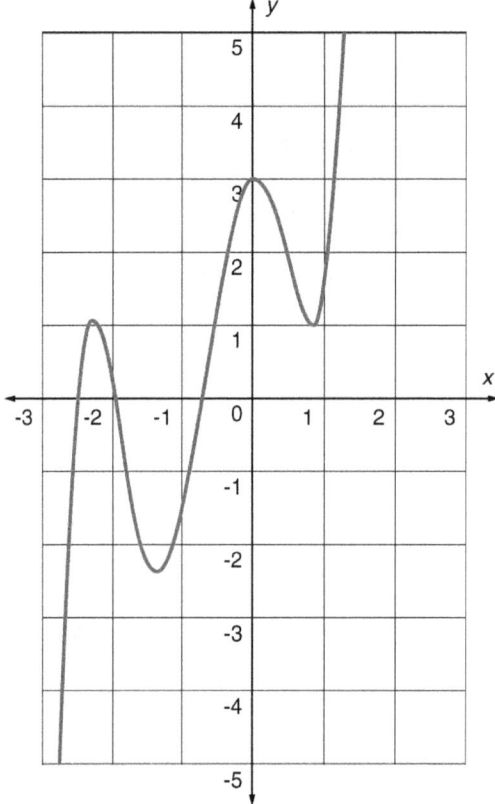

a. $y = x^5 + 3.5x^4 - 6.5x^2 + 0.5x + 3$
b. $y = x^5 - 3.5x^4 + 6.5x^2 - 0.5x - 3$
c. $y = 5x^4 - 6.5x^2 + 0.5x + 3$
d. $y = -5x^4 - 6.5x^2 + 0.5x + 3$

21. Solve for x, if $x^2 - 2x - 8 = 0$.

a. $2 \pm \frac{\sqrt{30}}{2}$

b. $2 \pm 4\sqrt{2}$

c. 1 ± 3

d. $4 \pm \sqrt{2}$

22. 200 dogs were randomly selected from a neighborhood in a local suburb. Of those 200, 42 were part German Shepherd, 21 were part Bulldog, and 12 were part Husky. If there are 1400 dogs in the entire suburb, approximately how many are expected to be part Bulldog?

Math 2

1. Store-brand coffee beans cost $1.23 per pound. A local coffee bean roaster charges $1.98 per $1\frac{1}{2}$ pounds. How much more would five pounds from the local roaster cost than five pounds of the store-brand coffee?
    a. $0.55
    b. $1.55
    c. $1.45
    d. $0.45

2. What is the equation for the line passing through the origin and the point $(2, 1)$?
    a. $y = 2x$
    b. $y = \frac{1}{2}x$
    c. $y = x - 2$
    d. $2y = x + 1$

3. Give a numerical expression for the following: "Six less than three times the sum of twice a number and one."
    a. $2x + 1 - 6$
    b. $3x + 1 - 6$
    c. $3(x + 1) - 6$
    d. $3(2x + 1) - 6$

4. A rectangle has long sides that are each 6 meters longer than the short sides. The perimeter of the rectangle is 36 meters. What is the length of one of the rectangle's long sides?
    a. 4 meters
    b. 6 meters
    c. 12 meters
    d. 18 meters

5. What is the slope of the equation $8x - 2y = 10$?
    a. 10
    b. 8
    c. -5
    d. 4

6. If $f(3) = 7$ and $f(7) = 24$, what is $f(x)$?
    a. $f(x) = \frac{17}{4}x - \frac{23}{4}$
    b. $f(x) = \frac{23}{4}x - \frac{17}{4}$
    c. $f(x) = 4x - 6$
    d. $f(x) = 6x - 4$

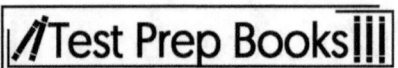

7. The equation $6x + 9y = 18$ is part of a system of two equations that has infinitely many solutions. Which of the following could be the second equation?
   a. $12x + 21y = 42$
   b. $x + y = 6$
   c. $8x + 16y = 24$
   d. $10x + 15y = 30$

8. What is the greatest possible value for y in the inequality $y \leq 8x - 19$ if $x = 4$?
   a. 11
   b. 17
   c. 9
   d. 13

9. Suppose you are shown a number line with the following description: There is an open dot on the number 15 and a closed dot on the number 35, and these dots are connected by a solid line. Which inequality represents the data shown on this number line?
   a. $x < 15 \cup x \geq 35$
   b. $x > 15 \cup x \leq 35$
   c. $15 < x \leq 35$
   d. $15 \leq x < 35$

10. The following functions intersect at which points?

$$y = x^2$$

$$y = x + 2$$

   a. $(-2,4); (1,1)$
   b. $(-1,1); (2,4)$
   c. $(1,1); (2,-4)$
   d. $(2,4); (-1,-1)$

11. What is the equation of a circle whose center is (1, 5) and radius is 4?
   a. $(x - 1)^2 + (y - 25)^2 = 4$
   b. $(x - 1)^2 + (y - 25)^2 = 16$
   c. $(x + 1)^2 + (y + 5)^2 = 16$
   d. $(x - 1)^2 + (y - 5)^2 = 16$

12. What is the volume of a cylinder, in terms of π, with a radius of 6 centimeters and a height of 2 centimeters?
   a. $36\pi \text{ cm}^3$
   b. $24\pi \text{ cm}^3$
   c. $72\pi \text{ cm}^3$
   d. $48\pi \text{ cm}^3$

13. Chuck wants to scale up his operations by a factor of 4. His current operational output can be defined with the expression $3x + 25$. Which of the following expressions represents Chuck's operational output after scaling up?
    a. $12 + 25$
    b. $12x + 100$
    c. $3x + 100$
    d. $4x + 30$

14. Which of the following expressions is equivalent to the expression $4(2x^2 + 12) - 2x(3x + 4) + 10$?
    a. $8x^2 - 6x + 50$
    b. $-6x + 58$
    c. $6x^2 + 6x + 50$
    d. $2x^2 - 8x + 58$

15. What are the polynomial roots of $x^2 + x - 2$?
    a. 1 and -2
    b. -1 and 2
    c. 2 and -2
    d. 9 and 13

16. If $f(x) = (x + 4)^2 + 10$, then what is $f(5)$?
    a. 35
    b. 81
    c. 91
    d. 19

17. For a group of 20 men, the median weight is 180 pounds, and the range is 30 pounds. If each man gains 10 pounds, which of the following would be true?
    a. The median weight will increase, and the range will remain the same.
    b. The median weight and range will both remain the same.
    c. The median weight will stay the same, and the range will increase.
    d. The median weight and range will both increase.

18. What's the probability of rolling a 6 exactly once in two rolls of a die?
    a. $\frac{1}{3}$
    b. $\frac{1}{36}$
    c. $\frac{1}{6}$
    d. $\frac{5}{18}$

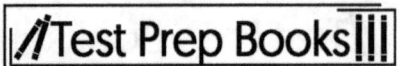

19. A right triangle has a hypotenuse of 10 inches, and one leg is 8 inches. How long is the other leg in inches?

20. Stacy interviews residents from her city who have an appointment in the next month to donate blood. They all want to increase their iron levels before giving blood. She randomly assigns these people to take either an iron supplement pill or a placebo pill, and the people do not know which type of pill they are taking. They have their iron levels measured before and after taking the supplements. Say Stacy finds the people who take the iron pill have a significant increase in iron levels, while the placebo group had unaffected iron levels. Based on this study, this result probably holds true for:
    a. All of the residents in Stacy's city
    b. Only the people participating in this test
    c. All people who will give blood
    d. All females in Stacy's city

21. Find the value(s) of x in the following nonlinear equation:

$$x^2 = 8x$$

   a. 8
   b. 0, 8
   c. 0
   d. No solution

22. Which set of points would make the following data set a linear function?

$$x: (1, 2, 3, 4, 5), y: (4, 8, 12, 16, 20)$$

   a. $x: 6, y: 24$
   b. $x: 6, y: 27$
   c. $x: 7, y: 23$
   d. $x: 8, y: 28$

Answer Explanations #1

Reading and Writing 1

1. B: Choice *B* is correct. Johnson states that men and women peacefully protested the denial of their rights as Americans. The search for freedom is mentioned, but this is not what was being protested, so Choice *A* is incorrect. People were assaulted and a man was killed during the protest, so neither of these could be what was being protested. Therefore, Choices *C* and *D* are incorrect.

2. C: The goal for this question is to select a sentence that not only affirms, or backs up, the selected statement, but could also appear after it and flow with the rest of the piece. Choice *A* is irrelevant to the sentence; just because new members earned scholarships doesn't necessarily mean that this was testament of Hampton's leadership or that this actually benefitted the NAACP. Choice *B* is very compelling. If Hampton got an award for the increase in numbers, this could bolster the idea that he was the direct cause of the rise in numbers and that he was of great value to the organization. However, it does not say directly that he was the cause of the increase and that this was extremely beneficial to the NAACP. Choice *C* is a much better choice than Choice *B*. Choice *C* mentions that the increase in members is unprecedented. Because there has never been this large an increase before, it can be concluded that this increase was most likely due to Hampton's contributions. Thus, Choice *C* is correct. Choice *D* does nothing for the underlined section.

3. C: Roosevelt notes that secrecy ensures an individual's right to vote as they choose. Choice *A* and Choice *D* may be true; public votes were known for their carnivalesque atmosphere, and private votes protect voters from violent confrontations with their political foes. However, these ideas are not stated in the passage. Choice *B* is incorrect as the opposite may be true. Privacy might increase the likelihood that, because the vote is secret, an individual can attest to voting one way but actually vote another without any accountability. This would make bribery a risk.

4. D: The graph shows the number of people (in millions) boarding United States flights between 1996 and 2005. In the first few months following the September 11 attacks, the number of passengers boarding US flights dropped to around 50 million, compared to around 70 million before the attacks. Therefore, the correct answer is Choice *D*. The graph does not show where the flights were redirected, the number of passengers that other countries received as a result of the redirected air travel, or the resulting flight schedule implications, making the other choices incorrect.

5. B: Choice *B* is the strongest revision, as adding *to explore* is very effective in both shortening the sentence and maintaining, even enhancing, the writer's point. Choice *A* is not technically incorrect, but it is overcomplicated. Choice *C* is a decent revision, but the sentence could still be more condensed and sharpened. Choice *D* fails to make the sentence more concise and inserts unnecessary commas.

6. A: Choice *A* is direct and clear, without any punctuation errors. Choice *B* is well written but too wordy. Choice *C* adds an unnecessary comma. Choice *D* is also well written but much less concise than Choice *A*.

7. D: Choice *D* is correct because the addition of finer details helps the reader understand exactly what Prometheus did and his impact: fire came with knowledge and power. Choice *A* lacks a comma after *fire*. Choice *B* inserts unnecessary commas since *people* is not part of the list *knowledge and power*. Choice *C*

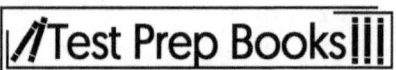

Answer Explanations #1

is a strong revision, but it could be confusing, hinting that the fire itself was knowledge and power, as opposed to symbolizing them.

8. C: Choice *C* is correct because it is clear and fits within the context of the passage. Choice *A* is incorrect because "We rejoiced as 'hackers'" does not explain what was meant by "hackers" or why it was a cause for rejoicing. Choice *B* is incorrect because it does not mention a solution being found and is therefore not specific enough. Additionally, it mentions technology, which is not a topic in the passage. Choice *D* is incorrect because it suggests that rejoicing is the way in which a solution was "hacked."

9. A: The word "however" best demonstrates that the second sentence is not what would be expected given the information in the first sentence. Choice *B* is incorrect because it suggests that the second sentence shares a parallel idea to what is presented in the previous statement. Choice *C* is incorrect because the sentiment is not restated. Choice *D* is incorrect because the previous statement is not a cause for the sentence in question.

10. A: While Choice *B* isn't necessarily wrong, it lacks the direct nature that the original sentence has. Also, by breaking up the sentences like this, the reader becomes confused because the connection between the Taliban's defeat and ongoing war is now separated by a second sentence that is not necessary. Choice *C* corrects this problem, but the fluidity of the sentence is marred because of the awkward construction of the first sentence. Choice *D* begins well but lacks the use of *was* before *overthrown*, which discombobulates the sentence. While *yet* provides an adequate transition for the next sentence, the term *however* is more appropriate. Thus, the original structure of the two sentences is correct, making Choice *A* the correct answer.

11. D: Out of context, Washington, D.C. being an island could mean many things. The meaning of the metaphor can be found in the sentences that precede and follow it, which mention isolation and a wide gap between the government and its citizens. Choice *A* is wrong because Carter is not mentioning an island to describe a vacation. This metaphor does not allude to resources, so Choice *B* is incorrect. Choice *C* implies that Americans have access to the "island" of government, but the real meaning is the opposite, that government has become unresponsive to citizens. Therefore, Choice *C* is incorrect.

12. C: It is easy to imagine that she may have felt either anger, Choice *A*, or fear, Choice *B*, but those are not expressed in the text. Choice *D* is incorrect because although the passage mentions that her appearance was haughty, it goes on to say that she likely felt agony, which is a synonym for anguish, Choice *C*.

13. A: Choice *A* has consistent parallel structure with the verbs *read, identify,* and *determine*. Choices *B* and *C* have faulty parallel structure with the words *determining* and *identifying*. Choice *D* has incorrect subject/verb agreement. The sentence should read, "Students have to read ... identify ... and determine."

14. B: Choice *B* is correct because the sentence is talking about a continuing process. Therefore, the best modification is to add the word *to* in front of *increase*. Choice *A* is incorrect because this modifier is missing. Choice *C* is incorrect because with the additional comma, the present tense of *increase* is inappropriate. Choice *D* makes more sense, but the tense is still not the best to use.

15. D: Choice *D* is the correct answer because *rather* acts as an interrupting word here and should be separated by commas. Choices *B* and *C* use commas incorrectly, breaking the flow of the sentence.

16. D: To fix the original sentence, either a comma must be added after the word *on* to separate the dependent clause from the independent clause, or the order of the clauses must be flipped. Choice *B* adds an unnecessary comma after the word *invested*. Choice *C* creates an incomplete sentence by adding a period after the dependent clause.

17. D: These sentences are written in a very casual style. In this case, the word *Easy* is used informally in place of the full sentence *The answer to that question is easy*. Therefore, it needs to be separated from the complete sentence *It's interest*. In addition to lacking this necessary punctuation, Choice *C* incorrectly changes the contraction *it's* to the possessive *its*.

18. A: Choice *B* incorrectly replaces the word *simply* with *simple* and adds an unnecessary comma. Choice *C* uses a comma where a semicolon is needed. Choice *D* adds an unnecessary comma.

19. C: Choice *C* is correct because the phrase *even likely* is a parenthetical element, which must be set off by commas. Choice *D* does not set off the phrase with commas. Choice *A* omits the second required comma, and Choice *B* misplaces it.

20. B: According to Carter, these examples are the shocks and tragedies that have gradually caused Americans to lose their faith and confidence in government and other institutions, such as schools and media. While there are references to previous presidents, it is not Carter's intention to grade their time in office, making Choice *A* incorrect. The future is not mentioned in these paragraphs, rendering Choice *C* incorrect. Expectations of Americans are not discussed in the passage. Rather, the passage mentions what Americans remember, what they were taught, who they respected, etc. For that reason, Choice *D* is incorrect.

21. D: *Transgression* most closely means *offense* in this excerpt. Obedience, or following the rules, is the opposite of transgression, making Choice *A* incorrect. The word *transgression* has a moral or legal connotation that is lacking in the word *disruption*, making Choice *B* incorrect. A *confession* is an admission of an offense, but it is not the transgression or offense itself, making Choice *C* incorrect.

22. D: The best substitution for the word *posterior* is *rear*. This answer can be drawn from realizing posterior legs means the opposite of "forward appendages." Also, the prefix *post-* means behind or after. While the word *strongest* fits in the sentence nicely, nothing implies that that particular set of legs is the strongest. This makes Choice *A* incorrect. *Anterior*, meaning front, is actually the antonym for the word *posterior*, so Choice *B* is wrong. *Ambulatory* is a word that could describe any pair of functioning legs and does not differentiate the hind legs from the front or middle, which makes Choice *C* incorrect.

23. C: *Convocation* means a gathering or a formal assembly. In this case, the people are summoning the leaders of government to an assembly. Based on context and conventional definitions of the words, Choices *A*, *B*, and *D* are incorrect.

24. A: The passage describes a situation and then explains the causes that led to it. Also, it utilizes cause and effect signal words, such as *reasons*, *factors*, *so*, and *as a result*. Choice *B* is incorrect because a compare and contrast order considers the similarities and differences of two or more things. Choice *C* is incorrect because spatial order describes where things are located in relation to each other. Finally, Choice *D* is incorrect because time order describes when things occurred chronologically.

25. D: Choice *A* is irrelevant. The argument's conclusion is that Hank is a professional writer. It does not matter where or for whom Hank's agent works. Choice *B* seems fairly strong at first glance. It feels

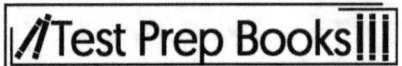

Answer Explanations #1

reasonable to say that being a professional writer requires representation. However, the argument would still be strong if being a professional writer did not require an agent. Hank would still be a professional writer. Choice C is irrelevant. Whether Hank is a professional writer does not depend on his reviews. Choice D is strong. Negate it to determine if the argument falls apart. If being a professional writer requires earning money, then Hank would not be a professional writer. The argument falls apart. Therefore, Choice D is the correct answer.

26. D: Choice D references the argument's main points—*Infinite Jest* is a modern classic, the book deserves its praise, and everybody should read it. In contrast, Choice A restates the author's conclusion. The correct answer to main point questions will often be closely related to the conclusion. Choice B restates a premise. Is the author's main point that *Infinite Jest* is a page-turner? No, he uses readers' obsession with the book as a premise. Choice C is definitely not the main point of the passage. It's a simple fact underlying the argument. It certainly cannot be considered the main point.

27. C: This reading comprehension question can be answered based on the second paragraph—scientists were concerned about astronauts' nutrition and began researching useful nutritional supplements. Choice A in particular is not true because it reverses the order of discovery (first NASA identified algae for astronaut use, and then it was further developed for use in baby food). Choices B and D are not uses of algae discussed in the article.

Reading and Writing 2

1. D: The objective for questions like this is to determine if a revision is possible within the choices and if it can adhere to the specific criteria of the question; in this case, we want the sentence to maintain the original meaning while being more concise, or shorter. Choice B can be eliminated as the meaning of the original sentence is split into two distinct sentences. The second of the two sentences is also incorrectly constructed. The clause "flooding occurs slowly or rapidly submerging" in Choice C is awkward and difficult to understand without the use of a comma after *rapidly*, making it a poor construction. Choice D is certainly more concise and correctly phrased, and it communicates the meaning of the message that flooding can overtake small areas as well as great lengths of land either slowly or very quickly. This rules out Choice A in the process.

2. B: By starting a new sentence, the run-on issue is eliminated, and a new line of reasoning can be seamlessly introduced, making Choice B correct. While Choice C fixes the run-on issue via a semicolon, a comma is still needed after *this*. Choice D contains a comma splice. The independent clauses must be separated by more than just a comma, even with the rearrangement of the second half of the sentence.

3. A: Choice A is correct; while the sentence seems long, it actually doesn't require any commas. The conjunction *that* successfully combines the two parts of the sentence without the need for additional punctuation. Choices B and C insert commas unnecessarily. Choice D alters the meaning of the original text by creating a new sentence, which is only a fragment.

4. B: Choice B correctly separates the section into two sentences and adds a comma after *Usually*. Choice A is incorrect because it is a run-on sentence. Choice C adds an extraneous comma, while Choice D makes the run-on issue worse and does not coincide with the overall structure of the sentence.

Answer Explanations #1

5. B: In Choice *B*, a colon is used to introduce an explanation. Colons can be used to introduce quotes, explanations, or lists. Additionally, the quote ends with the punctuation inside the quotes, unlike Choice *C*.

6. C: The word *civelized* should be spelled *civilized*. The words *distinguishes* and *creatures* are both spelled correctly.

7. D: This sentence must have a comma before *although* because it is connecting two independent clauses. Thus, Choices *B* and *C* are incorrect. Choice *A* is incorrect because the second sentence in the underlined section is a fragment.

8. B: Choice *B* is correct because the conjunction *and* is used to connect phrases that are to be used jointly, such as teachers working hard to help students "identify salient information" and to "think critically." The conjunctions *so*, *but*, and *nor* are incorrect in the context of this sentence.

9. C: The word *apprehension* most nearly means fear. The passage indicates that "assault is an unlawful and intentional act that causes reasonable fear/anxiety in another individual, either by an imminent threat or by initiating offensive contact." The creation of fear in another individual seems to be a property of assault.

10. D: A *rookery* is a colony of breeding birds. Although *rookery* could mean Choice *A*, houses in a slum area, it does not make sense in this context. Choices *B* and *C* are both incorrect, as this is not a place for hunters to trade tools or for wardens to trade stories.

11. B: Choice *B* is correct because *skill* is defined as having a certain aptitude for a given task. Choice *C* is incorrect because *work* does not directly denote "critical thinking, business skills, problem solving, and creativity." Choice *A* is incorrect because the word *care* doesn't fit into the context of the passage, and Choice *D*, *composition*, is incorrect because nothing in this statement points to the way in which something is structured.

12. C: One can reasonably infer that Gulliver is considerably larger than the children who were playing around him because multiple children could fit into his hand. Choice *A* is incorrect because there is no indication of stress in Gulliver's tone. Choices *B* and *D* aren't the best answers because, though Gulliver seems fond of his new acquaintances, he didn't travel there with the intentions of meeting new people, nor does he express a definite love for them in this particular portion of the text.

13. A: Choice *A* is consistent with the argument's logic. The argument asserts that the world powers' military alliances amounted to a delicate fuse and that the assassination merely lit it. The main point of the argument is that any event involving the military alliances would have led to a world war. Choice *B* runs counter to the argument's tone and reasoning. It can immediately be eliminated. Choice *C* is also clearly incorrect. At no point does the argument blame any single country or group of countries for starting World War I. Choice *D* is incorrect for the same reason as Choice *C*, so it can be eliminated.

14. C: We are looking for an inference—a conclusion that is reached on the basis of evidence and reasoning—from the passage that will likely explain why the famous children's author did not achieve her usual success with the new genre (despite the book's acclaim). Choice *A* is wrong because the statement is false according to the passage. Choice *B* is wrong because, although the passage says the author has a graduate degree on the subject, it would be an unrealistic leap to infer that she is the foremost expert on Antebellum America. Choice *D* is wrong because there is nothing in the passage to

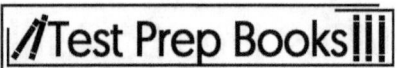

Answer Explanations #1

lead us to infer that people generally prefer a children's series to historical fiction. In contrast, Choice *C* can be logically inferred since the passage speaks of the great success of the children's series and the declaration that the fame of the author's name causes the children's books to "fly off the shelves." Thus, we can infer that she did not receive any bump from her name since she published the historical novel under a pseudonym, which makes Choice *C* correct.

15. D: Outspending other countries on education could have other benefits, but there is no reference to this in the passage, so Choice *A* is incorrect. Choice *B* is incorrect because the author does not mention corruption. Choice *C* is incorrect because there is nothing in the passage stating that the tests are not genuinely representative. Choice *D* is accurate because spending more money has not brought success. The United States already spends the most money, but the country is not excelling on these tests. Choice *D* is the correct answer.

16. C: The paragraph literally "presents a conundrum," explains the problem of partial understanding, and ends with more questions or inquiries. There is no solution offered in this paragraph, making Choices *A* and *B* incorrect. Choice *D* is incorrect because the paragraph does not begin with a definition.

17. C: This question is testing whether you can discern accurate conclusions from a timeline. Although the incorrect answer choices can seem correct, they cannot be confirmed from the information presented on the timeline. Choice *A* is incorrect; while it may be reasonable to assume that the timeline documents all major life events, we do not know for certain that Bell did not engage in any notable activities after founding the National Geographic Society. Choice *B* is incorrect because the timeline does not confirm that the school was in Canada; Bell actually started it in the United States. Choice *D* is incorrect because nothing on the timeline shows causation between the two events. Choice *C* is the only verifiable statement based on the timeline, so it must be the correct answer.

18. D: The passage directly states that the larger sensor is the main difference between the two cameras. Choices *A* and *B* may be true, but these answers do not identify the major difference between the two cameras. Choice *C* states the opposite of what the paragraph suggests is the best option for amateur photographers, so it is incorrect.

19. B: The main point of this passage is to show how tornadoes form. Choice *A* is off base because while the passage does mention that tornadoes are dangerous, it is not the main focus of the passage. While thunderstorms are mentioned, they are not compared to tornadoes, so Choice *C* is incorrect. Choice *D* is incorrect because the passage does not discuss what to do in the event of a tornado.

20. D: This question requires readers to understand the relevance of the given detail. In this case, the author mentions "costly and crucial equipment" before mentioning space suit visors, which are given as an example of something that is very valuable. Choice *A* is not correct because fashion is only related to sunglasses, not to NASA equipment. Choice *B* can be eliminated because it is simply not mentioned in the passage. While Choice *C* seems like it could be a true statement, it is also not relevant to what is being explained by the author.

21. A: The line "Beyond these signs of his activity, however, which I merely shared with all the readers of the daily press, I knew little of my former friend and companion," suggests that the narrator learned of the cases mentioned in the press, another name for the newspaper. Choice *B* is incorrect because there is no mention of police reports. Choices *C* and *D* are incorrect because the narrator admits that he has not had direct contact with Holmes or his cases for some time.

Answer Explanations #1

22. D: Choice *D* is the correct answer because it provides a tangible example of the work that NASA has done to improve commercial flight, helping airlines reduce surface congestion and save jet fuel. Choice *A* is incorrect because it does not provide an example of work NASA has done. Choice *B* is incorrect because it expands on the structure of the ATD project but does not state what it ultimately accomplished for flight. Choice *C* is incorrect because it only mentions tests of the tools and not the work NASA did on them or what they achieved.

23. A: Choice *A* is the correct answer because the text creates a cause-and-effect relationship in which *therefore* appropriately describes the relationship. The theme is a Renaissance fairytale, and people will be wearing a certain type of clothing. Choice *B* is incorrect because the sentences do not set up a comparison to suggest similarity. Choice *C* is incorrect because *moreover* means besides. The second sentence is a related matter, so that does not work. Choice *D* is incorrect because the word *because* would create a sentence fragment and incorrectly imply that the wedding's theme is based around what the guests are wearing, when it is actually the opposite.

24. B: Choice *B* is the correct answer because it makes sense in the context of the sentence. The planes were picked due to the specific criteria they met. For this reason, they were *specifically* chosen. Choice *A* is incorrect because *exceptionally* is not an appropriate word to convey that the planes were picked for a reason. Choice *C* is incorrect because *usually* would imply that this incident happened more than once, but it did not. Choice *D* is incorrect because the planes were picked for a reason that was necessary to a mission.

25. B: Choice *B* is the correct answer because the importance of the diners cannot be stressed enough. In other words, it is not possible to overly state their impact. It cannot be *overstated*. Choice *A* is incorrect because *understated* is the opposite of *overstated*. Choice *C* is incorrect because *outdone* would imply that there is some sort of competitive successor to the diner, which is not what the text is trying to say. Choice *D* is incorrect because the diner's importance can be understood when studying its history.

26. C: Choice *C* is the correct answer because it is true that human nails are not relevant to the overall discussion. Turtle shells are the main topic of the text. Therefore, it is unnecessary to bring up a comparison to human nails, and that sentence can be deleted. Choice *A* is incorrect because the two topics are not related enough for human nails to be a natural progression in discussion. Choice *B* is incorrect because human responsibility is not a topic of discussion in this text. Choice *D* is incorrect because although the information is accurate, it is not relevant to the overall text.

27. D: Choice *D* is the correct answer because it is the most appropriate word choice for this text. The language in this text is elevated and uses complex vocabulary. In this instance, the phrase *stick to* is not formal enough, which makes Choice *A* incorrect. *Adhere to* uses more formal vocabulary that fits the context of the text. Choice *B* is incorrect because the students are following rules, not laws. *Obey* has a connotation that there is an authority figure involved, which does not fit the context. Choice *C* is incorrect because the students are not agreeing or disagreeing with the conventions in this context. They are merely rules for the English language that will improve their academic success. Although it would not be a completely incorrect choice, *adhere to* is a better fit for the vocabulary featured.

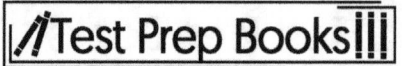

Answer Explanations #1

Math 1

1. B: To simplify this inequality, subtract 3 from both sides:

$$3 - 3 - \frac{1}{2}x \geq 2 - 3$$

$$-\frac{1}{2}x \geq -1$$

Then, multiply both sides by –2 (remembering this flips the direction of the inequality):

$$(-\frac{1}{2}x)(-2) \geq (-1)(-2)$$

$$x \leq 2.$$

2. C: First, find the total cost of the hat and jersey, then multiply by 0.5 to apply the 50% off:

$$(32.99 + 64.99) \times 0.5 = 48.99$$

Finally, calculate the sales tax of 6% (that is, 0.06) and add it to the total:

$$48.99 + (48.99 \times 0.06) = 51.93$$

3. D: The shape of the scatter plot is a parabola (U-shaped). This eliminates Choices A (a linear equation that produces a straight line) and C (an exponential equation that produces a smooth curve upward or downward). The value of a for a quadratic function in standard form ($y = ax^2 + bx + c$) indicates whether the parabola opens up (U-shaped) or opens down (upside-down U). A negative value for a produces a parabola that opens down; therefore, Choice B can also be eliminated.

4. A: The volume of a cylinder is $\pi r^2 h$. Plugging in the given values yields:

$$\pi \times (5 \text{ in})^2 \times 10 \text{ in} = 250\pi \text{ in}^3$$

5. B: The table shows values that are increasing exponentially. The differences between the inputs are the same, while the differences in the outputs are changing by a factor of 2. The values in the table can be modeled by the equation $f(x) = 2^x$.

6. A: To expand a squared binomial, it's necessary to use the first, outer, inner, last (FOIL) method.

$$(2x - 4y)(2x - 4y)$$

$$(2x)(2x) + (2x)(-4y) + (-4y)(2x) + (-4y)(-4y)$$

$$4x^2 - 8xy - 8xy + 16y^2$$

$$4x^2 - 16xy + 16y^2$$

Answer Explanations #1

7. B: The zeros of this function can be found by setting: $f(x)$ equal to 0 and solving for x.

$$0 = x^2 + 4$$

$$-4 = x^2$$

$$\sqrt{-4} = x$$

Taking the square root of a negative number results in an imaginary number, so the solution is:

$$x = \pm 2i$$

8. A: The common denominator here will be $4x$. Rewrite these fractions as

$$\frac{3}{x} + \frac{5u}{2x} - \frac{u}{4} = \frac{12}{4x} + \frac{10u}{4x} - \frac{ux}{4x} = \frac{12x + 10u - ux}{4x}$$

9. C: In this scenario, the variables are the number of sales and Karen's weekly pay. The weekly pay depends on the number of sales. Therefore, weekly pay is the dependent variable (y), and the number of sales is the independent variable (x). All four answer choices are in slope-intercept form, $y = mx + b$, so we just need to find m (the slope) and b (the y-intercept). We can calculate both by picking any two points, for example, $(2, 380)$ and $(4, 460)$.

The slope is given by $m = \frac{y_2 - y_1}{x_2 - x_1}$, so $m = \frac{460 - 380}{4 - 2} = 40$. This gives us the equation $y = 40x + b$. Now we can plug in the x and y values from our first point to find b. Since $380 = 40(2) + b$, we find $b = 300$. This means the equation is $y = 40x + 300$.

10. C: The area of the shaded region is the area of the square minus the area of the circle. The area of the circle is πr^2. The side of the square will be $2r$, so the area of the square will be $4r^2$. Therefore, the difference is:

$$4r^2 - \pi r^2 = (4 - \pi)r^2$$

11. B: Because this is not a right triangle, the SOHCAHTOA mnemonic can not be used. However, the law of cosines can be used:

$$c^2 = a^2 + b^2 - 2ab \cos C$$

$$c^2 = 19^2 + 26^2 - 2 \times 19 \times 26 \times \cos 42° = 302.773$$

Taking the square root and rounding to the nearest tenth results in $c = 17.4$.

12. C: Because the triangles are similar, the lengths of the corresponding sides are proportional. Therefore, these two relationships exist:

$$\frac{30 + x}{30} = \frac{22}{14}$$

$$\frac{y + 15}{y} = \frac{22}{14}$$

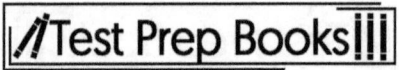

Answer Explanations #1

Using cross multiplication on the first proportion results in the equation:

$$14(30 + x) = 22 \times 30$$

When solved, this gives:

$$x \approx 17.1$$

Using cross multiplication on the second proportion results in the equation:

$$14(y + 15) = 22y$$

When solved, this gives:

$$y \approx 26.3$$

13. 30: The best way to solve this problem is by using a system of equations. We know that Jan bought $90 worth of apples ($a$) and oranges ($o$) at $1 and $2, respectively. That means our first equation is:

$$1(a) + 2(o) = 90$$

We also know that she bought an equal number of apples and oranges, which gives us our second equation: $a = o$. We can then replace a with o in the first equation to give:

$$1(o) + 2(o) = 90 \text{ or } 3(o) = 90$$

Solving for o yields:

$$o = 30$$

Thus, Jan bought 30 oranges (and 30 apples).

14. A: To solve for x in both equations, we need to remove y as a variable from one of them. We can do this by solving one equation for y, then inserting that solution in place of y in the other equation and solving for x there. This can be done starting with either equation, but for this example we will first solve $4x + 2y = 8$ for y. To solve it for y, we need to isolate that variable on one side, so start by subtracting $4x$ from both sides, which gives us $2y = 8 - 4x$. Now divide both sides by 2, which gives us $y = 4 - 2x$. We now insert our temporary solution for y into the other equation and solve for x. We start with $10x + 3(4 - 2x) = 15$. We can multiply 3 against everything inside the parentheses, which gives us $10x + 12 - 6x = 15$. Combining x variables and subtracting both sides by 12 gives us $4x = 3$. Finally, dividing both sides by 4 gives us our solution, $x = \frac{3}{4}$. This can be verified by inserting $x = \frac{3}{4}$ into both equations and solving for y; if both equations yield the same result for y, then our solution for x is correct.

15. B: To solve for x in both equations, we need to remove y as a variable from one of them. We can do this by solving one equation for y, then inserting that solution in place of y in the other equation and solving for x there. This can be done starting with either equation, but for this example we will first solve $\frac{2}{5}x + 5y = 18$ for y. To solve for y, we need to isolate that variable on one side, so start by subtracting $\frac{2}{5}x$ from both sides, which gives us $5y = 18 - \frac{2}{5}x$. Dividing both sides by 5 gives us $y = \frac{18}{5} -$

172

Answer Explanations #1

$\frac{2}{25}x$, which is our temporary y solution (remember that dividing by 5 is the same as multiplying by $\frac{1}{5}$). We can insert this temporary solution into the other equation and solve for x. We start with $x - 8\left(\frac{18}{5} - \frac{2}{25}x\right) = 4$. Remember that our multiplier for the parentheses expression is negative, so we multiply that expression by -8 to get $x - \frac{144}{5} + \frac{16}{25}x = 4$. At this point we need to get rid of our fractions since neither of them can be reduced further. This can be done by converting $-\frac{144}{5}$ into a fraction with a denominator of 25 first, then multiplying both sides of the equation in their entirety by 25 to remove the fractions. After these operations are done, we have the equation $25x - 720 + 16x = 100$. Combining x variables and adding 720 to both sides gives us $41x = 820$. Finally, dividing both sides by 41 gives us $x = \frac{820}{41}$, which is reducible to $x = 20$. This can be verified by inserting $x = 20$ into both equations and solving for y; if both equations yield the same result for y, then our solution for x is correct.

16. C: An x-intercept is a point where the graph crosses the x-axis. At this point, the value of y is 0. To determine if an equation has an x-intercept of -2, substitute -2 for x, and calculate the value of y. If the value of -2 for x corresponds with a y-value of 0, then the equation has an x-intercept of -2. The only answer choice that produces this result is Choice C.

$$0 = (-2)^2 + 5(-2) + 6$$

17. 4: Kristen bought four DVDs, which would cost a total of $4 \times \$15 = \$60$. She spent a total of $100, so she spent $100 - \$60 = \$40$ on CDs. Since they cost $10 each, she must have purchased $\$40 \div \$10 = 4$ CDs.

18. A: Simplify this to:

$$(4x^2 y^4)^{\frac{3}{2}} = 4^{\frac{3}{2}}(x^2)^{\frac{3}{2}}(y^4)^{\frac{3}{2}}$$

Now:

$$4^{\frac{3}{2}} = (\sqrt{4})^3 = 2^3 = 8$$

For the other terms, recall that the exponents must be multiplied, so this yields:

$$8x^{2 \cdot \frac{3}{2}} y^{4 \cdot \frac{3}{2}} = 8x^3 y^6$$

19. D: For manufacturing costs, there is a linear relationship between the cost to the company and the number produced, with a y-intercept given by the base cost of acquiring the means of production and a slope given by the cost to produce one unit. In this case, that base cost is $50,000, while the cost per unit is $40. So, $y = 40x + 50,000$.

20. A: The graph contains four turning points (where the curve changes from rising to falling or vice versa). This indicates that the degree of the function (highest exponent for the variable) is 5 because a function of degree n can have no more than $n - 1$ turning points, eliminating Choices C and D. The y-intercepts of the functions can be determined by substituting 0 for x and finding the value of y. The function for Choice A has a y-intercept of 3, and the function for Choice B has a y-intercept of -3. Therefore, Choice B is eliminated.

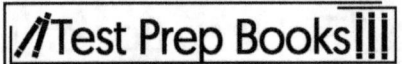

Answer Explanations #1

21. C: The quadratic formula can be used to solve this problem. Given the equation, use the values $a = 1$, $b = -2$, and $c = -8$.

$$x = \frac{-b \pm \sqrt{b^2 - 4ac}}{2a} = \frac{-(-2) \pm \sqrt{(-2)^2 - 4(1)(-8)}}{2(1)}$$

From here, simplify to solve for x.

$$x = \frac{2 \pm \sqrt{4 + 32}}{2} = \frac{2 \pm \sqrt{36}}{2} = \frac{2 \pm 6}{2} = 1 \pm 3$$

22. 147: First, calculate the percentage of dogs that are part Bulldog in the neighborhood.

$$\frac{21}{200} = 10.5\%$$

Then, multiply that percentage times the population size.

$$10.5\% \cdot 1400 = 0.105 \cdot 1400 = 147$$

Math 2

1. D: 5 pounds of store-brand coffee would cost $\frac{\$1.23}{1 \text{ lb}} \times 5 \text{ lbs} = \$6.15$. For 5 pounds of local coffee, the cost would be $\frac{\$1.98}{1.5 \text{ lbs}} \times 5 \text{ lbs} = \$6.60$. Calculate the price difference: $\$6.60 - \$6.15 = \$0.45$.

2. B: The origin is (0,0). The slope is given by:

$$m = \frac{y_2 - y_1}{x_2 - x_1} = \frac{1 - 0}{2 - 0} = \frac{1}{2}$$

The y-intercept will be 0, since it passes through the origin, $(0, 0)$. Using slope-intercept form, the equation for this line is:

$$y = \frac{1}{2}x$$

3. D: "Sum" means the result of addition, so "the sum of twice a number and one" can be written as 2x+1. Next, "three times the sum of twice a number and one" would be $3(2x + 1)$. Finally, "six less than three times the sum of twice a number and one" would be $3(2x + 1) - 6$.

4. C: Let's say the short side of the rectangle is x. The perimeter of the rectangle is the sum of all four sides. Thus, we get the following:

$$x + x + (x + 6) + (x + 6) = 36$$

$$4x + 12 = 36$$

$$4x = 24$$

$$x = 6$$

Answer Explanations #1

This is the length of the short side of the rectangle, so the long side is $6 + 6 = 12$ meters.

5. D: The slope can easily be found by converting the given equation into slope-intercept form, $y = mx + b$. Start by adding $2y$ to both sides, which results in $8x = 2y + 10$. Then subtract 10 from both sides, giving $8x - 10 = 2y$. We can safely swap both sides for readability, then divide both sides by 2, resulting in the slope-intercept equation $y = 4x - 5$. In this format, the slope is immediately identifiable as the multiplier on the x variable, so the slope is 4.

6. A: First, we need to determine the slope of the equation. We are given two points on the line, $(3, 7)$ and $(7, 24)$. The slope of the line can be calculated by finding the difference between the two y values and dividing that by the difference between the two x values. This looks like $\frac{y_2 - y_1}{x_2 - x_1}$. Inserting our values, we get $\frac{24 - 7}{7 - 3} = \frac{17}{4}$, so the slope of our line is $\frac{17}{4}$. Now we need to find the y-intercept by inserting one of our given points into the equation; for this example, we will insert the point $(3, 7)$. This gives us a starting point of $7 = \frac{17}{4}(3) + b$. Multiply $\frac{17}{4}$ by 3 to get $\frac{51}{4}$. Then, we need to convert 7 into a fraction with a denominator of 4 in order to combine it with $\frac{51}{4}$. This can be done by multiplying 7 by $\frac{4}{4}$ (a fraction equal to 1), which lets us represent 7 as $\frac{28}{4}$. Finally, subtract both sides by $\frac{51}{4}$ to get $b = -\frac{23}{4}$. With the slope and y-intercept found, we can represent $f(x)$ as $f(x) = \frac{17}{4}x - \frac{23}{4}$.

7. D: The equation $10x + 15y = 30$ is the only choice that maintains infinitely many solutions with the other equation, $6x + 9y = 18$. This is because both of these equations can be reduced to match each other exactly. $10x + 15y = 30$ can be divided by 5 to get $2x + 3y = 6$, and $6x + 9y = 18$ can be divided by 3 to get $2x + 3y = 6$. This means that both equations are essentially the same, so the system of these two equations has infinitely many solutions since the equations would be represented by the exact same line.

8. D: The greatest possible value occurs when y is equal to the value on the right side of the "less than or equal to" sign, so this inequality can be solved as if it were an equation. Inserting $x = 4$ gives $y \leq 8(4) - 19$. Multiplying 8 by 4 and subtracting 19 gives us $y \leq 13$. The greatest possible value for y in this inequality would be the value of 13 itself, so Choice *D* is correct.

9. C: The inequality described is a specific intersection between two criteria. The open dot on 15 means that 15 is not included as a valid solution, while the closed dot on 35 means that 35 is included. The correct expression of this inequality would be $15 < x \leq 35$.

10. B: In order to find where the two equations intersect, we must set them equal to each other and solve for x:

$$x^2 = x + 2$$

$$x^2 - x - 2 = 0$$

$$(x - 2)(x + 1) = 0$$

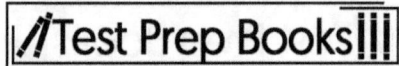

Answer Explanations #1

Now that we know that $x = 2$ and -1, we can plug those values into either of the equations to solve for their corresponding y-values:

$$y = (2)^2 = 4$$

$$y = (-1)^2 = 1$$

This means that the two equations intersect at $(2,4)$ and $(-1,1)$.

11. D: Subtract the center from the x- and y-values of the equation and square the radius on the right side of the equation. Choice A is not the correct answer because it fails to square the radius. Choice B is not the correct answer because it incorrectly squares the x- and y-values of the center. Choice C is not the correct answer because it incorrectly adds the x- and y-values of the center rather than subtracting them.

12. C: The volume of a cylinder is $\pi r^2 h$, and $\pi \times 6^2 \times 2$ is $72\,\pi$ cm³. Choice A is not the correct answer because that is only $6^2 \times \pi$. Choice B is not the correct answer because that is $2^2 \times 6 \times \pi$. Choice D is not the correct answer because that is $2^3 \times 6 \times \pi$.

13. B: To scale Chuck's operations up by a factor of 4, simply multiply 4 by his current operational output, $3x + 25$. This gives the equivalent expression $12x + 100$.

14. D: $2x^2 - 8x + 58$ is an equivalent expression. Start by distributing the terms of the original expression to the parentheses to remove them. This gives the expression $8x^2 + 48 - 6x^2 - 8x + 10$. From here, combine terms of a similar degree of x. The x^2 terms can be combined into $2x^2$, and the constants can be combined into 58. The $8x$ is left on its own, giving a final expression of $2x^2 - 8x + 58$.

15. A: Finding the roots means finding the values of x when y is zero. The quadratic formula could be used, but in this case, it is possible to factor by hand since the numbers -1 and 2 add to 1 and multiply to -2. Solving for each value gives the values $x = 1$ and $x = -2$.

16. C: To solve for $f(5)$, we insert 5 for x in the equation. $5 + 4$ is 9, which is then squared to get 81. $81 + 10$ is 91, so $f(5) = 91$.

17. A: If each man gains 10 pounds, every original data point will increase by 10 pounds. Therefore, the man with the original median will still have the median value, but that value will increase by 10. The smallest value and largest value will also increase by 10, so the difference between the two (the range) will remain the same.

18. D: If we roll a die twice, there are six possibilities for the first roll and six for the second roll, which gives $6 \times 6 = 36$ total possibilities. Now, how many ways are there to roll exactly one 6? We could get a 6 & 1, or 6 & 2, or 6 & 3, or 6 & 4, or 6 & 5. Furthermore, the 6 could come on the second roll; we could get a 1 & 6, or 2 & 6, or 3 & 6, or 4 & 6, or 5 & 6. Counting these up, we find a total of 10 different ways to roll exactly one 6. That means the event could happen in 10 out of 36 possible rolls, so the probability is $\frac{10}{36}$, which simplifies to $\frac{5}{18}$.

Answer Explanations #1

19. 6: The length of the other leg can be determined using the Pythagorean Theorem: $a^2+b^2 = c^2$, where a and b represent the lengths of the legs, and c is the length of the hypotenuse. Given that the hypotenuse (c) is 10 inches and one leg (a) is 8 inches, we can plug these values into the theorem:

$$(8)^2 + b^2 = (10)^2$$

$$64 + b^2 = 100$$

$$b^2 = 100 - 64 = 36$$

$$b = 6$$

Therefore, the length of the other leg is 6 inches.

20. B: This study was only for people who have upcoming appointments to have their blood drawn, so they have something in common. The sample of people was not a random sample of people from the city. Therefore, these results are only probable for those people in the sample group.

21. B: First, rearrange the equation to bring all terms to the same side:

$$x^2 - 8x = 0$$

Then, factor the quadratic expression:

$$x \times (x - 8) = 0$$

Separate the two equations by setting each factor equal to 0:

$$x = 0$$

$$x - 8 = 0$$

Simplify the bottom equation by isolating x:

$$x = 0$$

$$x = 8$$

Test both solutions to make sure they satisfy the equation:

$$0^2 = 8 \times 0$$

$$8^2 = 8 \times 8$$

Both 0 and 8 are valid solutions.

22. A: The linear rate of change is $\frac{4}{1}$. Choice A provides the correct ratio.

Practice Test #2

Reading and Writing 1

The next question is based on the following passage:

> In our time we have come to live with the moments of great crisis. Our lives have been marked with debate about great issues—issues of war and peace, issues of prosperity and depression. But rarely in any time does an issue lay bare the secret heart of America itself. Rarely are we met with a challenge, not to our growth or abundance, or our welfare or our security, but rather to the values, and the purposes, and the meaning of our beloved nation.

Except from Lyndon Johnson's "Address to Joint Session of Congress," March 15, 1965

1. How does Johnson suggest this issue is different from other debates?
    a. Other debates haven't led to protests.
    b. It is easier to solve.
    c. It is more difficult to solve.
    d. It concerns values.

The next question is based on the following passage:

> In the United States we have a capitalistic economy. That is because public opinion favors that type of economy under the conditions in which we live. But we have imposed certain restraints; for instance, we have antitrust laws. These are the legal evidence of the determination of the American people to maintain an economy of free competition and not to allow monopolies to take away the people's freedom.

Excerpt from Eleanor Roosevelt's "The Struggle for Human Rights," September 28, 1948

2. According to the passage, what is the goal of antitrust laws?
    a. To establish trust between governments and populations
    b. To encourage foreign investment in the American economy
    c. To foster economic competition
    d. To allow businesses to compete with the government

The next question is based on the following graphs:

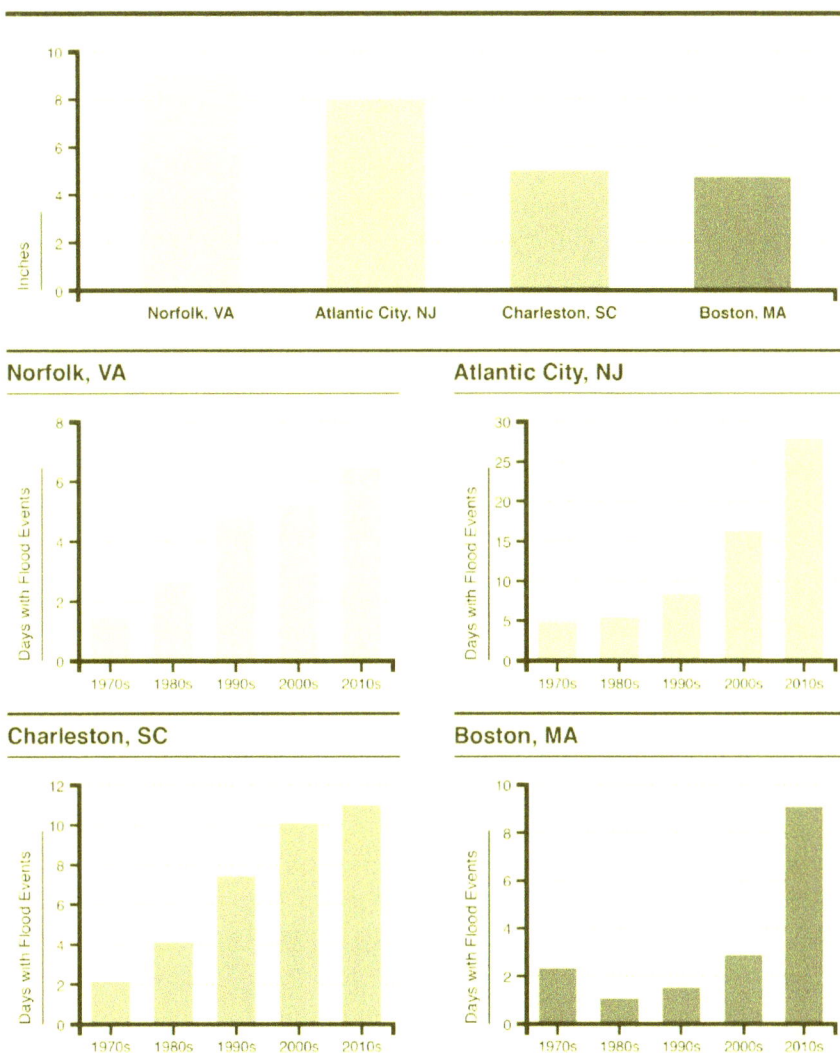

Global warming is the result of air pollution that prevents the Sun's radiation from being emitted back into space. Instead, the radiation is trapped in the Earth's atmosphere and results in global warming. The warming of the Earth has resulted in climate changes. As a result, floods have been occurring with increasing regularity. Some claim that the increased temperatures on Earth may cause the icebergs to melt. They fear that the melting of icebergs will cause the oceans levels to rise and flood coastal regions.

3. What information from the graphs could be used to support the claims found in the paragraph above?
   a. Between 1970–1980, Boston experienced an increase in the number of days with flood events.
   b. Between 1970–1980, Atlantic City, New Jersey did not experience an increase in the number of days with flood events.
   c. Since 1970, the number of days with floods has decreased in major coastal cities across America.
   d. Since 1970, sea levels have risen along the East Coast.

4. Which of the following would be the best choice for the underlined portion of the sentences below?

   For much of the early 19th century, when people first started studying dinosaur bones, the assumption was that they were simply giant lizards. <u>For the longest time this image was the prevailing view on dinosaurs,</u> until evidence indicated that they were more likely warm-blooded.

   a. NO CHANGE
   b. For the longest time this was the prevailing view on dinosaurs,
   c. For the longest time, this image, was the prevailing view on dinosaurs
   d. This was the prevailing image of dinosaurs

5. Which of the following would be the best choice for the sentence below?

   The temptation of the evil spirit Un-man ultimately takes over Weston and he is possessed.

   a. NO CHANGE
   b. Weston gives in to the temptation of the evil spirit Un-man and becomes possessed.
   c. Weston is possessed as a result of the temptation of the evil spirit Un-man ultimately, who takes over.
   d. The temptation of the evil spirit Un-man takes over Weston and he is possessed ultimately.

6. Which of the following would be the best choice for the underlined portion of the sentences below?

   I have to admit that when my father bought a recreational vehicle (RV), I thought he was making a huge mistake. I didn't really know anything about RVs, but I knew that my dad was as big a "city slicker" as there was. <u>In fact, I even thought he might have gone a little bit crazy.</u>

   a. NO CHANGE
   b. Move the sentence so that it comes before the preceding sentence.
   c. Move the sentence to the beginning of a new paragraph.
   d. Omit the sentence.

7. Which of the following would be the best choice for the underlined portion of the sentences below?

   Attaining a high level of expertise <u>allows</u> aircraft engineers to apply essential mathematical equations and scientific processes to aeronautical and aerospace issues or inventions. Without these skills, the engineers will not be able to function in their field.

   a. NO CHANGE
   b. inhibits
   c. requires
   d. should

8. Which of the following would be the best choice for the underlined portion of the sentence below?

   Although the passengers were successful in <u>diverging</u> the plane before it could reach its target, the plane crashed in a western Pennsylvania field and killed everyone on board.

   a. NO CHANGE
   b. diverting
   c. converging
   d. distracting

9. What word could be used in place of the underlined description?

   Hampton was born and raised in the Maywood neighborhood of Chicago, Illinois in 1948. <u>Gifted academically</u> and a natural athlete, he became a stellar baseball player in high school. After graduating from Proviso East High School in 1966, he later went on to study law at Triton Junior College.

   a. Vacuous
   b. Energetic
   c. Intelligent
   d. Athletic

The next question is based on the following passage:

   Experiment 80. Fill a test tube one-fourth full of cold water. Slowly stir in salt until no more will dissolve. Add half a teaspoonful more of salt than will dissolve. Dry the outside of the test tube and heat the salty water over the Bunsen burner. Will hot water dissolve things more readily or less readily than cold? Why do you wash dishes in hot water?

   Excerpt from "Common Science" by Carleton W. Washburne

10. What is the most likely result of Experiment 80?
    a. The heat is unable to dissolve the additional salt.
    b. Once heated, the additional salt dissolves completely.
    c. The additional salt prevents the water from heating up higher than room temperature.
    d. The heated salt-and-water solution could be used to wash dishes.

The next question is based on the following passage:

> In the morning before office hours, at noon when business was plenty and time scarce, at night under the face of the full city moon, by all lights and at all hours of solitude or concourse, the lawyer was to be found on his chosen post. "If he be Mr. Hyde," he had thought, "I should be Mr. Seek."

Excerpt from *The Strange Case of Dr. Jekyll and Mr. Hyde* by Robert Louis Stevenson

11. What can one reasonably conclude from the final comment of the passage above?
    a. The speaker is considering a name change.
    b. The speaker is experiencing an identity crisis.
    c. The speaker has mistakenly been looking for the wrong person.
    d. The speaker intends to continue to look for Hyde.

12. Which of the following would be the best choice for the underlined portion of the sentence below?

    With such a drastic range of traits, appearances and body types, dogs are one of the most variable and adaptable species on the planet.

    a. NO CHANGE
    b. drastic range of traits, appearances, and body types,
    c. drastic range of traits and appearances and body types,
    d. drastic range of traits, appearances, as well as body types,

13. Which of the following would be the best choice for the underlined portion of the sentence below?

    Therefore, the animal's chances to mate are increased and these useful genes are passed into their offspring.

    a. NO CHANGE
    b. genes are passed onto their offspring.
    c. genes are passed on to their offspring.
    d. genes are passed within their offspring.

Practice Test #2

The next question is based on the following passage:

I'm not alone when I say that it's hard to pay attention sometimes. I can't count how many times I've sat in a classroom, lecture, speech, or workshop and been bored to tears. Usually I turn to doodling in order to keep awake. This never really helps; I'm not much of an artist. Therefore, after giving up on drawing a masterpiece, I would just concentrate on keeping my eyes open and trying to be attentive. This didn't always work because I wasn't engaged in what was going on.

14. Which of the following would be the best choice for the underlined sentence below?

    Usually I turn to doodling in order to keep awake.

    a. NO CHANGE
    b. Usually, I turn to doodling in order to keep awake.
    c. Usually, I turn to doodling, in order, to keep awake.
    d. Usually, I turned to doodling in order to keep awakened.

15. Which of the following would be the best choice for the underlined sentence below?

    Everyone probably has had to at one time or another do this.

    a. NO CHANGE
    b. Everyone probably has had to, at one time. Do this.
    c. Everyone has probably had to do this at some time.
    d. At one time or another everyone probably has had to do this.

16. Which of the following would be the best choice for the underlined portion of the sentences below?

    Asking questions to the audience or class will make them a part of the topic at hand. Discussions that make people think about the content and how it applies to there lives world and future are key.

    a. NO CHANGE
    b. how it applies to their lives, world, and future are key.
    c. how it applied to there lives world and future are key.
    d. how it applies to their lives, world, and future, are key.

17. Which of the following would be the best choice for the underlined portion of the sentence below?

    Paleontologists know this sail exists and have ideas for the function of the sail however they are uncertain of which idea is the true function.

    a. NO CHANGE
    b. the sail however, they are uncertain of which idea is the true function.
    c. the sail however they are, uncertain, of which idea is the true function.
    d. the sail; however, they are uncertain of which idea is the true function.

The next question is based on the following passage:

How does soap make your hands clean?

Why will gasoline take a grease spot out of your clothes?

If we were to go back to our convenient imaginary switchboard to turn off another law, we should find near the heat switches, and not far from the chemistry ones, a switch labeled Solution. Suppose we turned it off:

The fishes in the sea are among the first creatures to be surprised by our action. For instantly all the salt in the ocean drops to the bottom like so much sand, and most saltwater fishes soon perish in the fresh water.

Excerpt from *Common Science* by Carleton W. Washburne

18. What effect does the author achieve by presenting the scenario above?
    a. Humor through a hypothetical situation
    b. Shock through a surprise twist
    c. Deception through misleading information
    d. Curiosity through growing suspense

The next question is based on the following excerpt:

We remember when the phrase "sound as a dollar" was an expression of absolute dependability…

Excerpt from "The Crisis of Confidence" by Jimmy Carter

19. Which phrase means the same thing as "sound as a dollar" as it's used in the paragraph above?
    a. Hands down
    b. Solid as a rock
    c. Piece of cake
    d. Fair and square

The next question is based on the following passage:

"Press your little finger on the spot. You see. The flower yawns immediately, the secret lock works. And you think the bumble bee does not know these things? Watch it in the garden and you will see how it can read the signs of the flowers. When it visits a snapdragon, it always alights on the yellow spot and nowhere else. The door opens, it enters. It twists and turns in the corolla and covers itself with pollen, with which it daubs the stigma. Having drunk the drop, it goes off to other flowers, forcing the opening of which it knows the secret thoroughly."

Excerpt from *The Storybook of Science* by Jean-Henri Fabre

20. In the paragraph above, what does the speaker imply when he says the "flower yawns"?
    a. The petals of the flower are opening up slowly.
    b. The flower is worn out from pollination and needs rest.
    c. The flower is expanding its surface area to absorb more carbon dioxide.
    d. The flower is having a difficult time regulating night and day.

The next question is based on the following passage:

> Once EPA researchers cut open the pipes and took the scales apart, they examined each layer of scale and the minerals that were present. Different minerals have different inherent solubilities which clued researchers in to which minerals may be dissolving into the water. EPA researchers looked at which minerals were predicted to form based on the modeling, and then looked at pipe scales found on the lead service lines from those systems to see which minerals really were forming.

21. What does the word *solubilities* mean in the paragraph above?
    a. Concentration levels
    b. Bonding strengths
    c. Levels of condensation
    d. Abilities to dissolve

22. Which of the following would be the best choice for the underlined portion of the sentence below?

    While all dogs descend through gray wolves, it's easy to notice that dog breeds come in a variety of shapes and sizes.

    a. NO CHANGE
    b. descend by gray wolves
    c. descend from gray wolves
    d. descended through gray wolves

The next question is based on the following passage:

> Vacationers looking for a perfect experience should opt out of Disney parks and try a trip on Disney Cruise Lines. While a park offers rides, characters, and show experiences, it also includes long lines, often very hot weather, and enormous crowds. A Disney Cruise, on the other hand, is a relaxing, luxurious vacation that includes many of the same experiences as the parks, minus the crowds and lines. The cruise has top-notch food, maid service, water slides, multiple pools, Broadway-quality shows, and daily character experiences for kids. There are also many activities, such as bingo, trivia contests, and dance parties that can entertain guests of all ages. The cruise even stops at Disney's private island for a beach barbecue with characters, water slides, and water sports. Those looking for the Disney experience without the hassle should book a Disney cruise.

23. The main purpose of this passage is to do which of the following?
    a. Explain how to book a Disney cruise.
    b. Show what Disney parks have to offer.
    c. Show why Disney parks are expensive.
    d. Compare Disney parks to a Disney cruise.

The next question is based on the following passage:

> What you see too often in Washington and elsewhere around the country is a system of government that seems incapable of action. You see a Congress twisted and pulled in

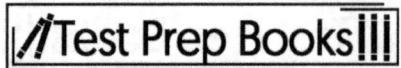

every direction by hundreds of well-financed and powerful special interests. You see every extreme position defended to the last vote, almost to the last breath by one unyielding group or another. You often see a balanced and a fair approach that demands sacrifice, a little sacrifice from everyone, abandoned like an orphan without support and without friends.

Often you see paralysis and stagnation and drift. You don't like it, and neither do I. What can we do?

First of all, we must face the truth, and then we can change our course. We simply must have faith in each other, faith in our ability to govern ourselves, and faith in the future of this Nation. Restoring that faith and that confidence to America is now the most important task we face. It is a true challenge of this generation of Americans.

Excerpt from "The Crisis of Confidence" by Jimmy Carter

24. What is the underlying message of Jimmy Carter's speech?
    a. There is no hope for the future of the United States.
    b. The American people have lost faith in their government.
    c. Finding the way again as a nation will be hard and will require facing difficult facts.
    d. America was once as great as other Western countries, but it no longer is.

The following exchange occurred after the baseball coach's team suffered a heartbreaking loss in the final inning:

Reporter: The team clearly did not rise to the challenge. I'm sure that getting zero hits in 20 at-bats with runners in scoring position hurt the team's chances at winning the game. What are your thoughts on this devastating loss?

Baseball Coach: Hitting with runners in scoring position was not the reason we lost this game. We made numerous errors in the field, and our pitchers gave out too many free passes. Also, we did not even need a hit with runners in scoring position. Many of those at-bats could have driven in the run by simply making contact. Our team did not deserve to win the game.

25. Which of the following best describes the main point of dispute between the reporter and baseball coach?
    a. The loss was heartbreaking.
    b. Getting zero hits in 20 at-bats with runners in scoring position caused the loss.
    c. Numerous errors in the field and pitchers giving too many free passes caused the loss.
    d. The team deserved to win the game.

The next question is based on the following passages:

Text 1: Thomas Hobbes was a philosopher who thought negatively of human nature. He believed that people naturally wish to dominate one another and are naturally at war with one another. Therefore, humans must give up their rights to their government, which has the task of protecting people from their worst desires.

Text 2: Philosopher John Locke is well known for arguing that humans are rational creatures that can act logically despite their emotions. He coined the term "natural law," which means that morals come from the human ability to reason. Due to this, the government should not be able to take away human rights. His philosophy is the basis for the U.S. Constitution.

26. Based on the texts, what are the two common themes that both philosophers focus on?
    a. Human nature and war
    b. Human nature and government
    c. Government and intelligence
    d. The United States and natural law

The next question is based on the following passages:

Text 1: The hikers on the expedition were told to observe the northern lights. Bright green light undulated across the sky and captivated the audience. The Native American tour guide told the story of how the northern lights were torches being carried by spirits. These spirits were lighting the way for souls that had recently passed on and needed guidance to the next life. Surviving relatives would appreciate the lights and speak to their loved ones as they traveled across the sky.

Text 2: The Sámi, the indigenous Finno-Ugric people of northern Scandinavia, watched as the green, red, and purple northern lights flickered across the night sky. Immediately, they hurried back to their tents without saying a word. The lights were a sign of the dead, and if the lights saw you, they would either steal you away or behead you!

27. Based on the texts, what can be assumed about these two cultures?
    a. The Native Americans and Sámi both look forward to the northern lights as an opportunity to connect with their loved ones.
    b. The Native Americans and Sámi people both believe in some form of afterlife and spirits.
    c. The two cultures have different views of the lights because they are different colors depending on the location.
    d. No assumptions can be made based on the information presented in these texts.

Reading and Writing 2

1. Which of the following would be the best choice for the underlined portion of the sentence below?

    Everyone has heard the <u>idea of the end justifying the means; that is be John's philosophy.</u>

    a. NO CHANGE
    b. idea of the end justifying the means; this is John's philosophy.
    c. idea of the end justifying the means, this is the philosophy of John.
    d. idea of the end justifying the means. That would be John's philosophy.

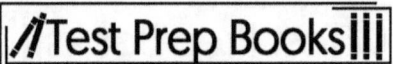

2. Which of the following would be the best choice for the underlined portion of the sentence below?

   What's clear about the news today is that the broader the media the more ways there are to tell a story.

   a. NO CHANGE
   b. What's clear, about the news today, is that the broader the media,
   c. What's clear about newscasting today is that the broader the media,
   d. The news today is broader than earlier media

3. Which of the following would be the best choice for the underlined portion of the sentence below?

   The diction of the story is also more precise and can be either straightforward or suggestive depending in earnest on the goal of the writer.

   a. NO CHANGE
   b. depending; in earnest on the goal of the writer.
   c. depending, in earnest, on the goal of the writer.
   d. the goal, in earnest, depending on the writer.

4. What edit to the underlined portion is needed to correct the following sentence?

   Education provides today's society with a vehicle for raising its children to be civil, decent human beings with something valuable to contribute to the world.

   a. NO CHANGE
   b. Education provide
   c. Education will provide
   d. Education providing

5. What edit to the underlined portion is needed to correct the following sentence?

   Being "civilized" humans means being "whole" humans. Education must address the minds, bodies, and souls of students. It would be detrimental to society, only meeting the needs of the mind, if our schools were myopic in their focus. As humans, we are multidimensional, multifaceted beings who need more than head knowledge to survive.

   a. NO CHANGE
   b. It would be detrimental to society if our schools were myopic in their focus, only meeting the needs of the mind.
   c. Only meeting needs of our mind, our schools were myopic in their focus, detrimental to society.
   d. Myopic is the focus of our schools, being detrimental to society for only meeting the needs of the mind.

6. What edit to the underlined portion is needed to correct the following sentence?

If teachers set high expectations for <u>there students</u>, the students will rise to that high level.

a. NO CHANGE
b. they're students
c. their students
d. thare students

The next question is based on the following passage:

You will judge for yourselves if I promise too much for the working man, when I say that he will stand by such an enterprise with the utmost of his patience, his perseverance, sense, and support; that I am sure he will need no charitable aid or condescending <u>patronage</u>; but will readily and cheerfully pay for the advantages which it confers; that he will prepare himself in individual cases where he feels that the adverse circumstances around him have rendered it necessary; in a word, that he will feel his responsibility like an honest man, and will most honestly and manfully discharge it.

From Charles Dickens' speech at the Birmingham and Midland Institute on December 30, 1853

7. Which word is most closely synonymous with the word *patronage* as it appears in the paragraph above?
a. Auspices
b. Aberration
c. Acerbic
d. Adulation

The next question is based on the following passage:

Two years ago, the secret discovery of several small, hidden colonies prompted William Dutcher, President of the National Association of Audubon Societies, and Mr. T. Gilbert Pearson, Secretary, to attempt the protection of those colonies. With a fund contributed for the purpose, wardens were hired and duly <u>commissioned</u>.

Excerpt from *Our Vanishing Wildlife* by William T. Hornaday

8. As it is used in the paragraph above, the word *commissioned* most nearly means:
a. Appointed
b. Compelled
c. Beguiled
d. Fortified

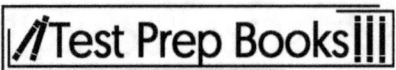

The next question is based on the following passage:

> Hampton's <u>charismatic</u> personality, organizational abilities, sheer determination, and rhetorical skills enabled him to quickly rise through the chapter's ranks.

9. What word is synonymous with the underlined description?
    a. Egotistical
    b. Obnoxious
    c. Chauvinistic
    d. Charming

Read the following opinions of two opposing politicians:

> Conservative politician: Social welfare programs are destroying our country. These programs are not only adding to the annual deficit, which increases the national debt, but they also discourage hard work. Our country must continue producing leaders who bootstrap their way to the top. None of our country's citizens truly need assistance from the government; rather, the assistance just makes things easier.
>
> Liberal politician: Our great country is founded on the principle of hope. The country is built on the backs of immigrants who came here with nothing, except for the hope of a better life. Our country is too wealthy not to provide basic necessities for the less fortunate. Recent immigrants, single mothers, and people who are elderly, disabled, or have historically been disenfranchised all require an ample safety net.

10. What is the main point of dispute between the politicians?
    a. Whether spending on social welfare programs increases the national debt
    b. Whether certain classes of people rely on social welfare programs to meet their basic needs
    c. Whether social welfare programs are necessary
    d. Whether the country's leaders have bootstrapped their way to the top

Practice Test #2

The next question is based on the following passage:

> This American government—what is it but a tradition, though a recent one, endeavoring to transmit itself unimpaired to posterity, but each instant losing some of its integrity? It has not the vitality and force of a single living man; for a single man can bend it to his will. It is a sort of wooden gun to the people themselves.
>
> Excerpt from *Civil Disobedience* by Henry David Thoreau

11. Which choice best summarizes the passage above?
    a. The government may be instituted to ensure the protections of freedoms, but this is weakened by the fact that it is easily manipulated by individuals.
    b. Unlike an individual, government is uncaring.
    c. Unlike an individual, government has no will, making it more prone to be used as a weapon against the people.
    d. American government is modeled after other traditions but has greater potential to be used to control people.

The next question is based on the following table:

Month	Average Low Temperature
January	43°F
February	47°F
March	56°F
April	60°F

A farmer has kept track of the average low temperatures for the first quarter of the year. He does this so that next year he'll know when to plant his crops. He is hoping to plant three crops: asparagus, potatoes, and spinach. Asparagus cannot withstand temperatures of 60°F or less. Potatoes grow best at temperatures above 55°F. Spinach does well in cold temperatures and can withstand temperatures as low as 40°F.

12. Based on the information provided in the chart and passage, which of the following statements is true?
    a. The farmer can grow asparagus in January, potatoes from February to April, and spinach every month.
    b. The farmer can grow spinach every month and potatoes in March and April, but he cannot grow asparagus.
    c. The farmer can grow asparagus every month, spinach in February, and potatoes in January and April.
    d. The farmer can grow potatoes in March and April but cannot grow any other crops.

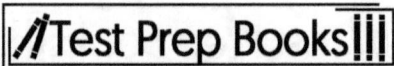

The next question is based on this Table of Contents from a government publication:

Contents

Frontispiece	2
Copyright, Restrictions, and Permissions Notice	4
Commissioners	5
Commission Staff	6
Letter From the Chairman	8
Executive Summary: Our Promise to Children	12
Introduction	17
Chapter 1: Confronting the Tragedy of Child Abuse and Neglect Fatalities	22
Section I: Populations in Need of Special Attention	36
Hillsborough County, Florida: Using Data to Improve Practice and Keep Children Safe	38
Chapter 2: Saving Children's Lives Today and Into the Future	42
Chapter 3: Addressing the Needs of American Indian/Alaska Native Children	52
Chapter 4: Reducing Child Abuse and Neglect Deaths in Disproportionately Affected Communities	60
Section II: Components of the Commission's National Strategy	68
Wichita, Kansas: Champions for Children	70
Chapter 5: Leadership and Accountability	74
Double Protection for Children: Connecting Law Enforcement and CPS	86
Chapter 6: Decisions Grounded in Better Data and Research	90
Salt River Pima-Maricopa Indian Community: Multiple Eyes on the Child	102
Chapter 7: Multidisciplinary Support for Families	106
Conclusion: Taking Our Recommendations Forward	120

Excerpt from *Within Our Reach: A National Strategy to Eliminate Child Abuse and Neglect Fatalities* by the Commission to Eliminate Child Abuse and Neglect Fatalities, 2016

13. After reading through the Table of Contents, what is the most likely purpose of this publication?
    a. To recommend different programs that can help children, such as the National School Lunch Program
    b. To provoke thought regarding the usefulness of government institutions
    c. To educate readers about child abuse and neglect, including how to address it
    d. To inform parents about how to care for their children

14. Which of the following is implicitly stated within the following sentence?

> This leaves a very small percentage available for drinking, yet we see millions of gallons of water wasted on watering huge lawns in deserts like Arizona, or on running dishwashers that are only half-full, or on filling all the personal pools in Los Angeles; meanwhile, people in Africa are dying of thirst.

   a. People run dishwashers that are not full.
   b. People in Africa are dying of thirst.
   c. People take water for granted.
   d. People should stop watering their lawns.

The next question is based on the following passage:

> I returned from the City about three o'clock on that May afternoon pretty well disgusted with life. I had been three months in the Old Country, and was fed up with it. If anyone had told me a year ago that I would have been feeling like that I should have laughed at him; but there was the fact. The weather made me liverish, the talk of the ordinary Englishman made me sick. I couldn't get enough exercise, and the amusements of London seemed as flat as soda-water that has been standing in the Sun. "Richard Hannay," I kept telling myself, "you have got into the wrong ditch, my friend, and you had better climb out."

> Excerpt from *The Thirty-Nine Steps* by John Buchan

15. What inference can be made from this text?
   a. The narrator hates the country and wishes to travel abroad.
   b. The narrator enjoys small talk with other regular people.
   c. The narrator feels extremely motivated to better his life.
   d. The narrator previously held a good opinion of the Old Country.

The next question is based on the following passage:

> Here seven years before, when she was twelve, she had made a hard choice to please her guardian--the old rancher whom she loved and called father, who had indeed been a father to her. That choice had been to go to school in Denver. Four years she had lived away from her beloved gray hills and black mountains. Only once since her return had she climbed to this height, and that occasion, too, was memorable as an unhappy hour. It had been three years ago. To-day girlish ordeals and griefs seemed back in the past: she was a woman at nineteen and face to face with the first great problem in her life.

> Excerpt from *The Mysterious Rider* by Zane Grey

16. What inference can be made from this text?
   a. The woman never wanted to leave the mountains.
   b. The woman only has positive memories of the location that she is at.
   c. The woman has struggled greatly in life.
   d. The woman resents the old rancher for making her go to school.

The next question is based on the following passage:

> World War II spanned from 1939 to 1945. The conflict included most major countries in the world, and there were two distinct groups. The Axis powers included Germany, Japan, and Italy, and the Allied powers included the United States, United Kingdom, and Soviet Union. Major events of the war included the Holocaust, Operation Doomsday, and the atomic bombings of Japan.

17. The author would like to include a sentence that emphasizes how deadly World War II was. Which choice best accomplishes this goal?
    a. The end of the war led to the creation of the United Nations, which has stopped further wars from happening through 72 different peacekeeping missions.
    b. The Treaty of Versailles created discontent in Germany, allowing Adolf Hitler to rise to power and kill six million Jewish people and five million non-Jewish people.
    c. It is estimated that between 70 million and 85 million people lost their lives as a result of the conflict.
    d. Land, air, and sea forces came together to storm the beaches of Normandy, France, where 24 warships and 155 other ships were sunk.

18. Which revision most effectively improves the structure of the following sentence?

    Michael Jordan is arguably the best basketball player of all time and he began his professional career with the Chicago Bulls in 1984.

    a. The Chicago Bulls drafted Michael Jordan, the best basketball player of all time, in 1984.
    b. The career of the best basketball player of all time, Michael Jordan, began with the Chicago Bulls in the year 1984 when he was drafted.
    c. In 1984, with the Chicago Bulls, Michael Jordan began his career as the best basketball player ever.
    d. Michael Jordan, who is arguably the best basketball player of all time, began his professional career with the Chicago Bulls in 1984.

The next question is based on the following passage:

> Railroads revolutionized the transportation of goods and people in the 19th century. The 19th century was the time of change known as the Industrial Revolution. As a part of the Industrial Revolution, the railroad paved the way for new opportunities with the connection of the two coasts of the United States. It also changed the economy to an extreme degree.

19. Which revision improves the conciseness of the text?
    a. NO CHANGE
    b. The Industrial Revolution, which took place in the 19th century, connected the two sides of the United States through the invention of the railroad. This brought new opportunities such as the long-range transportation of goods and people. It also changed the economy greatly.
    c. The Industrial Revolution of the 19th century connected the United States from coast to coast and provided the nation with new opportunities. It revolutionized the transportation of goods and people and caused major change within the economy.
    d. The 19th-century Industrial Revolution was a time of great change in the country. It brought about the widespread use of the railroad. Railroads spanned from both coasts of the nation and created new opportunities for everyone with the transportation of goods and people. This heavily affected the economy as well.

20. Which choice most effectively combines these two sentences?

    > The dishwasher was invented by a woman named Josephine Cochrane in 1886. She is credited with greatly improving kitchen efficiency for homes, restaurants, and hotels.

    a. The dishwasher was invented in 1886 by a woman named Josephine Cochrane, who is credited with greatly improving kitchen efficiency for homes, restaurants, and hotels.
    b. The dishwasher was invented in 1886 by a woman named Josephine Cochrane, which led to her receiving the credit for greatly improving kitchen efficiency for homes, restaurants, and hotels.
    c. Hotels, restaurants, and homes all saw great improvements to their kitchens' efficiency in 1886 due to the invention of the dishwasher by a woman named Josephine Cochrane.
    d. Josephine Cochrane was a woman who is credited with inventing the dishwasher in 1886 and improving the kitchen efficiency in homes, restaurants, and hotels.

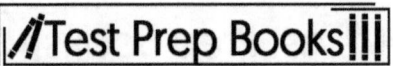

Practice Test #2

The next question is based on the following passage:

(1) The Orient Express is a luxury train service that has existed since 1883. (2) The famous train route traveled 1900 miles. (3) It spanned through numerous cities, such as Paris, Vienna, Budapest, and Istanbul. (4) It was featured in Agatha Christie's book, *Murder on the Orient Express*. (5) Although the Orient Express is not as popular as it once was, due to the invention of faster travel methods, it remains a nostalgic adventure for tourists with an appreciation for its history.

21. The author wishes to add the following sentence to the passage:

"This famous mystery novel added to the intrigue and allure of the luxurious experience."

The best placement for this sentence is:
   a. After Sentence 1
   b. After Sentence 2
   c. After Sentence 3
   d. After Sentence 4

The next question is based on the following passage:

Furious with the injustice of the scene before him, he clenched his fists and gritted his teeth. While he couldn't take action in the moment, he was prepared to write a _____ letter to the press about the politician's corruption.

22. Which word choice best completes the sentence to match the tone of the text?
   a. diplomatic
   b. compassionate
   c. pedantic
   d. scathing

23. What edit is needed to correct the following passage?

We must be unapologetic about expecting excellence from our students? Our very existence depends upon it.

   a. NO CHANGE
   b. We must be unapologetic about expecting excellence from our students, our very existence depends upon it.
   c. We must be unapologetic about expecting excellence from our students—our very existence depends upon it.
   d. We must be unapologetic about expecting excellence from our students our very existence depends upon it.

The next question is based on the following passages:

Text 1: According to a 2020 scientific study, there has been a 9 percent to 11 percent decline in the insect population per decade. Some insects have suffered even more. For example, in 1997, there were around 1.2 million western monarch butterflies. By 2019, that number had dwindled to just 30,000. According to the Smithsonian Institution, insect populations are vital to the pollination of plants that humans rely on.

Text 2: Farmer Joseph Wright has noticed that, over the last decade, bugs have become less of a problem for his crops due to pesticide use. As the years have passed, Wright has used increasingly powerful pesticides to ensure the best crop yield possible for the local grocery stores. However, he struggles to welcome enough bees for flower farming.

24. What is the main difference between these two texts?
    a. Text 1 seeks to persuade the audience, while Text 2 is purely factual.
    b. Text 1 uses informal language, while Text 2 is formal.
    c. Text 1 is made credible by statistical research, whereas Text 2 is anecdotal.
    d. Text 1 is excessively pedantic and is not as easy to understand as Text 1.

The next question is based on the following passages:

Text 1: In 1979, China introduced the one-child policy as a measure to curb its rapidly growing population. This policy imposed harsh penalties on families for having more than one child. At the time, China's population was around one billion people, and the nation grappled with resource shortages, including water and food. Notably, this policy had unintended consequences, leading to a highly imbalanced gender ratio, as male children were preferred for their ability to carry on the family name and inherit property as well as their societal responsibility to care for their parents in old age. In 2015, in response to an economic crisis made worse by declining birth rates, the policy was changed to allow families to have up to three children.

Text 2: Japan is currently confronting the pressing issue of a declining population, stemming from numerous societal factors. These include extraordinarily long work hours, a growing reluctance to marry, and an increasing number of women opting not to have children. The birth rate is concerning since the current population is aging, and the shrinking workforce struggles to generate sufficient tax revenue to support the economy and vital social systems, including healthcare. The country continues to grapple with the task of incentivizing young people to reproduce with monetary assistance and childcare services.

25. Based on the texts, what is the main way that China and Japan's population issues differ?
    a. China addressed its population issues through legislation and penalties, while Japan uses economic benefits and services to encourage change.
    b. China's plan to fix its population issues turned out to be a failure, while Japan's plan is highly effective.
    c. China's economy is struggling due to its restrictive policy choices, while Japan's economy is highly successful due to the focus on long work hours.
    d. China was forced to change its approach due to the imbalanced gender ratio, whereas Japan was forced to change its approach due to the aging population.

The next question is based on the following passage:

Frederick Douglass stands upon a pedestal; he has reached this lofty height through years of toil and strife, but it has been the strife of moral ideas; strife in the battle for human rights. No bitter memories come from this strife; no feelings of remorse can rise

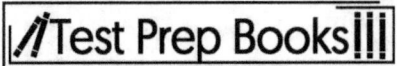

to cast their gloomy shadows over his soul; Douglass has now reached and passed the meridian of life, his co-laborers in the strife have now nearly all passed away. Garrison has gone, Gerritt Smith has gone, Giddings and Sumner have gone,—nearly all the early abolitionists are gone to their reward. The culmination of his life work has been reached; the object dear to his heart—the Emancipation of the slaves—has been accomplished, through the blessings of God; he stands facing the goal, already reached by his co-laborers, with a halo of peace about him, and nothing but serenity and gratitude must fill his breast.

Excerpt from Life and Times of Frederick Douglass *by Frederick Douglass*

26. Which choice best describes the purpose of the text?
    a. To argue that Frederick Douglass did more for abolitionism than anyone else
    b. To highlight Frederick Douglass's accomplishments in the face of great difficulty
    c. To compare Frederick Douglass with his co-laborers
    d. To detail the events of Frederick Douglass's childhood

The next question is based on the following passage:

The empire was unwieldy in size, and moreover it lacked any real bond of union. The various nations of which it was composed differed in language, in manners, and in habits of life. Each province was interested in its own local affairs, but was profoundly indifferent to the fate of the empire at large; and in time of war the soldiers were so little inclined to risk their lives for a monarch of whom they knew nothing that they only fought under compulsion, and often had to be driven with whips to face the enemy.

Excerpt from The Retreat of the Ten Thousand *by Professor C. Witt*

27. Which choice best describes the purpose of the text?
    a. To condemn the nations for not loving their empire
    b. To describe the relationship between the empire and its nations
    c. To celebrate the monarch for compelling the nations to fight
    d. To introduce the historical beginning of military conscription

Math 1

1. Which is the simplest form of the expression $(7n + 3n^3 + 3) + (8n + 5n^3 + 2n^4)$?
    a. $9n^4 + 15n - 2$
    b. $2n^4 + 5n^3 + 15n - 2$
    c. $9n^4 + 8n^3 + 15n$
    d. $2n^4 + 8n^3 + 15n + 3$

Practice Test #2

2. What is the solution for the following equation?

$$\frac{x^2 + x - 30}{x - 5} = 11$$

a. $x = -6$
b. There is no solution.
c. $x = 16$
d. $x = 5$

3. What are the center and radius of a circle with equation $4x^2 + 4y^2 - 16x - 24y + 51 = 0$?
   a. Center $(3,2)$ and radius $\frac{1}{2}$
   b. Center $(2,3)$ and radius $\frac{1}{2}$
   c. Center $(3,2)$ and radius $\frac{1}{4}$
   d. Center $(2,3)$ and radius $\frac{1}{4}$

4. Bill can make two wicker baskets every day. He already has some wicker baskets made. In five days, he will have a total of 17 wicker baskets. How many wicker baskets did he have before he started working on more?
   a. 10 baskets
   b. 13 baskets
   c. Five baskets
   d. Seven baskets

5. If $-3(x + 4) \geq x + 8$, what is the value of x?
   a. $x = 4$
   b. $x \geq 2$
   c. $x \geq -5$
   d. $x \leq -5$

6. Solve for X: $\frac{2X}{5} - 1 = 59$.

7. Paint Inc. charges $2,000 for painting the first 1,800 feet of trim on a house and an additional $1.00 per foot for each foot beyond that. How much would it cost to paint a house with 3,125 feet of trim?
   a. $3,125
   b. $2,000
   c. $5,125
   d. $3,325

8. Greg buys a $10 lunch with 5% sales tax. He leaves a $2 tip after paying his bill. How much money does he spend?
   a. $12.50
   b. $12.00
   c. $13.00
   d. $13.25

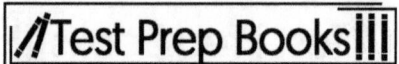

Practice Test #2

9. Suppose an investor deposits $1,200 into a bank account that accrues 1 percent interest per month. Assuming x represents the number of months since the deposit and y represents the money in the account, which of the following exponential functions models the scenario?
   a. $y = (0.01)(1{,}200^x)$
   b. $y = (1200)(0.01^x)$
   c. $y = (1.01)(1200^x)$
   d. $y = (1200)(1.01^x)$

10. Simplify: $(5x^2 - 3x + 4) - (2x^2 - 7)$
    a. x^5
    b. $3x^2 - 3x + 11$
    c. $3x^2 - 3x - 3$
    d. $x - 3$

11. Which of the following is a valid solution for both of the given equations?

$$9x + 12y = 54$$

$$6x - y = 12$$

   a. $(\frac{3}{5}, 5)$
   b. $(\frac{22}{9}, \frac{8}{3})$
   c. $(\frac{15}{2}, \frac{4}{3})$
   d. $(\frac{5}{3}, \frac{9}{2})$

12. Which of the following is a valid solution for both of the given equations?

$$x + 3y = 21$$

$$\frac{1}{3}x - 5y = 35$$

   a. $(14, -5)$
   b. $(-\frac{5}{4}, 15)$
   c. $(35, -\frac{14}{3})$
   d. $(-18, \frac{2}{5})$

13. What is the y-intercept of $y = x^{5/3} + (x - 3)(x + 1)$?
    a. 3.5
    b. 7.6
    c. -3
    d. -15.1

Practice Test #2

14. If $\sqrt{1+x} = 4$, what is x?

15. A line passes through the origin and through the point $(-3, 4)$. What is the slope of the line?
    a. $-\frac{4}{3}$
    b. $-\frac{3}{4}$
    c. $\frac{4}{3}$
    d. $\frac{3}{4}$

16. Given the value of a given stock at monthly intervals, which graph should be used to best represent the trend of the stock?
    a. Box plot
    b. Line plot
    c. Line graph
    d. Circle graph

17. A shipping box has a length of 8 inches, a width of 14 inches, and a height of 4 inches. If all three dimensions are doubled, what is the relationship between the volume of the new box and the volume of the original box?
    a. The volume of the new box is double the volume of the original box.
    b. The volume of the new box is four times as large as the volume of the original box.
    c. The volume of the new box is six times as large as the volume of the original box.
    d. The volume of the new box is eight times as large as the volume of the original box.

18. What is the simplified form of the expression $tan\theta\ cos\theta$?
    a. $sin\theta$
    b. 1
    c. $csc\theta$
    d. $\frac{1}{sec\theta}$

19. If $\overline{AE} = 4$, $\overline{AB} = 5$, and $\overline{AD} = 5$, what is the length of $\overline{AC}$? If necessary, round your answer to two decimal places.

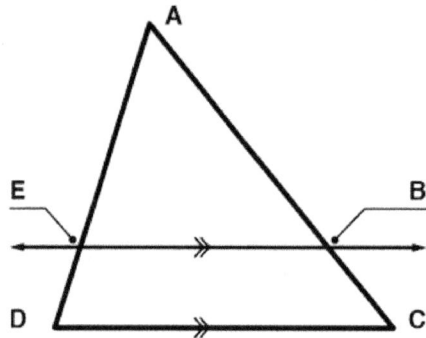

20. A randomly selected sample of 400 students at a high school (out of 1000 students) were asked if they would want to travel abroad for a semester in college. 26% of the 400 students surveyed answered affirmatively. Which of the following is true?
   a. 26% is a sample statistic.
   b. 26% is a population parameter.
   c. 26% is a margin of error.
   d. 26% is a standard deviation.

21. Which expression is equivalent to $(x \times 3)$?
   a. $9x \div 3$
   b. $3x \times 3$
   c. $3x \div 3$
   d. $3x \div 9$

22. Which set of points would make the following data set a linear function?

$$x: (7, 5, 3, 1, -1), y: (5, 6, 7, 8, 9)$$

   a. $x: 0, y: 10$
   b. $x: -2, y: 9$
   c. $x: 0, y: 9$
   d. $x: -3, y: 10$

Math 2

1. If $g(x) = x^3 - 3x^2 - 2x + 6$ and $f(x) = 2$, then what is $g(f(x))$?
   a. -26
   b. 6
   c. $2x^3 - 6x^2 - 4x + 12$
   d. -2

Practice Test #2

2. Solve for x: $9x - 32 = 49$
   a. $x = 7$
   b. $x = 9$
   c. $x = 13$
   d. $x = 15$

3. A shuffled deck of 52 cards contains four kings. One card is drawn, and it is not put back in the deck. Then, a second card is drawn. What's the probability that both cards are kings?
   a. $\frac{1}{169}$
   b. $\frac{1}{221}$
   c. $\frac{1}{13}$
   d. $\frac{4}{13}$

4. Patrick is planning seating arrangements for a party and is setting up tables that can each seat up to four people. It's estimated that between 25 and 45 people will attend the party and, while having empty seats is okay, the maximum number of tables that will comfortably fit in the room is 15. How many tables should Patrick set up to ensure that everyone will have a seat while avoiding setting out more tables than necessary?
   a. 12 tables
   b. 7 tables
   c. 11 tables
   d. 6 tables

5. If drawn, which of the following number lines would describe the inequalities $x < 3 \cup x > 7$?
   a. A number line with an open dot on 3 with a line pointing left and an open dot on 7 with a line pointing right
   b. A number line with a closed dot on 3 with a line pointing left and a closed dot on 7 with a line pointing right
   c. A number line with an open dot on 3 which is connected by a line to an open dot on 7
   d. A number line with a closed dot on 3 which is connected by a line to a closed dot on 7

6. Mom's car drove 72 miles in 90 minutes. There are 5,280 feet per mile. How fast did she drive in feet per second?
   a. 0.8 feet per second
   b. 48.9 feet per second
   c. 0.009 feet per second
   d. 70.4 feet per second

7. Jack lives 30 miles away from Jill's house. Starting from his house, he begins to drive directly away from Jill's house at a speed of 45 miles per hour. This can be represented with the equation $f(x) = ax + b$, where x represents how much time has passed in hours and a and b are constants. How far away is Jack from Jill's house after five hours?
   a. 225 miles
   b. 195 miles
   c. 205 miles
   d. 255 miles

8. What is the slope of this line?

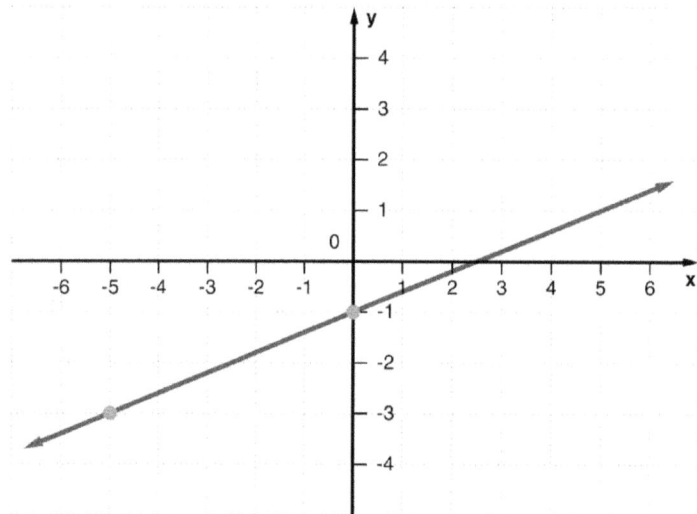

   a. 2
   b. $\frac{5}{2}$
   c. $\frac{1}{2}$
   d. $\frac{2}{5}$

9. The Robertson family drove to the beach for a vacation. During their 200-mile trip, they drove through two different highway roads, and it took a total of five hours. One highway had terrible traffic, and they only averaged 20 miles per hour. The other highway had much smoother traffic, and they averaged 70 miles per hour. If x is the time spent on the slower highway and y is the time spent on the faster highway, which system of equations best represents this situation?
   a. $20x + 70y = 200$
      $x + y = 5$
   b. $20x + 70y = 5$
      $x + y = 200$
   c. $70x + 20y = 200$
      $x + y = 5$
   d. $70x + 20y = 5$
      $x + y = 200$

10. If the sine of 60° = x, the cosine of what angle, in degrees, also equals x?

11. Sam is twice as old as his sister, Lisa. Their oldest brother, Ray, will be 25 in three years. If Lisa is 13 years younger than Ray, how old is Sam?

12. If $6t + 4 = 16$, what is t?
    a. 1
    b. 2
    c. 3
    d. 4

13. Which of the following expressions is equivalent to the expression $8(4x - 12)$?
    a. $2(16x - 48)$
    b. $3(9x - 17)$
    c. $4(8x - 16)$
    d. $12(6x - 18)$

14. The area of circle O is 49π m. What is the area of the sector formed by $\angle AOB$?

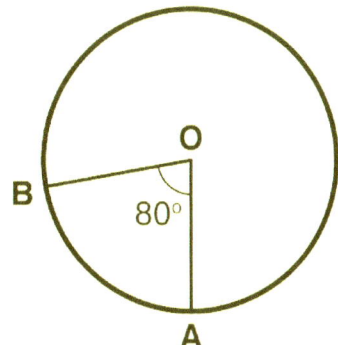

    a. 80π m
    b. 10.9π m
    c. 4.9π m
    d. 10π m

15. Find the volume of the following three-dimensional shape:

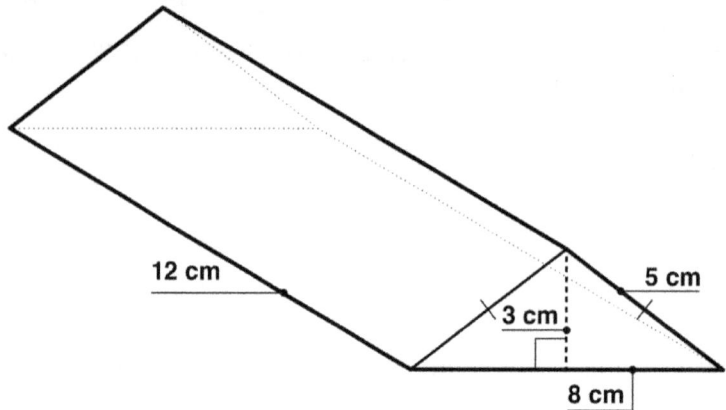

a. 240 cm³
b. 480 cm³
c. 144 cm³
d. 288 cm³

16. Ten students take a test. Five students get a 50. Four students get a 70. If the average score is 55, what was the last student's score?
a. 20
b. 40
c. 50
d. 60

17. A grocery store wants to know their customers' favorite brand of coffee, so they survey every 15th customer that walks in one day. What kind of sampling design is this?
a. Simple random
b. Systematic
c. Cluster
d. Convenience

18. Which set of points would make the following data set a linear function?

$$x: (-3, 0, 3, 6, 9), y: (6, 8, 10, 12, 14)$$

a. $x: 10, y: 16$
b. $x: 12, y: 15$
c. $x: 12, y: 16$
d. $x: 15, y: 16$

Practice Test #2

19. Find the value(s) of x in the following nonlinear equation:

$$x^2 = -9x$$

a. 9
b. 0
c. -9, 0
d. No solution

20. Which expression is equivalent to $(12x - 4)$?
    a. $4 \times (3x - 2)$
    b. $3 \times (4x - 1)$
    c. $(72x - 24) \div 6$
    d. $(12x - 4) \div 4$

21. Which set of points would make the following data set a linear function?

$$x: (7, 3, -1, -5, -9), y: (4, 6, 8, 10, 12)$$

a. $x: -14, y: 14$
b. $x: -13, y: 14$
c. $x: -12, y: 16$
d. $x: -13, y: 16$

22. Solve the following system of equations to determine where the lines intersect.

$$35x + 49y = 147$$

$$5x + 7y = 21$$

a. No solution
b. Infinite solutions
c. (5, 7)
d. (3, 5)

207

Answer Explanations #2

Reading and Writing 1

1. D: Johnson says that this challenge speaks "to the values, and the purposes, and the meaning of our beloved nation." There is no mention of other protests, Choice A, and there is no mention of whether those issues are easier, Choice B, or harder, Choice C, to solve, so those are not correct.

2. C: The passage states that antitrust laws maintain economic competition and prevent monopolies from limiting people's freedoms. Choice A is incorrect, as antitrust laws are intended to protect consumers, and while they contribute to a relationship between governments and populations, that's not their primary goal. Choice B is incorrect because Roosevelt does not mention foreign investment. Finally, businesses do compete with the government in certain industries, but that is not the purpose of antitrust laws, so Choice D is incorrect.

3. D: All of the cities included in the graphs are along the East Coast of the United States. All of the bars on the graphs show an increase in sea level or the number of days with flood events since 1970. Therefore, the author chose to include the graphs to support the claim that sea levels have risen along the East Coast since 1970, Choice D. Choice A is incorrect because the bar above 1970 on Boston's graph is longer than the graph's bar above 1980. Between 1970-1980, Boston experienced a decrease in the number of days with flood events. It's important to note that while there was a decrease from one decade to another, it does not negate the overall trend of an increase in flooding events. Choice B is incorrect because the bar above 1970 on Atlantic City's graph is shorter than the graph's bar above 1980. Therefore, between 1970-1980, Atlantic City experienced an increase in the number of days with flood events. Choice C is incorrect because the bars increase in height on all of the cities' graphs, showing an increase in the number of days with floods along the entire East Coast.

4. D: Choice D strengthens the overall sentence structure while condensing the number of words, making the subject of the sentence and the emphasis of the writer much clearer to the reader. In Choice A, the language is choppy and over-complicated. Choice B is better but lacks the reference to a specific image of dinosaurs. Choice C introduces an unnecessary comma.

5. B: Choice B is the best answer because it brings more clarity to the message of the sentence. Choice A, the original sentence, unnecessarily includes the word *ultimately* and leaves out a comma before the independent clause at the end. Choices C and D are awkward and wordy; therefore, neither is the best answer.

6. B: Leaving the sentence in place is incorrect because the father "going crazy" doesn't logically follow the fact that he was a "city slicker." Choice C is incorrect because the sentence in question is not an introductory sentence and does not transition smoothly into a new paragraph. Choice D is incorrect because the sentence doesn't necessarily need to be omitted since it logically follows the very first sentence in the passage.

7. A: *Allows* is the best choice for the sentence because attaining the high level of skill or expertise is what enables, or allows, the engineers to have the knowledge of mathematical equations and scientific processes that are essential to function in their field. Choice B, inhibits, would mean that the expertise stops the engineers' use of essential equations and processes, and it does not make sense grammatically in the sentence. Choice *C*, requires, suggests that the engineers must use essential equations and processes in order to attain high levels of expertise. This would only work if we were discussing learning, rather than applying, these skills. Choice *D*, should, does not make sense in the sentence.

8. B: Although *diverging* means to separate from the main route and go in a different direction, it is used awkwardly and unconventionally in this sentence. Therefore, Choice *A* is not the answer. Choice *B* is the correct answer because it implies that the passengers were able to cause a change in the plane's direction. *Converging* is incorrect because it implies that the plane met another in a central location. Although the passengers may have distracted terrorists on board the plane, they did not distract the plane itself; therefore, Choice *D* is incorrect.

9. C: To be "gifted" is to be talented. "Academically" refers to education. Therefore, Fred Hampton was intellectually talented, or intelligent. Choice *B* is incorrect because it refers to a level of energy or activity. Choice *A* is incorrect because *vacuous* means the opposite of being gifted academically. Choice *D* is incorrect because it refers to one's physical build and/or abilities.

10. B: After the experimenter is asked to add more salt than can be dissolved and then to use a Bunsen burner to heat the test tube, a logical result would be that the heat is an agent to dissolve the salt more readily. We can guess this from the rhetorical question that follows: "Why do you wash dishes in hot water?" This implies that heat helps things dissolve more easily. That also means that Choices *A* and *C* are incorrect. The mention of washing dishes does not suggest that the saltwater solution itself could be used to wash dishes, so Choice *D* is also incorrect.

11. D: The speaker invokes the game of hide and seek to indicate they will continue their search for Hyde. Choices *A* and *B* are not possible answers because the text doesn't refer to any name changes or an identity crisis. The text also makes no mention of a mistaken identity when referring to Hyde, so Choice *C* is also incorrect.

12. B: Choice *B* is correct because the Oxford comma is applied, clearly separating the specific terms. Choice *A* lacks this clarity. Choice *C* is correct but too wordy since commas can be easily applied. Choice *D* uses commas incorrectly.

13. C: Choice *C* correctly uses *on to*, describing the way genes are passed generationally. The use of *into* is inappropriate for this context, which makes Choice *A* incorrect. Choice *B* is close, but *onto* refers to something being placed on a surface. Choice *D* doesn't make logical sense.

14. B: Since the sentence can stand on its own without *Usually*, separating it from the rest of the sentence with a comma is correct. Choice *A* needs the comma after *Usually*, while Choice *C* uses commas incorrectly. Choice *D* is tempting, but changing *turn* and *awake* to *turned* and *awakened* does not fit.

15. C: This revision improves the awkward wording of the original sentence. Choice *B* adds an unnecessary comma and period. Choice *D* leaves out the required comma after the word *another*.

16. B: Choice *C* incorrectly changes *applies* to *applied*, fails to change *there* to *their*, and fails to add the necessary punctuation. Choice *D* incorrectly adds a comma between the subject (*Discussions that make people think about the content and how it applies to their lives, world, and future*) and the predicate (*are key*).

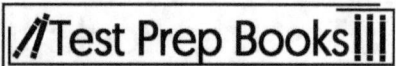

17. D: Choice *D* correctly applies a semicolon to introduce a new line of thought while remaining in a single sentence. The comma after *however* is also appropriately placed. Choice *A* is a run-on sentence. Choice *B* is incorrect because the single comma is not enough to fix the sentence. Choice *C* adds unnecessary commas around *uncertain*.

18. A: The author conjures up a world where there is an imaginary switchboard that can turn off the law of solutions, runs through an example where all saltwater fish die, and then decides the switchboard should be left alone. This is a comedic hypothetical to open the topic of solutions and emulsions. There is not an element of shock or surprise, making Choice *B* incorrect. Despite the fiction, all the information presented was logical and complete, which leaves Choice *C* incorrect. Since the author tells the reader exactly what happens when the Solution switch is turned off, there is no element of suspense, making Choice *D* incorrect.

19. B: Carter explains that the saying *sound as a dollar* ordinarily means something is dependable and reliable. *Solid as a rock* is another phrase that conveys dependability and reliability. *Hands down* refers to intensity or completeness; something that is "the best value, hands down," is absolutely the best value. The phrase *hands down* does not speak to dependability, making Choice *A* incorrect. Ease, not reliability, is the meaning behind the phrase *piece of cake*. This makes Choice *C* incorrect. Choice *D* is incorrect because getting something fair and square means it was earned honestly.

20. A: The author means the flower's petals open up slowly like a person yawning. "To open" or "to gape" is one of the meanings of the verb *yawn*. Choice *B* is incorrect because it focuses on the sleepiness of yawning, not the motion. Choice *C* is wrong because it inaccurately parallels how yawning allows people to receive more oxygen to their brains. There is no evidence to indicate the flower is having issues with regulating the time of day, making Choice *D* erroneous.

21. D: Based on the sentence it is used in, one can infer the meaning from the context. Later in the sentence, the writer uses the word *dissolve* in place of *solubility*. Choices *B* and *C* are both the opposite of the correct meaning and, therefore, incorrect. Choice *A* is the result of the dissolution and also incorrect.

22. C: Choice *C* correctly uses *from* to describe the fact that dogs are related to wolves. The word *through* is incorrectly used in the original sentence, so Choice *A* is incorrect. Choice *B* does not make sense. Choice *D* unnecessarily changes the verb tense in addition to incorrectly using *through*.

23. D: The passage compares Disney cruises with Disney parks. It does not discuss how to book a cruise, so Choice *A* is incorrect. Choice *B* is incorrect because, though the passage does mention some of the park attractions, it is not the main point. The passage does not mention the cost of either option, so Choice *C* is incorrect.

24. C: Jimmy Carter talks about how Americans are losing confidence in their government, their ability to self-govern, and democracy. He basically says America has lost its way and must find it again. That will be hard and will require facing the truth. In the last paragraph, he says that we need to change course and restore confidence and faith. Choice *A* is incorrect because Carter believes that faith can be restored, meaning there is hope for the future. Choice *B* only addresses part of the speech, so it is not the best answer. While Carter does reference other people in the Western world, that is irrelevant to the underlying message, making Choice *D* incorrect.

Answer Explanations #2

25. B: Choice A is not the main point of disagreement. The reporter calls the loss devastating, and there's no reason to believe that the coach would disagree with this assessment. Choice C is mentioned by the coach but not by the reporter. It is unclear whether the reporter would agree or disagree with this assessment, so this is not the main point dispute. Choice D is the opposite of what the coach said, and the passage does not state whether the reporter believes that the team deserved to win, so this is not the main point of dispute. Choice B is strong since both passages mention the at-bats with runners in scoring position. The reporter asserts that the team lost due to the team failing to get such a hit. In contrast, the coach identifies several other reasons for the loss, including fielding and pitching errors. Additionally, the coach disagrees that the team even needed a hit in those situations. Therefore, Choice B is the correct answer.

26. B: Choice B is correct because both philosophers focus on the topics of human nature and how it relates to government. Choice A is incorrect because only the Hobbes text mentions war. Choice C is incorrect because intelligence is not mentioned in either text. Choice D is incorrect because only the Locke text mentions the United States and natural law.

27. B: Choice B is correct because both cultures associate the northern lights with some form of spirit and with the dead carrying on after life. For the Native Americans, the lights are spirits that guide the recently deceased to the next life. For the Sámi, they are a sign of the dead and a dangerous force. Choice A is incorrect because the Sámi would not look forward to the lights since they mean danger. Choice C is incorrect because there is no indication that the color of the lights is connected to the cultural beliefs presented. Choice D is incorrect because some assumptions can be made about the cultural beliefs regarding spirits and the afterlife.

Reading and Writing 2

1. B: Choices A incorrectly adds *be*. Choice D use the wrong verb tense in the second clause. Choice C uses a comma where a semicolon is needed and rephrases the second clause awkwardly.

2. C: Choice C makes the specific distinction that the sentence is talking about the current state of broadcasting news (using the phrase *newscasting today*) instead of relying on the possibly confusing phrase *the news today*, which could be read as referring to a specific news story from today. Choice A does not clearly communicate this distinction. Choice C is also the only option to include the necessary comma at the end.

3. C: Choice C is the best answer because of how the commas are used to flank *in earnest*. This distinguishes the side thought (*in earnest*) from the rest of the sentence. Choice A needs punctuation. Choice B inserts a semicolon in a spot that doesn't make sense, resulting in a fragmented sentence and lost meaning. Choice D would make the sentence grammatically incorrect, and it is confusing due to its structure.

4. A: This passage is predominantly in the present tense, and the author is describing education as it currently is, so Choice A is the correct answer. Choice B is incorrect because the subject and verb do not agree; the singular subject "Education" should be paired with the singular verb "provides." Choice C is incorrect because the passage is in present tense, and "Education will provide" is future tense. Choice D doesn't make sense when placed in the sentence.

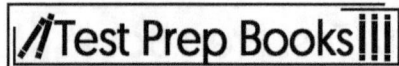

5. B: Choice B is correct because it provides clarity by describing what *myopic* means in context right after the word itself. Choice A is incorrect because the explanation of *myopic* comes before the word, making the structure awkward. Choices C and D are grammatically incorrect.

6. C: Choice C is the correct choice because the word *their* indicates possession, and the text is talking about "their students," or the students of someone. Choice A, *there*, describes where something is located. Choice B, *they're*, is a contraction and means *they are*. Choice D is not a word.

7. A: The word *patronage* most nearly means auspices, which means protection or support. Choice B, *aberration*, means *deformity* and does not make sense within the context of the sentence. Choice C, *acerbic*, means *bitter* and also does not make sense in the sentence. Choice D, *adulation*, is a positive word meaning *praise*, and thus does not fit with the word *condescending* in the sentence.

8. A: The word *commissioned* most nearly means *appointed*. Choice B, *compelled*, means forced. Choice C, *beguiled*, means entertained. Choice D, *fortified*, means defended.

9. D: An individual with a charismatic personality is charming and appealing to others. Therefore, Choice D is the correct answer. Choice A is incorrect because someone with an egotistical personality is conceited or self-serving. Choice B is incorrect because "obnoxious" is the opposite of charismatic. Choice C is incorrect because someone with a chauvinistic personality is aggressive or prejudiced against other groups of people.

10. C: Choice A is incorrect. The Conservative politician believes that spending on social welfare programs increases the national debt, but the Liberal politician does not address the cost of those programs. Choice B is incorrect because while the Liberal politician explicitly states that certain classes of people rely on social welfare programs, the Conservative politician does not mention certain classes of people. Choice C is correct. The dispute between the politicians is focused on whether social welfare programs are necessary. The Conservative politician states that citizens do not need assistance, that it just makes things easier. However, the Liberal politician points out that certain people require an ample safety net. Choice D is not the main point of dispute. Neither of the politicians discusses whether *all* of the nation's leaders have bootstrapped their way to the top.

11. A: Choice A is the most accurate summary of the main point of Thoreau's statement. Choice B is irrelevant. Choice C is also incorrect; Thoreau never personifies government. Also, this doesn't coincide with his wooden gun analogy. Choice D is compelling because of its language but doesn't define the statement.

12. B: Since spinach can grow in temperatures above 40°F and the lowest temperature on the chart is 43°F, it can be grown any month. Potatoes can only grow in March and April because that's when the temperatures are above 55°F. Asparagus cannot be grown in any month because it requires temperatures to be above 60°F. Choices A, C, and D all incorrectly identify one or more of these growing periods.

13. C: To understand the theme of the publication and determine its purpose, it is necessary to read some of the chapter titles. Some chapter titles include "Confronting the Tragedy of Child Abuse and Neglect Facilities" and "Reducing Child Abuse and Neglect Deaths in Disproportionately Affected Communities." Based on the evidence provided by these titles, we can infer that the common theme is child abuse reduction. This best aligns with Choice C.

Answer Explanations #2

14. C: Choice C is correct because people who waste water on lawns in the desert, run a half-full dishwasher, or fill their personal pools are not taking into account how much water they are using because they get an unlimited supply; therefore, they are taking it for granted. Choice A is incorrect because it is explicitly stated within the text: "running dishwashers that are only half full." Choice B is also explicitly stated: "meanwhile people in Africa are dying of thirst." Choice D is not implicitly stated within the sentence.

15. D: Choice D is the correct answer because the narrator states that if someone had told him a year ago that he would dislike the Old Country, he would not have believed them. Thus, it is reasonable to assume that he previously held a good opinion of the Old Country. Choice A is incorrect because there is nothing to suggest that the narrator wishes to travel abroad. Choice B is incorrect because the narrator states that he did not enjoy the talk of ordinary Englishmen. Choice C is incorrect because the narrator is displeased with life but does not express a strong motivation to better it.

16. A: According to the text, the woman did not leave the mountains because she wanted to but rather to please her guardian. The text refers to her "beloved" mountains and notes how long she lived away from them. This suggests that she never wanted to leave the mountains. Choice B is incorrect because the text mentions the woman's unhappy memories in the place. Choice C is incorrect because the text states she is currently facing the first major problem in her life. Choice D is incorrect because there is no indication of the woman having any negative feelings toward the old rancher.

17. C: Choice C is the correct answer because it is a fact that emphasizes how deadly the war was. The addition of casualties to the text stresses how many lives were lost. Choice A is incorrect because it explains what happened post-war and how the United Nations was a necessary creation. Choice B is incorrect because it explains a major factor in the beginning of the war and how many people were killed during the Holocaust. However, the Holocaust was just one event during the war, so it does not cover the entire scope of deadliness. Choice D is incorrect because it provides information about a specific event during the war and how that event damaged ships, but it does not encompass the overall deadliness of the war.

18. D: Choice D is the correct answer because it makes the sentence structure easier to read. It uses commas to break up information into logical segments. It also maintains the original order of information in the sentence. Choice A is incorrect because it makes the Bulls the subject of the sentence rather than Michael Jordan. Choice B is incorrect because it changes the subject of the sentence to Michaels Jordan's career rather than Michael Jordan himself. Choice C is incorrect because it changes the structure of the sentence, and it does not flow as well.

19. C: Choice C is the correct answer because it improves the concision of the text. It provides all of the relevant information while getting rid of excessive wordiness by combining sentences. Choice A is incorrect because there is an appropriate choice that is more concise than the original. Choice B is incorrect because it does not combine any sentences to become more concise. Choice D is incorrect because it is just as long as the original text and does not improve concision.

20. A: Choice A is the correct answer because it effectively combines the two sentences in a way that flows seamlessly. It retains all of the relevant facts that are presented in the original sentences. It combines them effectively with a comma and a conjunction. Choice B is incorrect because, although it adds a comma and a conjunction, it also adds an excessive amount of wording to do the same job as

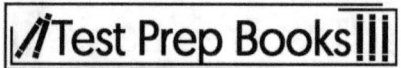

Answer Explanations #2

Choice A. Choices C and D are incorrect because they change the order of the information provided, changing the main subject of the text.

21. D: Choice D is the correct answer because the sentence in question is continuing the discussion about Christie's novel, which takes place in the fourth sentence. Therefore, the best place to put this line is after the sentence about the novel. Choices A, B, and C would be premature because the novel has not been mentioned yet.

22. D: Choice D is the correct answer because *scathing* is the best word to describe the tone of the text. The character in the text is angry that he has witnessed corruption. His body language and determination tell readers that his letter to the press will most likely be negative in nature and fueled by his rage. Choice A is incorrect because his anger would stop the letter from being *diplomatic*. Choice B is incorrect because there is nothing to suggest that the man is feeling *compassionate*. Choice C is incorrect because readers have no basis to believe that the letter would be *pedantic.*

23. C: Choice C is correct because it uses an em dash. Em dashes are versatile. They can separate phrases that would otherwise be in parentheses, or they can stand in for a semicolon. In this case, a semicolon would be another decent choice for this punctuation mark because the second sentence expands upon the first sentence. Choice A is incorrect because the statement is not a question. Choice B is incorrect because adding a comma here would create a comma splice. Choice D is incorrect because this creates a run-on sentence since the two sentences are independent clauses.

24. C: Choice C is the correct answer because Text 1's approach to the topic of the dwindling insect population is citing statistics and credible sources. Text 2 is the anecdotal experience of one farmer who is contributing to the insect decline through pesticides. Choice A is incorrect because Text 1 is only presenting facts; it is not attempting to persuade the audience of anything. Choice B is incorrect because Text 1 is not informal. Choice D is incorrect because, while Text 1 uses formal language, it does not use pedantic language that is difficult to understand.

25. A: Choice A is the correct answer because the main difference in the information provided is the methods that each country has used to address its population issues. China chose to enforce laws and give fines to those who did not comply. Japan does not have any legislation but instead chooses to encourage its citizens through providing money and helpful services to families. Choice B is incorrect because China's plan to decrease the birth rate worked—it just happened to go too far the other way and create a new issue. Japan's plan is not yet highly effective because the country is still actively dealing with the issue. Choice C is incorrect because, although it is true that China's policy caused economic issues further down the line, Japan's economy is suffering as well. This is stated in the sentence that mentions that there is not enough tax revenue. Choice D is incorrect because China's policy did not change solely because of the gender imbalance. It was primarily due to the economic crisis mentioned in the last sentence of Text 1.

26. B: Choice B is the correct answer because the purpose of this text is to highlight Frederick Douglass's accomplishments despite the strife that he experienced. He contributed to his life's mission of seeing slaves emancipated. Choice A is incorrect because Frederick Douglass's efforts are not compared against anyone else's. Choice C is incorrect because the co-laborers are mentioned only to say that they have passed on and faced God, just as Douglass will. Choice D is incorrect because Douglass's childhood is not mentioned.

Answer Explanations #2

27. B: Choice B is the correct answer because the purpose of the text is to explain how the nations exist within the empire but are not socially or culturally tied to it. Choice A is incorrect because the text is written with a neutral tone and does not give an opinion on the nations or empire. Choice C is incorrect because the monarch is mentioned neutrally without the author's opinion on their actions. Choice D is incorrect because there is no indication in the passage that this was the historical start of conscription.

Math 1

1. D: The expression is simplified by collecting like terms. Terms with the same variable and exponent are like terms, and their coefficients can be added.

2. B: We can try to solve the equation by factoring the numerator into $(x + 6)(x - 5)$. Since $(x - 5)$ is on the top and bottom, that factor cancels out. This leaves the equation $x + 6 = 11$. Solving the equation gives the answer $x = 5$. When this value is substituted back into the equation, it yields a zero in the denominator of the fraction. Since this is undefined, there is no solution.

3. B: The technique of completing the square must be used to change the equation below into the standard equation of a circle:

$$4x^2 + 4y^2 - 16x - 24y + 51 = 0$$

First, the constant must be moved to the right-hand side of the equals sign, and each term must be divided by the coefficient of the x^2-term (which is 4). The x- and y- terms must be grouped together to obtain:

$$x^2 - 4x + y^2 - 6y = -\frac{51}{4}$$

Then, the process of completing the square must be completed for each variable. This gives:

$$(x^2 - 4x + 4) + (y^2 - 6y + 9) = -\frac{51}{4} + 4 + 9$$

The equation can be written as:

$$(x - 2)^2 + (y - 3)^2 = \frac{1}{4}$$

Therefore, the center of the circle is $(2, 3)$, and the radius is:

$$\sqrt{\frac{1}{4}} = \frac{1}{2}$$

4. D: Bill's progress in making wicker baskets can be visualized as a linear equation using slope-intercept form. Let $y =$ how many wicker baskets Bill has, and let $x =$ how many days have passed. He can make two wicker baskets per day, so the slope of the line is 2. The information we want to know is the y-intercept value, which we can find by inserting $x = 5$ and $y = 17$ and then solving for the unknown y-intercept. The equation starts as $17 = 2(5) + b$. Multiply 2 by 5 to get 10, then subtract 10 from both sides, resulting in $7 = b$. The y-intercept is 7, meaning that Bill had seven baskets before he started working on more.

5. D: Solve a linear inequality in a similar way to solving a linear equation. First, start by distributing the −3 on the left side of the inequality.

$$-3x - 12 \geq x + 8$$

Then, add 12 to both sides.

$$-3x \geq x + 20$$

Next, subtract x from both sides.

$$-4x \geq 20$$

Finally, divide both sides of the inequality by –4. Don't forget to flip the inequality sign because you are dividing by a negative number.

$$x \leq -5$$

6. 150: Set up the initial equation.

$$\frac{2x}{5} - 1 = 59$$

Add 1 to both sides.

$$\frac{2x}{5} - 1 + 1 = 59 + 1$$

$$\frac{2x}{5} = 60$$

Multiply both sides by 5/2.

$$\frac{2x}{5} \times \frac{5}{2} = 60 \times \frac{5}{2}$$

$$x = 150$$

7. D: Find how many feet are left after the first 1,800 ft:

$$3,125 \text{ ft} - 1,800 \text{ ft} = 1,325 \text{ ft}$$

At $1 per foot, this part will cost $1,325. Add this to the $2,000 for the first 1,800 ft to get the total cost:

$$\$2,000 + \$1,325 = \$3,325$$

8. A: The tip is not taxed, so he pays 5% tax only on the $10. To find 5% of $10, calculate $0.05 \times \$10 = \$0.50$. Add up $10 + $0.50 + $2 to get $12.50.

9. D: Exponential functions can be written in the form: $y = a \times b^x$. The equation for an exponential function can be written given the y-intercept (a) and the growth rate (b). The y-intercept is the output (y) when the input (x) equals zero. It can be thought of as an "original value," or starting point. The value of b is the rate at which the original value increases ($b > 1$) or decreases ($b < 1$). In this scenario, the y-intercept, a, would be $1200, and the growth rate, b, would be 1.01 (100% of the original value combined with 1% interest, or $100\% + 1\% = 101\% = 1.01$).

10. B: The first pair of parentheses is unnecessary, and we can delete the second pair after distributing the −1 in front of them:

$$(5x^2 - 3x + 4) - 1(2x^2 - 7) = 5x^2 - 3x + 4 - 2x^2 + 7$$

Next, like terms are combined by adding the coefficients of the same variables with the same exponents, while keeping the variables and their powers unchanged:

$$5x^2 - 3x + 4 - 2x^2 + 7 = 3x^2 - 3x + 11$$

11. B: To find the solution, we first need to solve one equation for y, then insert that temporary solution in place of y in the other equation to solve for x. Then, we can insert our x solution into either equation and solve for y. We can also solve for the variables in the reverse order or start with either equation, but for this example, we will start by solving $9x + 12y = 54$ for y. Start by subtracting $9x$ from both sides of the equation, which gives us $12y = 54 - 9x$. Then, divide both sides by 12 to get our temporary solution for y, which is $y = \frac{54}{12} - \frac{9}{12}x$. We can insert this temporary solution into the other equation and solve for x there, so we start with $6x - \left(\frac{54}{12} - \frac{9}{12}x\right) = 12$. Remember that we need to multiply the -1 outside the parentheses against the inside, so we get $6x - \frac{54}{12} + \frac{9}{12}x = 12$. We can remove the fractions from this equation by multiplying everything by 12, which gives us $72x - 54 + 9x = 144$. Combining x variables and adding 54 to both sides gives us $81x = 198$. Finally, dividing both sides by 81 gives us $x = \frac{198}{81}$, which can be reduced to $x = \frac{22}{9}$. Now we can insert $x = \frac{22}{9}$ into either equation and solve for y; for this example, we will insert it into the first equation. We start with $9\left(\frac{22}{9}\right) + 12y = 54$. The multiplication cancels out the fraction, which gives us $22 + 12y = 54$. Subtracting 22 from both sides gives us $12y = 32$. Finally, dividing both sides by 12 gives us $y = \frac{32}{12}$, which can be reduced to $y = \frac{8}{3}$. This means our final solution is Choice B: $\left(\frac{22}{9}, \frac{8}{3}\right)$.

12. C: To find the solution, we first need to solve one equation for y, then insert that temporary solution in place of y in the other equation to solve for x. Then, we can insert our x solution into either equation, and solve for y. We can also solve for the variables in the reverse order or start with either equation, but for this example, we will start by solving $x + 3y = 21$ for y. Start by subtracting x from both sides of the equation, which gives us $3y = 21 - x$. Then, divide both sides by 3, which gives us a temporary solution for y, which is $y = 7 - \frac{1}{3}x$. We can insert this temporary solution into the other equation and solve for x there, so we start with $\frac{1}{3}x - 5\left(7 - \frac{1}{3}x\right) = 35$. Multiplying -5 against everything inside the parentheses gives us $\frac{1}{3}x - 35 + \frac{5}{3}x = 35$. Combining x variables and adding 35 to both sides gives us $\frac{6}{3}x = 70$. $\frac{6}{3}$ can be reduced to 2, so we have $2x = 70$. Dividing both sides by 2 gives us $x = 35$. Now we can insert $x = 35$ into either equation and solve for y; for this example, we will insert it into the first

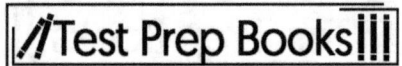

equation. We start with $35 + 3y = 21$. Subtracting 35 from both sides gives us $3y = -14$. Dividing both sides by 3 gives us $y = -\frac{14}{3}$. With this, our final solution is Choice C: $\left(35, -\frac{14}{3}\right)$.

13. C: To find the y-intercept, substitute zero for x, which gives us:

$$y = 0^{\frac{5}{3}} + (0-3)(0+1) = 0 + (-3)(1) = -3$$

14. 15: Start by squaring both sides to get $1 + x = 16$. Then, subtract 1 from both sides to get $x = 15$.

15. A: The slope is given by:

$$m = \frac{y_2 - y_1}{x_2 - x_1} = \frac{0-4}{0-(-3)} = -\frac{4}{3}$$

16. C: The scenario involves data consisting of two variables: month and stock value. Box plots display data consisting of values for one variable. Therefore, a box plot is not an appropriate choice. Both line plots and circle graphs are used to display frequencies within categorical data. Neither can be used for the given scenario. Line graphs display two numerical variables on a coordinate grid and show trends among the variables.

17. D: The formula for finding the volume of a rectangular prism is $V = l \times w \times h$, where l is the length, w is the width, and h is the height. The volume of the original box is calculated:

$$V = 8 \text{ in} \times 14 \text{ in} \times 4 \text{ in} = 448 \text{ in}^3$$

The volume of the new box is calculated:

$$V = 16 \text{ in} \times 28 \text{ in} \times 8 \text{ in} = 3{,}584 \text{ in}^3$$

The volume of the new box divided by the volume of the old box equals 8.

18. A: Using the trigonometric identity $\tan(\theta) = \frac{\sin(\theta)}{\cos(\theta)}$, the expression becomes $\frac{\sin\theta}{\cos\theta} \cos\theta$. The factors that are the same on the top and bottom cancel out, leaving the simplified expression $\sin\theta$.

19. 6.25: If a line is parallel to a side of a triangle and intersects the other two sides of the triangle, it separates the sides into corresponding segments of proportional lengths. To solve, set up a proportion:

$$\frac{AE}{AD} = \frac{AB}{AC} \rightarrow \frac{4}{5} = \frac{5}{x}$$

Cross multiplying yields:

$$4x = 25 \rightarrow x = 6.25$$

20. A: The entire high school was not surveyed, so this is a sample statistic and not a population statistic. 26% is actually the sample proportion.

21. A: When simplified, $x \times 3$ equals $3x$.

Choice A, $9x \div 3$, equals $3x$.

Answer Explanations #2

Choice B, $3x \times 3$, equals $9x$.

Choice C, $3x \div 3$, equals x.

Choice D, $3x \div 9$, equals $0.33x$.

22. D: The linear rate of change is $\frac{1}{-2}$. Choice D provides the correct ratio.

Math 2

1. D: This problem involves a composition function, where one function is plugged into the other function. In this case, the $f(x)$ function is plugged into the $g(x)$ function for each x value. Since f(x)=2, the composition equation becomes:

$$g(f(x)) = g(2) = (2)^3 - 3(2)^2 - 2(2) + 6$$

Simplifying the equation gives the answer:

$$g(f(x)) = 8 - 3(4) - 2(2) + 6$$

$$g(f(x)) = 8 - 12 - 4 + 6$$

$$g(f(x)) = -2$$

2. B: To solve for x, it must be isolated on one side of the equation. Start by adding 32 to both sides of the equation, which results in $9x = 81$. Then, divide both sides of the equation by 9, which gives the final result, $x = 9$.

3. B: For the first card drawn, the probability of a king being pulled is $\frac{4}{52}$. Since this card isn't replaced, if a king is drawn first, the probability of a king being drawn second is $\frac{3}{51}$. The probability of a king being drawn in both the first and second draw is the product of the two probabilities:

$$\frac{4}{52} \times \frac{3}{51} = \frac{12}{2,652}$$

To reduce this fraction, divide the top and bottom by 12 to get $\frac{1}{221}$.

4. A: Since Patrick wants to ensure that there are enough tables to ensure that everyone will have a seat, he will have to set out enough tables to seat 45 people. Since each table seats four people, dividing 45 by 4 will return the number of tables needed, which is 11.25 tables. This is rounded up to 12 since Patrick can only set out tables in whole number increments, making Choice A correct.

5. A: The correct answer is Choice A. Choices B and D use closed dots, which are used to represent $\leq$ or $\geq$, so they are incorrect. The inequalities go in separate directions but are combined by a union (∪). Therefore, Choice C is incorrect since it instead represents the inequalities in the wrong directions.

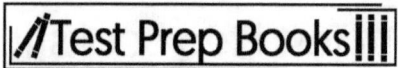

Answer Explanations #2

6. D: This problem can be solved by using unit conversion. The initial units are miles per minute. The final units need to be feet per second. Converting miles to feet uses the equivalence statement 1 mi = 5,280 ft. Converting minutes to seconds uses the equivalence statement 1 min = 60 s. Setting up the ratios to convert the units is shown in the following equation:

$$\frac{72 \text{ mi}}{90 \text{ min}} \times \frac{1 \text{ min}}{60 \text{ s}} \times \frac{5{,}280 \text{ ft}}{1 \text{ mi}} = \frac{380{,}160 \text{ ft}}{5{,}400 \text{ s}} = 70.4 \frac{\text{ft}}{\text{s}}$$

The initial units cancel out, and the new units are left.

7. D: We can use the information provided to fill in values for a and b in the equation $f(x) = ax + b$. Jack starts his travel already at a distance of 30 miles from Jill's house, so we can insert 30 for b. He is traveling at a rate of 45 miles per hour, and since x represents the number of hours Jack has been traveling, we can insert 45 for a. This gives us an equation of $f(x) = 45x + 30$. Now, in order to find out how far Jack has traveled after five hours, we evaluate $f(5)$ by inserting 5 for x. This gives us $f(5) = 45(5) + 30$. Multiplying 45 and 5 together gives 225, and adding 30 onto that gives 255. So, after five hours of travel, Jack is 255 miles away from Jill's house.

8. D: The slope is given by the change in y divided by the change in x. Specifically, it's:

$$slope = \frac{y_2 - y_1}{x_2 - x_1}$$

The first point is $(-5, -3)$, and the second point is $(0, -1)$. Work from left to right when identifying coordinates. Thus, the point on the left is point 1 $(-5, -3)$ and the point on the right is point 2 $(0, -1)$.

Now we just need to plug those numbers into the equation:

$$slope = \frac{-1 - (-3)}{0 - (-5)}$$

It can be simplified to:

$$slope = \frac{-1 + 3}{0 + 5}$$

$$slope = \frac{2}{5}$$

9. A: The correct system of equations is Choice A. $20x + 70y = 200$ represents the miles traveled during the five-hour time frame since x represents the number of hours spent on the slower highway and y represents the number of hours spent on the faster highway. $x + y = 5$ represents the combination of hours the Robertson family spent on the slow and fast highways.

10. 30: When x and y are complementary angles, the sine of x is equal to the cosine of y. The complementary angle of 60 degrees is $90 - 60 = 30$ degrees. Therefore, the answer is 30 degrees.

11. 18: If Ray will be 25 in three years, then he is currently 22. The problem states that Lisa is 13 years younger than Ray, so she must be 9. Sam's age is twice that, which means that the correct answer is 18.

12. B: First, subtract 4 from each side. This yields $6t = 12$. Now, divide both sides by 6 to obtain $t = 2$.

Answer Explanations #2

13. A: $8(4x - 12)$ and $2(16x - 48)$ are equivalent expressions. In the first expression, 8 can be represented as 2×4, allowing us to distribute the 4 inside the parentheses, while the 2 remains outside, which gives us $2(16x - 48)$.

14. B: Given the area of the circle, the radius can be found using the formula $A = \pi r^2$. In this case, $49\pi = \pi r^2$, which yields $r = 7$ m. A central angle is equal to the degree measure of the arc it inscribes; therefore, $\angle x = 80°$. The area of a sector can be found using the formula:

$$A = \frac{\theta}{360°} \times \pi r^2$$

In this case:

$$A = \frac{80°}{360°} \times \pi (7)^2 = 10.9\pi \text{ m}$$

15. C: This is a triangular prism, and its volume is equal to the area of the triangle times the length. The triangle has an area of $\frac{1}{2} \times base \times height = \frac{1}{2}(8 \text{ cm})(3 \text{ cm}) = 12 \text{ cm}^2$. The length of the prism is 12 cm. Therefore, the volume of the shape is $12 \text{ cm}^2 \times 12 \text{ cm} = 144 \text{ cm}^3$.

16. A: Let the unknown score be x. The average will be:

$$\frac{5 \times 50 + 4 \times 70 + x}{10} = \frac{530 + x}{10} = 55$$

Multiply both sides by 10 to get $530 + x = 550$, or $x = 20$.

17. B: This is a systematic sample since there is a set interval over which the participants are selected. Specifically, every 15th customer is surveyed.

18. C: The linear rate of change is $\frac{2}{3}$. Choice C provides the correct ratio.

19. C: First, rearrange the equation to bring all terms to the same side:

$$x^2 + 9x = 0$$

Then, factor the quadratic expression:

$$x \times (x + 9) = 0$$

Separate the two equations by setting each factor equal to 0s:

$$x = 0$$

$$x + 9 = 0$$

Simplify the bottom equation by isolating x:

$$x = 0$$

$$x = -9$$

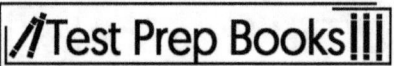

Answer Explanations #2

Test both solutions to make sure they satisfy the equation:

$$0^2 = 9 \times 0$$

$$-9^2 = 9 \times -9$$

Both 0 and -9 are valid solutions.

20. C: $12x - 4$ can be simplified with a common denominator, but it is not necessary to do so in this case, as the goal is to find an equivalent expression. The expression can be identified by multiplying or dividing the numbers inside the parentheses by the number outside the parentheses.

Choice C, $(72x - 24) \div 6$, equals $12x - 4$.

Choice A, $4 \times (3x - 2)$, equals $12x - 8$.

Choice B, $3 \times (4x - 1)$, equals $12x - 3$.

Choice D, $(12x - 4) \div 4$, equals $3x - 1$.

21. B: The linear rate of change is $\frac{2}{-4}$. Choice B provides the correct ratio.

22. B: Simplifying the top equation by dividing by 7 gives $5x + 7y = 21$, which is exactly the same as the bottom equation. This is thus a dependent system, and the problem has infinite solutions.

PSAT Practice Tests #3–#7

To keep the size of this book manageable, save paper, and provide a digital test-taking experience, practice tests 3–7 can be found online. Scan the QR code or go to this link to access it:

testprepbooks.com/online387/psat

The first time you access the tests, you will need to register as a "new user" and verify your email address.

If you have any issues, please email support@testprepbooks.com

Dear PSAT Test Taker,

Thank you for purchasing this study guide for your PSAT exam. We hope that we exceeded your expectations.

Our goal in creating this study guide was to cover all of the topics that you will see on the test. We also strove to make our practice questions as similar as possible to what you will encounter on test day. With that being said, if you found something that you feel was not up to your standards, please send us an email and let us know.

We would also like to let you know about other books in our catalog that may interest you.

SAT

This can be found on Amazon: amazon.com/dp/1637754051

ACT

amazon.com/dp/1637758596

ACCUPLACER

amazon.com/dp/1637756356

CLEP College Composition

amazon.com/dp/163775129X

We have study guides in a wide variety of fields. If the one you are looking for isn't listed above, then try searching for it on Amazon or send us an email.

Thanks Again and Happy Testing!
Product Development Team
info@studyguideteam.com

Online Resources

Included with your purchase are multiple online resources. This includes the practice tests in an interactive format and a convenient study timer to help you manage your time.

Scan the QR code or go to this link to access this content:

testprepbooks.com/online387/psat

The first time you access the page, you will need to register as a "new user" and verify your email address.

If you have any issues, please email support@testprepbooks.com.

Thank you for letting us be a part of your studying journey!

www.ingramcontent.com/pod-product-compliance
Lightning Source LLC
Chambersburg PA
CBHW060313240426
43661CB00059B/2744